Contents

BOOKKEEPING—
The Basis of Accounting

Students' Text

E. D. Agyeman
Emile Woolf and Agyeman
School of Accountancy
Accra

and

A. W. Brindley
Redbridge Technical College
Romford

McGRAW-HILL Book Company (UK) Limited

London · New York · St. Louis · San Francisco · Auckland · Bogotá · Guatemala
Hamburg · Johannesburg · Lisbon · Madrid · Mexico · Montreal · New Delhi · Panama
Paris · San Juan · São Paulo · Singapore · Sydney · Tokyo · Toronto

Published by McGRAW-HILL Book Company (UK) Limited

MAIDENHEAD · BERKSHIRE · ENGLAND

Redbridge Technical College
Romford

British Library Cataloguing in Publication Data

Agyeman, E D
  Bookkeeping: Students' text.–(McGraw-Hill business education courses).
  1. Bookkeeping
  I. Title   II. Brindley, A W
  657'.2   HF5635

  ISBN 0-07-084604-9

2345 WC&S 82310

PRINTED AND BOUND IN GREAT BRITAIN

Foreword to the Series

Course structures devised by the Business Education Council present an exciting new challenge to lecturers, students and authors alike. The council has considered it no longer appropriate to educate for a career in business by means of academic disciplines which, however appropriate in themselves, were brought into at best a loose interrelationship, and which were capable of being taught in a fashion, academically sound, but perhaps insufficiently applied to the situations which students might find in the business world.

The new course structure identifies, at all levels (General, National, Higher National), four important Central Themes, an understanding of which, it is argued, is central to all business education, and which underlie all academic disciplines. These Central Themes are Money (including the most efficient use of the resources which money can buy); People (and their human relationships as producers and consumers); Communication (embracing a much wider concept than mere 'Business English'); and Numeracy (not just 'Business Mathematics' but a logical and numerate approach to business problems). Additionally, the BEC philosophy is that academic disciplines must be interrelated if they are to be meaningful in the solution of business problems.

An important aim of the BEC course structure at both General and National level is therefore:

> to encourage the development of the understanding and skills implicit in the Central Themes, with particular emphasis on the improvement of the student's standards of literacy and numeracy.

A further aim at General level is:

> to develop basic work competence through practical assignments which relate the knowledge, skills and understanding derived from various parts of the course to business situations.

This, at National level, becomes:

> to develop the student's ability to interrelate knowledge, skills, and understanding from various parts of the course through practical assignments derived from business contexts.

The modular course structure itself encourages this interrelationship by breaking down traditional subject barriers. The exciting new challenge to authors and lecturers is to adopt the BEC philosophy without abandoning the integrity or the essential content of subject disciplines. Side by side with Common Core Modules, applicable to all students at a particular level, run Board Core Modules and Option Modules. There is a need to integrate subject matter both within and across the modules in order to produce a coherent pattern of study. This must be just as relevant for students ending their studies at this point as for those progressing to a higher BEC level or to examinations for and membership of professional bodies. The challenge to students is to grasp the intricacies of interwoven Central Themes, subjects and modules and to emerge with the knowledge, skills and understanding which will enable them to solve practical problems.

All the authors in this series have met the challenge in their own way. Each has, however, covered the general objectives and the learning objectives of the relevant BEC module in a way which makes for a logical teaching and learning progression, while bearing in mind the need for interconnections between the modules. Books at both General and National level stand, not only in their own right, but as part of a package. They contain their own assignments designed to integrate subject disciplines within the module and based on practical example. Books in the same series also contain common cross-modular assignments in order to carry integration still further.

The consulting editor and the authors are well aware that there is no unique solution to the challenge posed by the BEC course structure. Some people would advocate throwing caution to the winds and abandoning much that was good and relevant in the existing schemes, would seek out change for the sake of change. Others would attempt to mould BEC courses to their own skills and teaching methods, thus frustrating change altogether. We have decided on what we believe to be a sensible middle way; our approach seeks to enable teachers to plan and present the new course structures effectively, thus enabling students to learn more easily and above all, to consider BEC courses relevant to their jobs and careers.

Preface

This book has been planned primarily as a bookkeeping textbook, with emphasis on records, documents and accounting books. Many students following business courses are required to study accounting—and in so doing are given a cursory look at the records and documents which form the basis of the accounting systems. Other students will be studying bookkeeping since the skill learned will provide immediate job opportunities; yet young students who come to this subject from school often find bookkeeping confusing, because of its totally new terminology and new concepts and their own lack of practical business experience.

This book is intended for all students who, new to the subject, intend to learn bookkeeping, including those who will be taking the first level bookkeeping examinations of all examining institutes—in particular, the General Level of the Business Education Council, the London Chamber of Commerce, Royal Society of Arts, and West African Examinations Council.

Students are expected to imagine themselves working for 'Joe', the owner of a small business, who will explain the use of documents and books and who lays down certain rules to remember. As the business grows, so does the number of books and records required.

Questions are set at the end of each chapter. Some questions have answers at the back of the book. Other questions, prefixed 'NA', do not have answers and it is hoped that teachers of students following courses in schools and at colleges will use these questions for classwork and homework assignments.

We wish to acknowledge the permission to use examination papers given by the Associated Examining Board, the London Chamber of Commerce, the Royal Society of Arts and the East Midland Educational Union. Also we acknowledge the permission of Kalamazoo Ltd. and Lloyds Bank Ltd. for the use of documents as illustrations.

A *Teacher's Handbook* with additional exercises is published separately. The book contains teaching notes, additional teaching material and supplementary exercises. ISBN: 084605-70

ix

Discrimination between the sexes

In a book on the subject of bookkeeping, using the terminology and current practice of the business world, it has not been possible to eliminate the use of gender and retain a fluent text. The reader is asked to accept that in the majority of cases a deliberate distinction between the sexes is not implied.

1. Introduction

Joe Wynn is starting a new business and he wants you to work for him. A part of your job will be to keep the records of the money he spends and the money he receives. Do not worry—Joe has been in business a long time and he knows what details he expects you to record. He is the owner and he naturally wants to know whether or not his business is becoming successful. One thing he needs to know is how much profit he is making—or how much of a loss, if the business does not go very well. Joe is going to teach you some rules about the records you will be keeping—and these are important. Joe's new business is selling carpets. He is just starting, so there is not a lot of trade to begin with and all you have to do is to put down the money he spends on carpets and what he receives from the sales. To do this you need a *Cash Book*. Joe wants you to use a simple Cash Book; in fact, it could be a small note book. If you go into your local stationers and ask them to let you look at the Cash Books they stock, you will be surprised at the large number of different sizes, thicknesses, and colours. Also, the pages can be ruled in different columns. But you must remember one thing that Joe tells you: whatever book you use, remember that every sum of money spent you put down on the right-hand side of the book, and every sum of money received you put down on the left-hand side of the book. Let me show you. Open your Cash Book at the first double page. This is page 1.

Why do you think we have page 1 on both sides? Because both receipts *and* payments are recorded on the same page—receipts on one half of the page, payments on the other half. Note the headings. If you have not got a note book or a

1	RECEIPTS	PAYMENTS	1

proper Cash Book, use a piece of paper with a line drawn down the middle—one side for receipts and the other for payments.

Joe's Rule
No. 1
Receipts are always on the left.
Payments are always on the right.

Now, if Joe asks you these questions what would you say?

1.01 Why would it be better to use a proper Cash Book rather than pieces of paper?

1.02 Who else is going to look at the Cash Book apart from me and you?

1.03 Why is it important to put the figures down neatly under each other?

1.04 At the end of each day I am going to check that the amount in the till is the same as the amount you show in the Cash Book. If the two amounts do not agree, what will happen?

Look at the back of the book to see what answers Joe would give.

Joe expects his bookkeeper to be neat and tidy, to be able to do arithmetic, and to write legibly (so that other people can read his figures and letters), and he asks you to do the following to see just how good you are.

1.05 Write down these amounts in a column on a piece of paper and add up the column.

Forty-nine pounds 89 pence; seventy-six pounds 53 pence; one hundred and sixty-two pounds 40 pence; one thousand and nineteen pounds 75 pence; four hundred and fifty-three pounds 18 pence.

1.06 From your answer to **1.05** take away the following three amounts.

Fifty-four pounds 68 pence; twelve pounds 35 pence; eighty-seven pounds 6 pence.

1.07 Add the columns down and rows across.

	Column 1	Column 2	Total
Row 1	10.07	11.30	21 37
Row 2	4.03	74.56	78.59
Row 3	6.91	68.95	75 86
Row 4	3.28	25.74	29 02
Total	24.29	180 55	204.84

1.08 Now add the total column down and the two column totals across. They should be the same.

2

Do the same as for **1.07** and **1.08** with the following table: **1.09**

	1	2	3	Total
1	91.83	17.89	65.73	*175.45*
2	74.68	23.56	148.19	*246.43*
3	28.51	34.67	172.45	*235.63*
4	13.92	118.24	56.82	*188.98*
Total	*208.94*	*194.36*	*443.19*	*846.49*

The last question was difficult—particularly adding across. But you must always practise your adding up. If you want to pass an examination it is better for you to be able to do the arithmetic correctly. To help you to do this, the pages of any book used in bookkeeping are ruled with columns for pounds (£) and pence (p). If you ever have to use a book or paper without printed columns then rule some columns yourself—it makes your work so much neater. Look at the example below.

1	RECEIPTS	FOLIO	£	P	DATE	PAYMENTS	FOLIO	£	P	1
DATE	DETAILS				DATE	DETAILS				

Many small shopkeepers use a simply ruled Cash Book such as this one. The words and signs are not usually printed—you can write them in yourself on your own paper. We can use this for Joe's business. Joe will tell you what the narrow column headed 'Folio' is for later on, when you have got used to entering the books.

2. The Cash Account

Take a quick look at page 3 again—you will see how a Cash Book is ruled. The Cash Book is the book in which the *Cash Account* is kept. 'An account', explains Joe, 'is a record of similar transactions.' You have to write down the cash receipts and payments side by side, in order to find out the amount of cash that still remains. By the way, Account has an abbreviation: A/c. So you may write as a heading on the top of the book *Cash A/c.*

The source of receipts and payments

Receipts Most of the receipts that Joe will require you to record will come from sales of carpets and rugs. When the customer buys something in the shop, Joe (or you) will make out a receipt for the customer, as evidence that the customer has paid. The *Receipt Book* has a carbon copy so that you can make a note of the money received from the sale in the Cash Book, after the customer has left with his receipt.

Customer's Copy

	No. 33
Customer's Name Date	

Goods	Price
1 Rug	12·50
2 metres Axminster	
@ £4 per metre	8·00
Total	20·50
Signature of Assistant	

Receipt of Sale	No. 33
Customer's Name Date	

Goods	Price
1 Rug	12·50
2 metres Axminster	
@ £4 per metre	8·00
Total	20·50
Signature of Assistant	

Note You must often have received a similar receipt when you purchased goods yourself. In some large stores, and indeed smaller shops such as your local greengrocer, you

4

do not receive a receipt—so how does the shop manager, or owner, know how much money has been taken during the day? See answer to question **2.01**.

Very many payments are made by a business—wages, rent, rates, postage, petrol, repairs, advertising, purchases, and so on. Whatever amount of cash is paid out, it must be recorded in the Cash Book, together with details of what the cash has been spent on. Let Joe explain.

I have to visit suppliers to buy carpets and also have to pay your wages and all expenses connected with this shop and warehouse. Whatever is spent must have a bill or receipt to prove that it is genuine. So when I send you down to the local shops to buy stationery or groceries, make sure you get a receipt. Put all the receipts together in a file in date order and enter the Cash Book from these receipts. Here are today's customers' receipts and bills I have paid—so I will show you how to enter them in the Cash Book.

No. 33—£20.50; No. 34—£56.81; No. 35—£14.25; No. 36—£92.50; No. 37—£86.42; No. 38—£17.68.

Purchases £55.00; Petrol £3.85; Stationery £4.15; Purchases £40.00; Window cleaning £0.75; Carriage £2.75; Electric light bulbs £3.80; Purchases £80.00.

Cash Account

19–8				19–8				
Sept 20	Sales		20·50	Sept 20	Purchases			55·00
	Sales		56·81		Petrol			3·85
	Sales		14·25		Stationery			4·15
	Sales		92·50		Purchases			40·00
	Sales		86·42		Window cleaning			0·75
	Sales		17·68		Carriage			2·75
					Electric Light bulbs			3·80
					Purchases			80·00
					Balance	c/d		97·86
			288·16					288·16
Sept. 20	Balance	b/d	97·86					

Note the following points.

1 Always enter the date.
2 On the receiving side, all receipts from customers during the day are recorded as sales.
3 Whatever has been spent has shown against it the details of what it was spent upon (*see* **Purchases of goods for resale** on page 6).

4   The balance of £97.86 shows by how much the receipts exceed the payments and represents what should be left in the till.

5   The account is always balanced using the same layout as above.

Joe's Rule No. 2

The *cash balance* is the excess of the receipts over the payments.

Purchases of goods for resale

When Joe buys carpets and rugs to sell in his business, he records what he pays for them in the Cash Account and writes down 'Purchases'. You may think he ought to write 'Carpets' or 'Rugs', or whatever description is correct. Let Joe explain.

What I will need to find out, sooner or later, is the profit (or loss) that I have made. To do this I shall need to be able to compare what I have bought with what I have sold. Whatever I buy to resell, be it carpets, rugs, or any of the small items that go with carpets, they are all recorded as *purchases*. Remember that *purchases* are *goods purchased for resale*.

Assets

If I buy something that I will *not* be reselling—for example, a carpet cutting machine, or some display rollers, or a motor van which I shall retain for use in the business—you must show in the Cash Book exactly what has been bought. Items such as these, which I shall use in the business, are called *assets*.

2.02   Which of the following are assets?

(a) Office desk and chair.
(b) Cash in the till.
(c) Postage expenses.
(d) Petrol expenses.
(e) Warehouse racking.
(f) Warehouse heating expenses.

Balancing the Cash Account

Cash itself is an asset. If you have any cash in your pocket, then it is one of your own assets. If you look at the Cash Account drawn up by Joe, you will see that all the cash received from sales is added together on the left-hand side of the account.

Payments of cash reduce that asset, and so all the payments added together will give the amount to be taken from the total of the receipts. These calculations are made using *complementary arithmetic*.

Example   Look at this example: $5 + 3 + Q = 12$. What must Q equal?

Lay out the problem as follows:

$$\begin{array}{r} 5 \\ +\ 3 \\ +\ Q \\ \hline =\ 12 \\ \hline\hline \end{array}$$

Rather than add 5 and 3 to make 8, which you then deduct from 12, to give the answer 4, you should say to yourself: 5 and 3 are 8, what should be *added* to 8 to make the total 12? Answer 4.

Here is a longer example:

$$\begin{array}{r} 10 \\ +27 \\ +\ 5 \\ +\ 9 \\ +\ Q \\ \hline 86 \\ \hline\hline \end{array}$$

35

What must Q equal for the column to total 86?

Step 1 Add up the units column. Say to yourself: 0 plus 7 (equals 7) plus 5 (equals 12) plus 9 (equals 21).

What must I add to 21 to result in a 6 at the end of the total? (the 6 at the end of 86). Answer—add 5. Therefore 21 plus 5 equals 26. Write down the 5 you have added in the units column.

$$\begin{array}{r} 10 \\ +27 \\ +\ 5 \\ +\ 9 \\ +\ 5 \\ \hline 86 \\ \hline\hline \end{array}$$

The units column now adds to 26.

Step 2 Carry forward the 2 into the tens column (representing the twenty). Add up the tens column—carry forward of 2 plus 1 plus 2 equals 5. What must I add to 5 to

7

result in the total of 8? Answer 3. Write this in the tens column.

$$
\begin{array}{r}
10 \\
+27 \\
+\ 5 \\
+\ 9 \\
+35 \\
\hline
=86 \\
\hline
\end{array}
$$

2.03   Try these questions.

	(a)	(b)	(c)	(d)
	11	14	27	49.15
	9	2	92	3.71
	8	19	16	8.42
	5	7	48	9.13
	4	23	5	6.18
Balance =	12	= 29	= 15	= 39·51
	49	94	203	116.10

Always practise complementary arithmetic in balancing accounts. You may have difficulty where two sides look to be about the same amount, since the clue to complementary arithmetic is to add, first, the side with the largest amount (which in the case of the Cash Account is always the left-hand side). You can always use a pencil to write in the total of each side as follows.

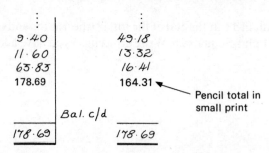

Bal. b/d.

Note   You have probably realized by now that the following are essential to your bookkeeping work: pen, pencil, rubber, and ruler. Until you have gained confidence, always use a pencil for totalling and balancing. Always use a ruler to balance and underline account headings. Neatness is very important.

2.04   Using complementary arithmetic, calculate the balances on the following Cash Accounts:

<table>
<tr><td colspan="2">(a)
Cash Account</td><td colspan="2">(b)
Cash Account</td></tr>
<tr><td>12.00
14.00
8.00
5.00</td><td>16.00
3.00
20·00 ✓

Bal. c/d</td><td>25.00
22.00
9.00
37.00</td><td>8.00
15.00
47.00
23·00 ✓
Bal. c/d</td></tr>
<tr><td>39.00</td><td>39.00</td><td>93.00</td><td>93.00</td></tr>
<tr><td>Bal. b/d</td><td></td><td>Bal. b/d</td><td></td></tr>
</table>

<table>
<tr><td colspan="2">(c)
Cash Account</td><td colspan="2">(d)
Cash Account</td></tr>
<tr><td>47.00
31.00
19.00
7.00
63.00</td><td>36.00
4.00
28.00
1.00
98·00 ✓
Bal. c/d</td><td>32.00
76.00
9.50
17.00
3.00
45.00</td><td>13.00
7.00
22.00
35.00
1.00
Bal. c/d 104·50 ✓</td></tr>
<tr><td>167.00</td><td>167.00</td><td>182·50</td><td>182·50</td></tr>
<tr><td>Bal. b/d</td><td></td><td>Bal. b/d</td><td></td></tr>
</table>

<table>
<tr><td colspan="2">(e)
Cash Account</td><td colspan="2">(f)
Cash Account</td></tr>
<tr><td>17.25
86.40
93.30
11.10
16.45</td><td>3.50
8.40
17.30
6.20
9.60
3.10
Bal. c/d</td><td>11.48
32.91
173.86
49.74</td><td>33.93
11.47
3.84
6.55
7.93
20.00
Bal. c/d 185·57</td></tr>
<tr><td>224·50</td><td>224·50</td><td>267·99</td><td>267·99</td></tr>
<tr><td>Bal. b/d</td><td></td><td>Bal. b/d</td><td>184·27</td></tr>
</table>

Ruling off an account

Turn back to page 5 and look at the Cash Account. Joe totalled the receipts to £288.16. This total was carried across on the same line to the payments side of the account. By complementary arithmetic Joe worked out the balance of £97.86. Remember that, although the balance is first written on the *payments* side, it represents the amount by which the receipts *exceed* the payments—and the bookkeeping way of writing this is to show the calculated balance as *balance c/d* (carried down), and the amount of cash actually in the till—as the asset—is also shown, as *balance b/d* (brought down) on the left-hand side. This is the amount in the till to which will be added the next receipts from sales.

If the payments on the Cash Account had exactly equalled the receipts, there would be no balance—both sides would total the same amount and would be *ruled off* with no balance shown, as follows.

Cash Account

Sales	49.00	Purchases	98.00
Sales	82.00	Stationery	2.61
Sales	14.61	Wages	45.00
	145.61		145.61

This is most unlikely; you will almost always have a balance on the Cash Account. The balance will also always be on the left-hand side. Why? As Joe says: if you receive £10 and put it in your pocket—how much of it can you spend? You can spend any amount up to £10. If you do spend it all, you have got nothing left—*but you can't spend more than £10.* It is the same with the Cash Account you are keeping. I can always take out everything there is—but I can't take out of the till more than is in the till. If you ever balance the Cash Account and the result is a balance which shows you have spent more than you have received—you have made an error and you must check all your transactions and also your arithmetic.

Drawings
When the owner of a business requires some money for his own use then he may take cash out of the till for himself. This is a payment and is recorded in the Cash Account in the same way as other payments. In the detail column is recorded 'Drawings' and this means that the owner has withdrawn the sum shown.

2.05 If you had to pay a bill by obtaining a postal order from the local Post Office, how would this be treated in the Cash Account?

Bookkeeping terminology

Debit This term is used to denote an entry on the left-hand side of an account. Sales receipts are debited to the Cash Account. When written in a record book or account, the term debit is abbreviated to Dr.

Credit This term is used to denote an entry on the right-hand side of an account. Cash purchases and expenses are credited to the Cash Account. This term has an abbreviation also: Cr.

Debit balance A debit balance denotes that the debit entries in an account exceed the credit entries. The balance (or surplus of debits over credits) appears on the debit side.

Credit balance If a credit balance arises on an account it will be shown on the right-hand side of the account.

10

Look at the Cash Account on page 5. Is the balance of £97.86 a debit balance or a credit balance?

2.06

A debtor is a person who owes money to the business. The balance on his account will be a debit balance.

Debtor

A creditor is someone to whom we (i.e., the business) owe money. The balance on his account will be a credit balance.

Creditor

3. The Bank Account

Why a bank account?

So far you have only handled and recorded cash paid or received. In practice, the majority of firms use a *bank account* for paying bills—apart from cash payments on small items such as bus fares, groceries, window cleaning, and so on. The advantage of a bank account is that actual cash is not handled in the business and there is no danger of cash being stolen or lost. Imagine the problem if Woolworths tried to pay cash to the delivery drivers of vehicles delivering goods to their premises. A great deal of money would have to be kept handy to pay them—and think of the dangers in this.

Types of bank account

Two main types of account are offered by a bank and often a business uses both of them. The main one would be the *current account*. The current account will be opened after the bank has taken up references on the business (and the owner), and the client (the name given by the bank to its customer) will then be given a cheque book and a bank paying-in book. See pages 15 and 16.

Amounts paid in have to be recorded in the bank paying-in book, on both the slip and its counterfoil—so that when the bank removes the slip, you (the client) still have the counterfoil and this is the document from which the Bank Account in your books is entered. We must now keep a Bank Account similar to the Cash Account, recording amounts paid into and withdrawn from the bank. All withdrawals are made from the bank account by means of a cheque. A cheque is simply an order to your bank to pay a sum of money to the person you name on the cheque. (By putting your own name on the cheque you withdraw cash for yourself.)

A current account allows the client to draw money out on demand—but the bank does not pay interest on the balance in the account. The bank will send you a statement of your account periodically, or upon request, and this is a copy of the client account in the bank's records. It enables the client to check that his own Bank Account kept in his own Bank Book corresponds to the one kept by the bank. (This job is called *bank reconciliation* and you will learn this in chapter 20.)

This is a savings account and will be used by a business to save its surplus cash. The bank will pay interest on balances kept in this account and payments into it, like payments into a current account, are recorded in a paying-in book. Cheques are not used to withdraw amounts to pay bills because money is normally withdrawn only by presenting the passbook.

Deposit account

Let Joe explain how you will enter this.

Current account

Entries follow the same system as the Cash Account: amounts paid into the bank are debits and withdrawals are credits. Often transfers are made between the Bank Account and our Cash Account, since cash received is first recorded in the Cash Account. Cash taken out of the business and banked will therefore have two entries:

Dr. Bank Account. (Money is paid into bank.)
Cr. Cash Account. (Cash is paid out.)

Of course, if we run out of ready cash and have to withdraw some money from the bank, the entries are reversed:

Dr. Cash Account
Cr. Bank Account.

(These are called *contra* entries—but more of this later.)

There is one important point concerning the Bank Account that differs from the Cash Account. With cash, we can only pay out the cash actually received, but with a Bank Account it is possible to withdraw more money than has been put into the account. This must be done with the permission of the bank manager, who may allow us to overdraw. An overdraft is really a loan—but instead of handing a specific sum of money to us, we are given permission to overdraw to the amount required. Look at this simple illustration.

Bank Account

Sept.	Total receipts	1,294	Sept.	Total withdrawals	1,594
	Balance c/d	300			
		1,594			1,594

How does it differ from, say, a Cash Account? The difference is that the balance is a *credit balance*. This means that the amount of £300 is owed to the bank. This is a *liability* of the business. You will recall that cash is an asset, whether in the Cash Account or the Bank Account. But if we take out more cash from the Bank Account than the amount paid in, not only have we *not* got the money but we owe the difference to the bank.

An amount owed by the business is a liability. An overdraft is a liability.

Liabilities

13

3.01 Give examples of other liabilities of the business.

Entering the Bank Account
Joe explains further how you are to keep the Bank Account.

This account is ruled in the same way as the Cash Account, and the same details are recorded. There is one additional detail which may be entered: the cheque number of the payment made. Look at this cheque book: the first three counterfoils show:

Cheque No. 5981234 Sept. 20 £3 for petrol.
Cheque No. 5981235 Sept. 20 £22 for carpets.
Cheque No. 5981236 Sept. 21 £12 for printing.

We do not have the cheques—they have been given to the suppliers. The cheque counterfoils should have the details of the payments written upon them. They will be entered as follows.

Bank Account

Sept. 20	Petrol	5981234	3.00
	Purchases	35	22.00
21	Printing	36	12.00

I would like you to enter the cheque numbers; later on I will show you how useful it is in reconciling the account with the bank statement.

Joe's Rule No. 3 A credit balance on the Bank Account means that we have overdrawn and this amount represents a liability of our business. Therefore a debit balance must represent an asset, since this is the money we have in the bank.

Drawings You know from chapter 2 that money taken out of the business for the owner's private use is called Drawings. Whether it is cash that is withdrawn or money taken out of the Bank Account, the detail to be shown is Drawings. (Do not confuse drawings with contra entries, which are transfers from cash to bank or *vice versa*—as shown in chapter 10, page 72).

Receipts and payments other than cheques
Receipts The bank may add amounts to our account for interest or dividends received by them on our behalf—or payments made directly to the bank by someone who owes money to our business. These are by an instruction to the bank known as a *standing order* or by another method called *credit transfer*. These are payments *into* the bank and therefore the Bank Account is debited in the Bank Book.

Payments 1 *Standing order* If our business requires to pay a regular sum of money we can authorize our bank to pay this amount, whenever required, without making out a cheque. The payment is made direct to the bank account of the person to whom we are paying that sum.

2 *Direct debit* This works in a similar way to a standing order. The payments can be made without writing out a cheque.

3 *Credit transfer* This enables us to pay several bills by using only one cheque.

4 Our bank will deduct amounts from our account for *service charges* and any *interest on overdrafts*.

In all four cases above, the amount paid is credited to our Bank Account in the Bank Book. This can only be done when we receive our bank statement. See page 19.

If a Postal Order were received instead of a cheque, how would it be treated in the accounts?   **3.02**

A specimen blank cheque

By completing a cheque and sending it to the person to whom we owe money, we save ourselves the job of actually taking or sending cash to him. In fact, the banks perform the transfer of money from our bank to his bank safely. Attached to the left-hand side of the cheque and bound into the cheque book is the counterfoil which is completed at the same time, and from which we can enter our cash book.

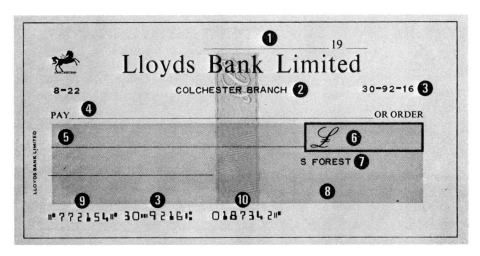

SPECIMEN BLANK CHEQUE

(1) Date; (2) Name of the account-holding branch; (3) The sorting code number of Colchester Branch; (4) Payee's name—the person to whom you are paying the cheque; (5) The amount in words; (6) The amount in figures; (7) The name of the account; (8) Signature; (9) The cheque number; (10) The account number.

A specimen completed cheque

(1) Always write in ink or ball-pen—*never* pencil; (2) Write out the amount of cheque in both words and figures—this gives us a double check on the amount you want to be paid, and prevents alteration of your cheques (particularly the figures); (3) Draw lines through any unused spaces (so that no-one can add anything to the amount you want to pay out); (4) Sign your cheque with your usual signature; (5) Don't forget to complete the counterfoil—this is your record of what you've paid out, to whom and when; (6) Crossings—most cheque books we issue are 'crossed' which gives you a lot of protection. If an 'open' cheque fell into the hands of a dishonest person, he might take it to a branch of Lloyds Bank and obtain cash for it. If your cheque had been 'crossed' then it would have had to be paid into a bank account.

A specimen current account credit slip

This form is completed when putting money into our current account. We can either complete loose slips, which have a counterfoil attached in the same way as cheques and counterfoils, or we can have a book of credit slips which have duplicates made by the use of carbon paper.

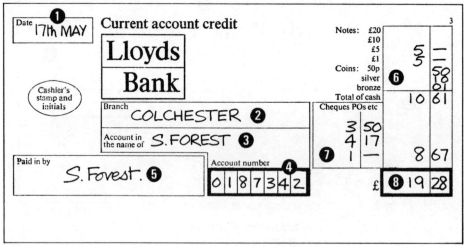

(1) Date; (2) Name of account holding branch (as at (2) on specimen cheque); (3) Account name (as at (7) on specimen cheque); (4) Account number (as at (10) on specimen cheque); (5) Signature of person paying the money in; (6) Breakdown of cash paid in; (7) Amounts of cheques paid in; (8) Total of the credit to the account (cash and cheques).

16

A bank statement

There are several important points to note.

1 The account looks different from the account you have seen in the Bank Book being used by our business. This has three columns: Payments, Receipts, and a Balance column showing a running balance total.
2 Amounts paid *into* our account are shown as a receipt with the particulars of 'Credit'. (In the bank's books we are a creditor for the amount paid into our account. The bank owes the money it holds to the clients for whom it is acting as banker.)
3 Payments made by the bank on our behalf show the amount and the cheque number.
4 S/O shows a standing order payment.
5 DIV is a dividend received.
6 D/D shows a direct debit payment.
7 Bank Giro Credit shows the amount paid into our account at a branch of the bank other than the one at which our account is kept.

Enter the following in the Cash Account and Bank Account. Balance both accounts at the end of March and carry down the balances.   **3.03**

Mar.	1	Received a loan of £500 from A. Smith and paid it into the bank.
	2	Paid rent by cheque £25.
	3	Transferred £80 to the cash till.
	4	Paid office cleaner £15 in cash.
	5	Purchased goods by cheque £385.
	6	Cash sales £72.
	8	Paid cash for stationery £14.
	10	Cash sales £116.
	11	Paid cash for goods for resale £100.
	12	Transferred £129 to the bank from the cash till.
	13	The owner drew a cheque for £15 for his own use.

Open a Bank Account and Cash Account and enter the balance on 1 April. Then enter the transaction and balance at the end of the month.   **3.04**

Apr.	1	Balance at bank £455; Cash balance £75.
	2	Paid wages in cash £48 and window cleaner £2.
	4	Received a Postal Order for £16 for sales.
	5	Paid a cheque value £86 to J. Walker.
	7	Withdrew £50 cash from bank (for office use).
	8	Paid wages in cash £49, groceries £3.
	10	The owner withdrew £20 as drawings from bank.
	14	Cash sales to date £163. Transferred £179 to bank.
	15	Received a cheque from F. Taylor for £64.

20	Paid the telephone bill by cheque £31.
22	Cash sales to date £192.
24	Drawings by the owner £25 in cash.
28	Transferred £175 cash to the bank.

NA 3.05   Complete the Cash Account and Bank Account for the month of January.

Jan. 15	Balance at bank £562.00.
	Balance in cash £14.50.
16	£85.00 withdrawn from bank.
17	Wages paid in cash £57.50.
17	Petrol paid in cash £4.85.
18	Dividends received of £17.25 were paid direct to the bank account.
19	Received a cheque from P. Kaylor £49.70.
20	The owner withdrew £30.00 cash.
21	Cash sales to date £142.60.
24	Shop fittings purchased by cheque £43.25.
25	Cash sales to date £63.00.
25	Paid cash of £112.75 into the bank.
28	The owner withdrew £50.00 by cheque.
29	Received a cheque value £25.00 from R. Wood.
30	Payment by standing order for mailing machine rental £15.50.
30	The bank made a charge of £14.50 for services.

NA 3.06   Complete the Cash Account and Bank Account for the month of February.

Feb. 21	Balance at bank £98.50 (credit).
	Balance in cash £15.25 (debit).
22	Cash sales £108.15.
22	Rent paid in cash £25.00.
23	The owner withdrew cash £15.00 for his own use.
24	£50.00 was paid into the bank.
25	A loan of £1,000 was received from H.P. Finance Co. Ltd and paid into the bank.
26	A motor van was purchased by cheque, £1,250.00.
28	£35.00 was paid direct to the bank by standing order from P. Spencer.

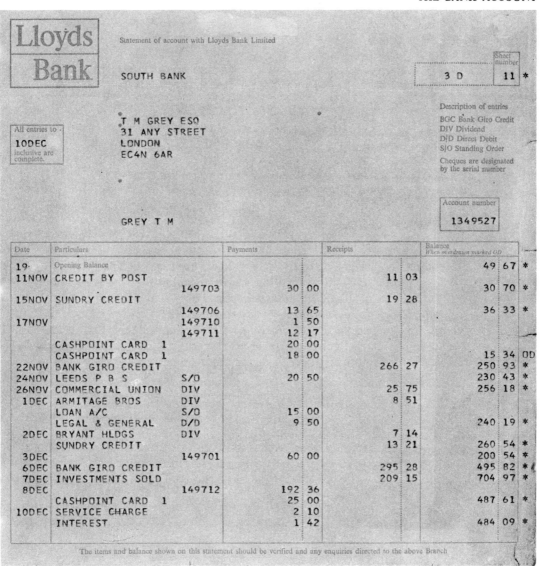

Sample bank statement

4. Credit Sales

Recording credit sales

(This chapter requires you to be able to calculate percentages. If you are not sure of your ability to do this, look first at the section in this chapter headed Percentages and try the exercises.)

Joe's business—selling carpets to hotels, business firms, and other similar organizations—requires him to sell on credit. This means that each sale involves an invoice being prepared. An invoice is simply the bill that the seller sends to the buyer, showing details of the goods supplied, the price, any discounts, and any extra costs (such as insurance, transport and containers) that the buyer must pay. Printed on the invoice there will be the *terms of trade* which show the conditions under which the seller supplies the goods—for example, that the seller will allow the buyer a cash discount for prompt payment of the amount owing.

Joe hands a bundle of copy invoices to you—look at the top one and listen to what Joe says.

Joe Wynn Carpet Dealer 14/15 Bow Road		INVOICE TO: Inv. No. 32 STAR HOTEL QUAYSIDE BOOLE Date June 1		
Goods		Qty.	Unit Price	Total Price
Axminster A4		10 metres	£5·00	50·00
Wilton A1		5 "	£6·00	30·00
				80·00
Less Trade Discount		at 25%		20·00
				60·00
Terms E. & O.E.				

Copy invoice

20

1 The top copy of each invoice has been sent to the customer. These are our file copies.
2 E. & O.E. means Errors and Omissions Excepted. We reserve the right to correct any errors, should there be any.

The customer's name and the invoice total need to be entered in the Sales Day Book. I call it the Sales Day Book, but other firms may call it the Sales Book or the Sales Journal. This book is needed to record credit sales and is described as a *book of original entry* (or *prime entry*). This is how it should be entered—I'll do the first one to show you.

SALES DAY BOOK

(Invoice Total column)

Date	Customer and Details	Folio	£ p	£ p
19-7 Jun. 1	Star Hotel Inv. No. 32			60·00

(Normal usage—note that only the date, name, invoice number and total are entered.)

I do it like this—but I'll show you how it is sometimes entered somewhat differently:

Date	Customer and Details	Folio	£ p	£ p
19-7 Jun.1	Star Hotel Inv. No. 32			
	Axminster 10 metres		50·00	
	Wilton 5 "		30·00	
			80·00	
	Less Trade Discount at 25%		20·00	60·00

(Examination requirement)

Students should note that some examination questions set on this topic will require you to demonstrate the second method—which shows the details on the invoices copied into the Sales Day Book. *Please read all examination questions carefully.*

21

Now you have seen the first invoice entered, copy the entry into your own Sales Day Book and then enter the rest of the invoices.

4.01 Invoice No. 33 Sales to A.B.C. Carpets Ltd.
15 metres of Wilton A3 @ £6 per metre.
10 metres of Wilton A2 @ £7 per metre.
Invoice No. 34 Sales to Poplar Treads Ltd.
5 metres of cord @ £4 per metre
35 metres of underlay @ 50p per metre.
All less 50 per cent. trade discount.
Invoice No. 35 Sales to Sounds International Ltd.
14 metres Cordex @ £5 per metre less 20 per cent trade discount.
10 metres Cordex @ £4 per metre less 25 per cent trade discount.

4.02 Add up the amounts you have entered in the Invoice Total column and write the sum underneath the last entry.

Percentages You should be able to work out discounts which are expressed as percentages. The following calculation can be used.
(a) 25% (25 per cent) = 25 out of a hundred = $\frac{25}{100}$ (as a fraction)
in other words 25% = one quarter ($\frac{1}{4}$).
Therefore 25% of £80 = one quarter of £80 = £20.
To do the calculation you can write

$$\frac{25}{100} \times \frac{£80}{1} = \frac{2{,}000}{100} = £20$$

Cancellation of the fraction will enable you to do the calculation more quickly, e.g.

$$\frac{25}{100}{}^{1}_{4} \times 80 = \frac{80}{4} = £20$$

(b) Convert the percentage into a decimal fraction and multiply the amount by the decimal fraction,
e.g.   25% = $\frac{25}{100}$ = 0.25
Therefore 25% of £80 = £80 × 0.25
(using long multiplication) = £20

Try the following exercises.
4.03 (a) Calculate   50% of £180; £95; £143.
(b) Calculate   25% of £160; £125; £73.
(c) Calculate 12$\frac{1}{2}$% of £160; £125; £73.
(d) Calculate   15% of £200; £130; £85.
(e) Calculate 2$\frac{1}{2}$% of £50; £20; £2.
(f) Calculate   5% of £45; £12; £2.50.

(a) Calculate   10% of £11.00; £118.00.   **4.04**
(b) Calculate   25% of £44; £120; £98.40.
(c) Calculate   33⅓% of £66; £72; £18.90.
(d) Calculate   45% of £70; £90; £130.

Open the Cash Book, Bank Book and enter these balances.   **NA 4.05**

June 1   Cash £42.50 (Dr), Bank £1,240 (Dr).
          Enter the following transactions in the two books above and the Sales Day Book.
       2   Purchased goods by cheque £395.00.
       4   Sold goods on credit to P.P. Berry for £125.00 net and T.T. Edwards £200.00 less 40 per cent trade discount.
       5   Paid sundry expenses in cash: stationery 95p; fares 42p; office sundries £1.45.
       8   Cash sales to date £342.00.
       9   Paid £300.00 into bank.
      12   Owner withdrew £50 from the bank.
      15   Sold goods on credit to S.S. Jenkins £84 less 25 per cent trade discount; plus £10.00 for a returnable carton.
      19   Made a loan to F. Wood £100.00—giving a cheque.
      24   Cash sales to date £450.00.
      25   Paid all cash in hand into bank.

Balance the Cash and Bank Accounts and total the Sales Day Book.

Trade discount

On Invoice No. 32 a *trade discount* of 25 per cent was shown. It represents a reduction in the selling price or an allowance made by the seller to the buyer. It is usually allowed only on transactions between businesses 'in the trade'—i.e., the manufacturer will allow it to the wholesaler, the wholesaler will allow it to the retailer. The retailer will sell it at a *net price*—i.c., a price without any reduction. Between traders, the trade discount can represent the profit that the buyer will make on reselling the goods.

When entering invoices in the Sales Day Book, you will see from the illustration on page 24 that only the net total of the invoice is shown in the final column. It is this net amount that is owed by the customer. Our business may purchase goods and receive a trade discount from our supplier. This will be explained in chapter 11.

Quantity discount (or bulk discount)

This is a reduction in the selling price because the buyer has purchased a large quantity. The discount can increase as the quantity purchased increases. Suppliers will usually quote the rates of discount on the price lists they supply to customers. You are aware that the large stores and multiple shops often sell products at a price lower than the smaller shops. This is often because they can buy very large quantities from the manufacturer—and thus obtain substantial discounts. This lower buying price is then passed on to the customer in the form of lower selling prices.

SALES DAY BOOK

DATE	CUSTOMER AND DETAILS		FOLIO	£	p	£	p
Jun. 1.	Star Hotel	Inv. No.32				60 · 00	
	Eagle Ins. Co.	33				89 · 75	
	Talyor Stores	34				149 · 83	
	Woodman & Son	35				61 · 90	
	Harper & Co. Ltd.	36				187 · 60	
	Wilson Bros	37				348 · 00	
	Boothroyd	38				75 · 00	
	Cannon~Taylor	39				143 · 00	
Jun.30	Total Sales					1,115 · 08	

Charges for containers

Firms that manufacture expensive or large products usually have to pack them very carefully. Liquids have to be kept in barrels or other containers, wire has to be coiled onto drums, and so on. Such containers can be very expensive, and it is usual to charge customers for the container as well as the product. This charge may be refundable on the return of the container. The charge is added to the net price of the goods on the invoice, so the net invoice charge entered in the Sales Day Book is for goods and containers. If the customer does return the container and is eligible for a refund, a separate record must be made of the returns, and this is explained in chapter 13.

Documents

Invoice (Inv) Prepared by the seller and sent to his customer, it shows the goods sold, with descriptions, quantities, prices, and trade discounts. It may include additional charges—for insurance, carriage, and containers. It then shows the total amount due to the seller.

If the customer has been undercharged on the invoice (due to error) the seller can send a *debit note*. It is used to debit the account of the customer in the same way as an invoice. It is recorded in the books and entered in exactly the same way as an invoice.

Debit note (D/N)

To finish this chapter look at Joe's fourth rule.

The Sales Day Book records *credit sales only* and the net total shown on sales invoices is the actual value of sales.

Joe's Rule No. 4

5. Sales Ledger (or Debtors Ledger)

The Sales Ledger records the amounts due to us from debtors—customers to whom we have sold goods on credit. You will probably say that the Sales Day Book that was discussed in the previous chapter records the same amounts. It does—but the invoices entered in that book are in strict date/number order. It does not show us how much a customer owes us for sales and chargeable containers, how much he has paid, and when he paid, what value of goods and containers he sent back to us (if any), or whether we gave him a discount for prompt payment of his bills. All these details are recorded in his account in the ledger. Let Joe explain.

Each customer has a separate page in the Sales Ledger to record the details of all the transactions between us. These details represent the *account* of the customer—so the Sales Ledger contains records of all customers who have bought goods on credit. Let me show you one of the accounts—and see ledger reference number—S1.

Sounds International Ltd. Account   S1

Date	Details	Folio	£ p	Date	Details	Folio	£ p
19-7							
Mar 1	Sales	SDB33	49·00				
Jul. 14	Sales	SDB48	171·00				

These are debit entries and show what is owed to us.

Look at these two items: Date and Folio. The date is that shown on the invoice; he owes us money because we have sold goods to him and the Folio column shows the page number in the Sales Day Book in which this invoice is recorded.

5.01   One part of the bookkeeper's job is to *post* the entries made in books of original entry to the ledger accounts. Can you remember the three books of original entry so far discussed?

By the way, *posting* is the bookkeeping term for transferring the details of a transaction from the book of original entry (where the very first book record is made) into the ledger account.

Two of the three books of original entry so far discussed are also Accounts. Can you remember which ones?

5.02

You must remember that the Sales Ledger does *not* show the sales made by the business—it only records the accounts of debtors—that is why an alternative name for this ledger is the *Debtors Ledger* (it contains the personal accounts of debtors). It may also be described as one of the *personal ledgers*—i.e., a ledger containing personal accounts. There are some things you must learn about debtors' accounts. First, a debtor owes us money and, since that money really belongs to us, it is an asset. So, *debtors* are *assets*. Second, an asset appears on the debit side of the account. (Debtors could be called 'debitors'—useful to remember that.) Third, the value of the asset is the debit balance on the account. You should be able to remember how to balance an account. Let us balance Sounds International Ltd. account.

Method 1 Proper balancing   *Method 2(a)* Pencil totals

Sounds Int. Account

Mar. 1 Sales 49·00	Bal. c/d 220·00	Mar 1 Sales 49·00
July 14 Sales 171·00		July 14 Sales 171·00
		220.00
220·00	220·00	
July 15 Bal b/d 220·00		

Method 2(b) Pencil totals when the account has both debit and credit entries

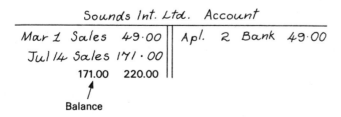

Sounds Int. Ltd. Account

Mar 1 Sales 49·00	Apl. 2 Bank 49·00
Jul 14 Sales 171·00	
171.00 220.00	

↑
Balance

Procedure   This is the procedure for dealing with credit sales.

Step 1   Prepare invoices and send top copy to customer.

Step 2   From copy invoices enter the Sales Day Book.

Step 3   Post the entries in the Sales Day Book to the ledger accounts, entering the folio references in both books.

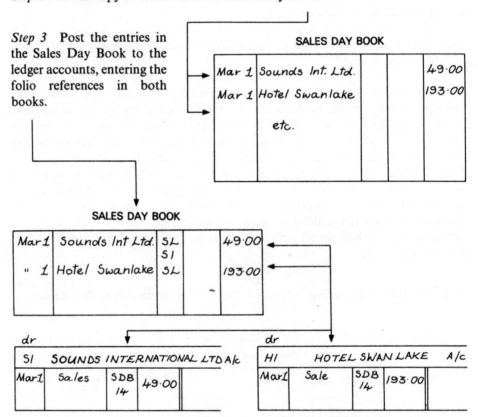

Books and accounts

The Sales Day Book is *not* an account. It does not show the balances owing by customers and it does not show the balance of sales made. It is a *memorandum book*—and from the weekly or monthly totals we can record the total sales credit in a *Sales Account.*

Joe's Rule No. 5   Customers' accounts are debited with the value of credit sales made to them, by posting the entries from the Sales Day Book.

Books of original entry

There is another important rule that needs to be learned. In the previous chapter and in the illustrations in this chapter, you have seen that the very first record of credit

28

sales is made in the Sales Day Book. The entry in the accounts is then made from the Sales Day Book. A similar procedure is adopted for *all* other transactions: that is, the *first* record of the transaction will be made in a book of original entry.

The first record of any transaction must be made in a book of original entry.

Joe's Rule No. 6

Let me give you an example that you know already. If cash sales are made, where do we record the receipt of cash? In the Cash Book. Therefore the Cash Book must be a book of original entry. If we pay a cheque for some petrol that we buy while delivering carpets, where does the first record of that expense appear? In the Bank Book. So the Bank Book is also a book of original entry. The other books of original entry that you will have to learn are

the Bought Day Book   (chapter 11)
the Sales Returns Book   (chapter 13)
the Purchases Returns Book (chapter 13)
the Journal   (chapter 19)
the Petty Cash Book   (chapter 21)

Now try the following exercises, remembering always to read the instructions carefully.

5.03

Enter the following transactions in your Sales Day Book, total the Sales Day Book, and post to the ledger accounts. (Use the same ledger accounts for **5.03**, **5.04**, and **5.05**.)

Apr. 1   Sold on credit to Sounds International Ltd.:
            5 metres Axminster A1 carpets @ £5 per metre
            $7\frac{1}{2}$ metres Wilton carpet @ £4 per metre
            14 metres underfelt @ £1.50 per metre.

Apr. 1   Sold on credit to Hotel Swanlake:
            2 doz. rugs @ £1.50 each
            30 door mats @ 70p each
            50 metres cleaning rugs @ 30p per metre.

5.04

Apr. 10   Sold on credit to Bow Office Furnishers Ltd.:
            25 metres Wilton carpet @ £4 per metre
            25 metres underfelt @ £1.50 per metre
            10 5-litre tins paint @ £3.40 per tin.

Apr. 10   Sold on credit to Hotel Swanlake:
            20 door mats @ 70p each
            8 tins paint @ £3.40 per tin
            3 tins emulsion paint @ £2.20 per tin.

5.05   Apr. 26   Sold to Metro Shopfitters & Furnishers Ltd. on credit:
16 tins gloss paint @ £3.15 per tin
80 metres furnishing material @ £4.10 per metre
17 metres Axminster carpet @ £5 per metre
Assorted end of range furnishing materials for £120.
We allowed them 20 per cent trade discount.
Returnable containers were charged at £15.00.

                 Apr. 27   Sold to Bow Office Furnishers Ltd.:
25 tins wood polish @ 60p per tin
40 tins carpet shampoo @ £2.50 per tin
120 metres furnishing material @ £4.10 per metre.
We allowed them 20 per cent trade discount.
Returnable containers were charged at £12.50.

Save the ledger accounts you have entered for **5.03**, **5.04**, and **5.05**. You will need them for the next chapter.

6. Receipts from Debtors

Now we are going to use the Cash Book, the Bank Book, and also the Sales Ledger. Debtors owe us money and when they pay, either by cheque or cash, the receipt of that payment is recorded in the Cash Account or Bank Account, on the debit side (it *increases* our asset of cash). The asset of cash goes up, but the asset of debtors goes down; therefore we must reduce the debtor's account. Look at the account of Sounds International Ltd.

Sounds International Ltd. Account

Mar. 1	Sales	SDB 14	49.00				

When we receive payment of the debt of £49.00, where should the entry be made to show that Sounds International have paid their debt? It can't be put on the debit side because that would make it appear that we were owed £98.00—therefore it *must* be entered on the credit side, as follows.

Sounds International Ltd. Account

Mar. 1	Sales	SDB 14	49.00	Apr. 2	Bank	BB 3	49.00

There is now no balance on this account. Note that the credit entry shows the date that the payment was received and entered in the Bank Book, that it was a cheque paid into the bank, and the Folio column shows the Bank Book page on which it is recorded.

Remember: the cheque was received and recorded in the *Bank Book*, which is the book of original entry, and only then was it posted to the ledger account. If we had received payment in cash, it would be debited to the Cash Account (and then credited to the ledger account of Sounds International Ltd.). You must learn the rule below.

Receipts from debtors are entered in the Cash Account (or Bank Account) as a debit and in the debtor's personal account in the Sales Ledger as a credit.

Joe's Rule No. 7

31

Rule No. 7 illustrates a principle which you have already learned regarding the Cash Book and Bank Book, that value received is debited and value given is credited. A quick look back at the Bank Book will show this. But the rule is now being extended to include value given by debtors; after all, when they pay, they give money to us. The receipt by us is recorded as a debit entry and their payment is recorded as a credit entry. These are the two aspects of each transaction—and each transaction must be both debited and credited. This is the principle of *double entry*, about which you will hear a lot more. One other point to look at and remember: each account has a Detail column. In this column is written the title of the account in which the second of the two entries appears. The following example should make it clear.

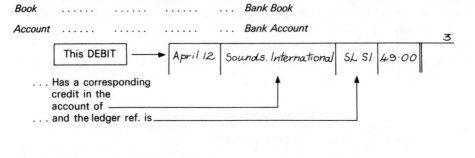

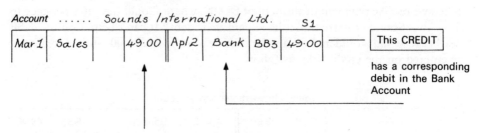

6.01 In which account is the corresponding credit entry for this debit?

When you have worked out the answer to **6.01** you will say that you haven't learned that account yet. And also, which ledger is that account kept in? Before explaining it in detail, try the following exercises.

6.02 Take out the ledger accounts you have prepared for exercises **5.03**, **5.04**, and **5.05**, and the Cash Book and Bank Book. The following payments are received; enter the receipts in the appropriate book (Cash or Bank) and post to the debtors' accounts. Balance the debtor's account.

Apr. 15 Received from Sounds International Ltd. a cheque for £76.00.
     16 Received from Hotel Swanlake a cheque for £72.00.
     19 Received from Hotel Swanlake cash £47.80.
     27 Bow Office Furnishers Ltd. paid us £171.50 by cheque.

Enter the following transactions in the appropriate record books and post to the **6.03**
ledger.

May	1	Sold to James Garner on credit assorted rugs for £16.85.
	2	Sold for cash 12 metres Wilton carpet @ £4 per metre.
	2	Sold for cash 10 tins paint @ £2.80 each.
	6	Received a cheque for £400.00 from Office Furnishers Ltd.
	12	Sold the following on credit to Office Furnishers Ltd.:

Office Furnishers Ltd. (May 12):
50 door mats @ 70p each.
25 tins paint @ £2.50 each.
12 metres cleaning rug @ 45p per metre.
We allow them 20 per cent trade discount.

May 16 Sold assorted furnishing materials for cash £16.50.

May 18 Shop Fitters Ltd. paid us £473.00 by cheque.

May 21 Sold on credit to Shop Fitters Ltd.:
6 paint brushes @ £1.15 each.
10 metres Axminster A1 @ £6.15 per metre.
No discount was allowed.

May 23 Sold on credit to W. Ing.:
20 metres Axminster A1 at £6.35 per metre.
40 metres Axminster SA1 at £7.80 per metre.
Trade discount of 25 per cent was allowed.
A charge of £20 was made for supporting containers.

The Sales Account

To keep an accurate record of sales, a separate account must be opened to record both cash sales and credit sales. Applying the principle of double entry to cash sales, we received cash because we sold (or gave) value of stock.

The bookkeeping entries are:

Debit Cash Account: Credit Sales Account.

Applying the same principle to credit sales, the bookkeeping entries are:

Debit the Customer's Account (the customer received the value): Credit Sales Account.

Look at the following ledger entries.

Cash Account

Oct.	3	Sales	48.00
	10	Sales	31.00

A. Customer Account

Oct.	5	Sales	92.00

B. Customer Account

Oct. 15	Sales	137.50	

C. Customer Account

Oct. 8	Sales	73.50	

These accounts are *asset* accounts. Cash is what actually exists. Debtors record the amount owing to the business.

Sales Account

	Oct. 3	Cash	48.00
	5	A. Customer	92.00
	8	C. Customer	73.50
	10	Cash	31.00
	15	B. Customer	137.50

This account is an *income* account—it shows the sales that the business has made. Cash sales and credit sales are both 'income'—after all, the customer will pay us cash in due course. The Sales Account records the selling price of stock sold.

Applying **Joe's Rule No. 6:** Cash sales are recorded in the Cash Book; credit sales are recorded in the Sales Day Book; and payments received are recorded in the Cash or Bank Book.

Returnable containers

If returnable containers have been charged to a customer, then the customer's account has been debited with the amount and the charge made added to the sales figure in the Sales Account. In practice it may be credited to a Container Account, but this is dealt with in more detail later on (see page 36). When the customer returns the containers, he needs to be refunded with the amount originally charged, if he has paid the original bill. If he has not paid, then his account is credited in order to reduce the amount owing to us.

Now: we *receive* the container, he *gives* it. So which account do we debit? The answer is: a *Sales Returns Account*. The Sales Returns Account represents the value of the sales previously made, now returned to us. Exactly the same treatment is given to goods that are actually returned which the customer may have found damaged or incorrect.

The book of original entry to record returns, of both goods and containers, is the *Sales Returns Book*, and this is explained in detail later; but look at the example of the ledger entries below.

If we sell goods to S. Hoe value £28.00:

Debit S. Hoe's account: Credit Sales Account.

If S. Hoe returns the goods as unsatisfactory and we allow full credit (i.e., full refund):

Credit S. Hoe's account: Debit Sales Returns Account.

A simple rule to learn: if sales are credits (recorded in the Sales Account) then sales returns are debits (recorded in the Sales Returns Account). After all, sales *returns* are the opposite to sales.

If a shop customer, who had paid cash for his goods, returned to the shop and he was refunded his money, what would the two ledger entries be?

6.04

Statement of account

If we look at a debtor's account in the Sales Ledger we should be able to see exactly what the latest position is regarding how much is owed to us. Like many firms, we send a copy of the account to the customer—thereby pointing out exactly what we

The Progressive Company (Wholesale) Limited
Hardware Factors and General Wholesalers

Progressive Works
Anytown
England
Telephone: Any 500
Telegrams: Speeds England
VAT Registered no. 64070

WARD & Co. LTD,
Long Row, CALNE,
Wilts.
SN11 001

Statement
Date

Date	Ref no	Details	VAT		Debit		Credit		Balance	
Sept. 1		A/c Rendered							357	22
Sept. 2	919	Goods	1	75	17	50			376	47
Sept. 3	987	Goods		97	9	75			387	19
Sept. 7	413	Cash					357	22	29	97
Sept. 8	1079	Goods	3	95	39	48			73	40
Sept. 18	1189	Goods	6	67	66	70			146	77

Kalamazoo
FB-10B-690504-7½x6½

Last amount in the balance column is the amount owing

believe the position is regarding his account. The copy we make is called a *statement*. It shows what transactions have taken place since the previous statement. The customer may not receive goods despatched to him and we may not receive payments made by him. His accounts may show different figures to those on our statement—through the statement, these errors are quickly detected.

A typical statement is shown on page 35.

Look at this example.

A statement is sent to 'The TV Centre' on 30 September.

Sept. 10	Goods Inv. No. 97	45.00	
Sept. 18	Goods Inv. No. 100	21.00	
		———	66.00
	E. & O.E.		

2   During October, sales are made to The TV Centre of £83.50 on 22 October and a cheque is received for £45.00 on 24 October. Invoice No. 102 included a £5 charge for a returnable container. This was returned on 29 October and the full amount of £5 was allowed.

3   The statement sent on 31 October will be:

Balance			66.00
Oct. 22	Goods Inv. No. 102	83.50	83.50
		———	———
			149.50
Oct. 24	Payment received		45.00
			———
			104.50
Oct. 29	Container refunded		5.00
			———
			99.50
	E. & O.E.		

Look at the illustration on the next page.

It shows a different way of keeping a ledger account. Instead of two columns to record debits and credits, three columns are used. One is for debits, one for credits,

Three-column ledger accounts

NAME WARD & Co. LTD.   ACCOUNT NO.
ADDRESS Long Row, CALN, Wilts SN11 001   CR. £500

DATE	REF. NO.	DETAILS	VAT		DEBIT	CREDIT	BALANCE	OLD BALANCE
		Bal. B/fwd.					129 50	
Aug 19	827	Goods		35	3 51		133 36	129 50
Aug 21	841	Goods	10	04	100 43		243 83	133 36
Aug 23	852	Goods	5	26	52 62		301 71	243 83
Aug 28	878	Goods	1	72	17 23		320 66	301 71
Aug 28	864	Goods	3	32	33 24		357 22	320 66
Sept 2	919	Goods	1	75	17 50		376 47	357 22
Sept 3	987	Goods		97	9 75		387 19	376 47
Sept 7	413	Cash				357 22	29 97	387 19
Sept 8	1079	Goods	3	95	39 48		73 40	29 97
Sept 18	1189	Goods	6	67	66 70		146 77	73 40

and the third one is to maintain a running balance of the account. Look at this example of the account for The TV Centre.

Usual ledger account
The TV Centre Account   T3

Sept. 10	Sales	45.00	Sept. 30	Bal. c/d		66.00
18	Sales	21.00				
		66.00				66.00
Oct. 1	Bal. b/d	66.00	Oct. 24	Bank		45.00
22	Sales	83.50	29	Returns		5.00
			31	Bal. c/d		99.50
		149.50				149.50
Nov. 1	Bal. b/d	99.50				

This is the usual method of handwritten accounts in ledgers, and is used in this textbook.

Three-column ledger account
The TV Centre Account

		Dr	Cr	Bal.
Sept. 10	Sales	45.00		45.00
18	Sales	21.00		66.00
Oct. 22	Sales	83.50		149.50
24	Bank		45.00	104.50
29	Returns		5.00	99.50

This type of account is found in systems using accounting machines and is also commonly used in handwritten business systems such as Kalamazoo.

6.05 Draw up a statement to be sent to S. Heep at the end of December from the following details.

Nov. 30   Balance owing to us £144.00.
Dec. 5   Invoice No. A/6142 for goods sold—net value £65.00.
       8   Cheque received from S. Heep value £5.00.
      14   Invoice No. A/6167 for goods sold—gross value £80, less 20 per cent trade discount. Containers charged at £7.50.
      16   Debit note sent to correct invoice No. A/6167 which should have shown a gross value of £90.
      29   Cheque received from S. Heep in respect of Invoice No. A/6142.

6.06 From the following information prepare the account of G. Oat as it would appear in the Sales Ledger of F. Harmer and Co., balance the account, and bring down the balance on 1 June.

May 1   Balance due to F. Harmer & Co. £78.00.
     6   Sales to Oat £48.00 net.
     8   Harmer & Co. charged Oat £14.00 for returnable containers.
    15   Harmer & Co. received the containers returned by Oat and they allowed credit in full.
    24   Oat sent a cheque for the balance due on 1 May.
    28   Purchases by Oat of goods at a catalogue price of £80 less 15 per cent trade discount.

NA 6.07 Prepare a three-column Sales Ledger Account for T. Ree as it would appear in the books of A. Wood after the following transactions.

Nov. 1   Balance due to A. Wood £42.00.
         Wood sold goods to Ree at a catalogue price of £250.00 less 25 per cent trade discount. A charge of £22 was also made for containers.

Nov. 5   Ree returned goods at a catalogue price of £50.
     18   Ree returned the containers and was allowed a credit of £16.00.
     24   Purchases by Ree of £86.75 net.
     28   Ree paid the amount due on 1 November.

7. Nominal (or General) Ledger

The Sales or Debtors Ledger keeps debtors' accounts. The Creditors or Bought Ledger keeps creditors' accounts (see chapter 12). Therefore a Nominal (or General) Ledger keeps nominal accounts. But what are these? First, can you remember the definition of an account?

If you can you will know that the *Cash Account* keeps a record of *cash in hand*; and the *Bank Account* keeps a record of the *cash in the bank*. P. E. Smith's Account keeps a record of our transactions with P. E. Smith.

7.01   Therefore, what name would we give to an account that keeps a record of:

(a) rent   (e) sales

(b) wages   (f) insurance

(c) motor running expenses   (g) discounts allowed

(d) fixtures and fittings   (h) rent received.

So far the only records you have of expenses paid are in the Cash Book and the Bank Book. If you wish to find out how much you have paid during the year for a particular expense, say motor running expenses (petrol, maintenance, repairs, licences, taxes), you would have to look through the whole of the Cash Book and Bank Book and add up all the individual entries. This would be a long and tedious job. The double entry principle, already explained, enables you to solve this problem.

The principle of double entry

Remember that the bookkeeper is working on behalf of a business, that is, his employer. All transactions are therefore considered from the viewpoint of the business in whose books the transactions are being recorded. The next important rule is that each and every transaction has two aspects—both a giving and a receiving one. Joe will have to explain.

We never pay money out unless we receive something in exchange. It may be stock, or it may be other assets, such as fixtures, cabinets, display stands, or motor vehicles. Even if we pay wages, we receive the services of the employee. If we pay rent, we receive the use of the premises; if we pay bank charges, we receive the use of the banking facilities.

What we must do is to record both the giving and the receiving aspects of each transaction. You already know how to record the giving aspect.

Just to remind you: if we pay out £950 for a display cabinet and we pay by cheque, how is the payment recorded?

7.02

But that entry only records the giving aspect. In order to record the fact that we have *received* the *value* of a display cabinet, it must be entered also into a separate account, called the Fixtures and Fittings Account. (Chairs, desks, cabinets, and similar assets are usually entered into this one account rather than opening separate accounts.) I have already told you that values given are credited (e.g., a payment of cash is credited in the Cash Account) and that values received are debited (for example, cash received is debited in the Cash Account). Now you must learn that this rule applies to *all* transactions; value received is debited and value given is credited. A simple rule, but one you must remember.

For every debit entry there is a corresponding credit entry in another account.

Joe's Rule No. 8

Look at the illustration on page 42. Imagine the accountant who is inspecting the books opening the Cash Book at page 18. He can see that certain entries in the book have been posted to the nominal accounts in the ledger because there is a folio reference in the Folio column of the Cash Book. The three credit entries on 5 March do not have such reference numbers and therefore they have yet to be posted to the ledger. One point should be made clear regarding the value of sales of 1 March of £248. We received the money, and therefore *debit* the Cash Account. We only received the money from a customer because we gave that value of stock to the customer. The value represents our sales price of the stock and is therefore recorded in the Sales Account.

Suggest the nominal accounts to which the payments made on 5 March should be posted.

7.03

Nominal accounts are those that record expenses and incomes. You are familiar with expenses, but are perhaps not aware that a business may receive income from sources other than sales. For example: rent received from subletting a part of its property; dividends on investments; interest on bank deposits; insurance claims; and sale of assets.

Nominal accounts

This name is given to those accounts that record real assets—machinery, buildings, vehicles, office equipment, and so on. These accounts are often kept in the Nominal Ledger although large businesses will keep them all in a separate Asset Ledger.

Real accounts

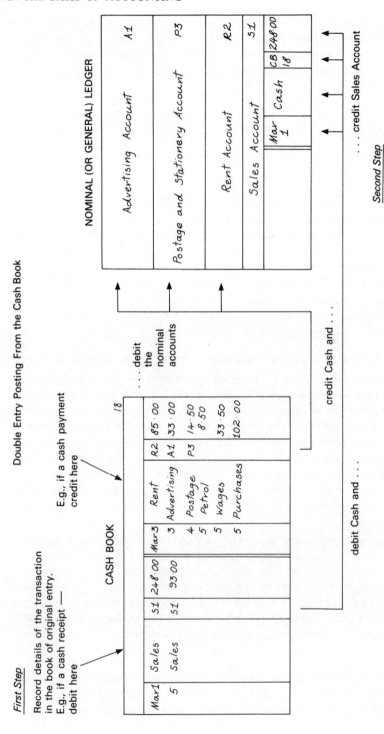

Double Entry Posting From the Cash Book

First Step

Record details of the transaction in the book of original entry. E.g., if a cash receipt — debit here

E.g., if a cash payment credit here

In posting details—copy the date, and the amount; enter *Cash* in the Detail column (this is the name of the account where the 'other' entry appears); enter the Cash Book folio reference page number; enter the nominal account folio reference number in the Folio column of the Cash Account.

These are accounts of people with whom our business deals—mainly customers and suppliers.

Double entry from the Sales Day Book

The illustration below shows the double entries required to record sales on credit. The person buying the goods—the debtor—must have his account debited, while the value of the sales made must be credited to the Sales Account. The first record, as you remember from chapter 4, is made by entering the details of the sale from the

Posting of Sales Invoices

STEP 1   Enter the Sales Day Book from copy invoices

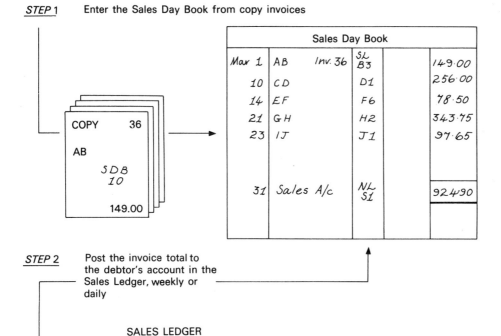

Sales Day Book				
Mar 1	AB	Inv. 36	SL B3	149·00
10	CD		D1	256·00
14	EF		F6	78·50
21	GH		H2	343·75
23	IJ		J1	97·65
31	Sales A/c		NL S1	924·90

COPY   36

AB

SDB 10

149.00

STEP 2   Post the invoice total to the debtor's account in the Sales Ledger, weekly or daily

SALES LEDGER

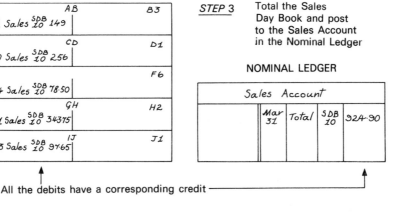

AB		B3
Mar1 Sales SDB10 149		

CD		D1
Mar10 Sales SDB10 256		

		F6
Mar14 Sales SDB10 78·50		

GH		H2
Mar21 Sales SDB10 343·75		

IJ		J1
Mar23 Sales SDB10 97·65		

STEP 3   Total the Sales Day Book and post to the Sales Account in the Nominal Ledger

NOMINAL LEDGER

Sales Account				
		Mar 31	Total	SDB 10 924·90

All the debits have a corresponding credit ─────────

copy invoice (Step 1). Remembering that the Sales Day Book is *not* an account, but only a memorandum book, the debtor's account will be debited (Step 2) and the Sales Account will be credited (Step 3) with the total of all the sales.

Do these exercises

7.04 Enter the name of the account to be debited and the account to be credited for these transactions.

	Account to be	
	debited	*credited*
(a) Purchased a motor van, paying by cheque	M V	Bank
(b) Purchased carpets for resale, paying cash	Stock	Cash
(c) Paid rent by cheque	Rent	Bank
(d) Sales for cash	– Cash	– Sales
(e) Sold goods on credit to A. Smith	– DL	– Sales
(f) Sold goods on credit to P. Taylor	– DL	– Sales
(g) Paid insurance by cheque	Ins	Bank
(h) Paid wages by cash	Wage	Cash
(i) Owner withdrew cash	Drawing	Cash

7.05 Give the name of the ledger in which the following accounts will be kept.

(a) Sales. – Sale
(b) Purchases. – Purchases
(c) A. Smith—debtor. – Debtors
(d) Machinery and Plant. – Asset
(e) Wages. – Nomal

(f) Commissions Received.
(g) Losses on till takings.
(h) Discounts. – Nomal
(i) D. Jones—creditor. – Creditor

7.06 (a) Using the Cash Book, Bank Book, Sales Day Book, Sales Ledger, and General Ledger, enter the following transactions for May. As soon as you have recorded the transactions in a book of original entry, you should post the details to the ledger account.

(b) At the end of the month, total the Sales Day Book and post to the nominal account. Balance the Cash Book, Bank Book, and Sales Ledger accounts.

Mar.	1	Cash sales £148.00.
	2	Paid cash into bank £100.00.
		Paid wages in cash £22.00.
	3	Paid printing expenses in cash £15.50.
	4	Cash sales £95.00.
		Sold goods on credit to P. Brown £48.75.
	5	Paid rent by cheque £48.00.
		Sold goods on credit to A. Shaw £65.25.
	8	P. Brown paid his account by cheque, paying £48.00 in full settlement.

Mar. 10   Cash sales £173.60.
             Paid wages in cash £22.00.
             Paid cash into bank £110.00.
- 14   Sold goods on credit to M. Miller £36.50.
- 18   Paid cash for shop display stand £18.90.
- 19   Sold goods on credit to A. Shaw £42.30.
- 21   Paid for purchases by cheque £265.00.
- 23   Cash sales £162.00.
             Paid wages in cash £44.00.
- 24   Miller returned goods valued £8.00 and was allowed full credit.
- 26   M. Miller paid £20 on account by cheque.
- 28   The owner drew £10 cash for his own use.

(c) Make a list of the accounts with debit balances and a list of those with credit balances. Total each list. If your double entry has been correct, the two lists should agree.

In the illustration on page 43 Invoice No. 36 has SDB 10 written on the front. What is this?   **7.07**

Purchase of assets on credit

So far we have purchased everything for cash. Many purchases are made on credit—that is, purchased now with the intention of paying later. A record must be made immediately after the purchase is made. In the case of assets we need to record the fact that the item now belongs to us and also that we owe that value to the supplier.

The rules learned apply as follows.

1 We receive the value of the asset—therefore debit the Asset Account.
2 The supplier 'gives' the value of the asset—therefore credit the supplier's account.

Sooner or later we will have to pay the supplier, and when that happens:

3 We give the cash—therefore credit the Cash (or Bank) Account.
4 The supplier receives the cash—therefore debit his account.

On 1 May we buy a pair of scales from Measure Right Ltd. at a cost of £58 and on 30 May we pay the bill by cheque. The ledger entries are: **Example**

Shop Fixtures Account

May 1   Measure Right   58.00

Measure Right Ltd. Account

May 30 Bank 58.00 | May 1 Shop fixtures 58.00

Bank Account

	May 30	Measure Right Ltd.	58.00

Between 1 May and 30 May the account of Measure Right Ltd. had a credit balance. He was a *creditor* (someone to whom we owed money). Creditors are liabilities.

Asset purchases in a book of original entry

In chapter 5 (**Joe's Rule No. 6**) you were told that all transactions should go through a book of original entry—and this includes the purchase and sale of assets. If assets were purchased for cash, then the payment would be first recorded in the Cash Book or Bank Book (both books of original entry) and posted to the asset account in the ledger. Assets purchased on credit are first entered in either the Journal or the analysed Bought Day Book. Since both of these books are dealt with at a later stage, you must assume, for the time being, that entries for assets purchased on credit are entered directly to the two ledger accounts concerned, that is—debit the asset account and credit the supplier's account.

Capital expenditure

Assets purchased are going to be used in the business. No doubt they will wear out eventually, but they will be kept until such time as they are no longer useful. All expenditure on assets to be retained in business for a long period of time (i.e. fixed assets) is called *capital expenditure*.

Revenue expenditure

Expenses incurred in operating the daily affairs of the business—such as rent, wages, travelling, insurance, advertising, and so on—are called *revenue expenditure*.

Capital and revenue expenditure are further considered in chapter 17.

7.08

Enter the name of the account to be debited and the account to be credited for the following transactions. (Use a sheet of paper for writing your answer.)

Account to be
debited   credited

(a) Motor van purchased on credit from R. A. Garage Ltd.
(b) Display cabinets purchased on credit from Shop Fitters Ltd.
(c) Cheque paid to Shop Fitters Ltd.
(d) Cash deposit paid to B. Worth for purchase of office desk.
(e) Cheque received for the sale of old office equipment.

7.09

Enter the following details into the Cash Book, Bank Book, and Sales Day Book and make the double entry posting to the Sales Ledger and General Ledger.

			£
Apr.	1	Balance at bank	400.00 (credit)
		Cash balance	50.00 (debit)
	2	Cash sales	175.00
	5	Purchased warehouse racks on credit from Rackhams Ltd.	285.00
		Paid a deposit to Rackhams by cheque	50.00
	7	Sold goods on credit to M. Miller	45.00
		P. White	85.00
	9	Paid wages in cash	77.00
	10	Purchased loading truck on credit from Forklifts Ltd.	1,950.00
		Paid a deposit by cheque to Forklifts Ltd.	150.00
	12	Received a cheque from M. Miller	45.00
	14	Paid by cheque the balance on Rackhams' account	
	15	Paid all cash in hand into the bank	
	16	Sold goods on credit to P. White	56.00
		S. Bond	19.50
		Cash sales	167.40
		Paid wages in cash	75.80
	18	Standing order payment for office machine rental	18.70
	19	Credit transfer receipt from P. White	85.00
	20	The owner drew a cheque	35.00
	21	Credit sales to P. Carter	88.75
		F. Taylor	28.45
	22	Paid cheque, on account, to Forklifts Ltd.	100.00
	23	Cash sales to date	342.90
		Paid wages in cash	78.65
	28	The owner drew cash	40.00
	30	Bank made interest charge	28.50

Which of the following items are revenue expenditure and which are capital expenditure?   **NA 7.10**

(a) Office desks and chairs.
(b) Repairs to plant and machinery.
(c) Motor vans.
(d) Painting the factory.
(e) Spare parts for factory machinery.
(f) A new piece of equipment that will enable a machine to be more efficient.
(g) A stock of stationery bought for the office.
(h) A new business sign to be displayed outside the factory.

Nominal accounts for cash discounts

Cash discounts are given to encourage a debtor to pay his bills promptly. By so doing he is entitled to reduce the bill by the agreed amount. These discounts are quite different from *trade discounts*. The invoice sent by the supplier will usually contain details of the *terms of trade*. These contain the conditions under which the supplier is selling goods to the buyer. If a discount is to be offered, it will state this on the invoice. For example: 'Terms—$2\frac{1}{2}$ per cent 7 days'. This means that the debtor can deduct $2\frac{1}{2}$ per cent from the invoice total if he pays within 7 days. Look at the effect on the accounts in the example below.

Example

A sells to B goods costing £100 and offers a cash discount, for prompt payment, of 5 per cent within 7 days.

In A's books the account for B will be:

	B's Account		
Sales	SDB 3	100.00	

If B pays the amount due within the period for claiming discount, he will send A a cheque for £95 (£100 less 5 per cent discount). Since a cheque for £95 has been received, it will be debited to the Bank Account and posted to the credit side of B's account. B's account now becomes:

	B's Account				
Sales	SDB 3	100.00	Bank	BB 8	95.00

It still appears, from B's account, that he owes £5 to A. This is not true, so the £5 must be taken out of B's account by entering the discount as a credit and posting the discount to a Discount Allowed Account (as a debit). A has allowed a discount to B and therefore A has made the loss of £5. The final position is:

	B's Account					B1
Sales	SDB 3	100.00	Bank	BB 8	95.00	
			Discount allowed	GL D3	5.00	

	Discount Allowed Account			D3
B's Account	SL B1	5.00		

What would the entries be in B's books?

The records in B's books show:

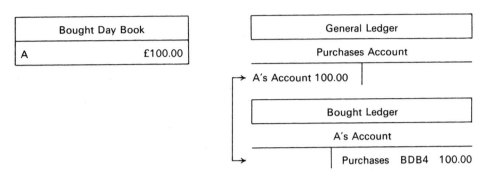

Bought Day Book	
A	£100.00

General Ledger
Purchases Account
A's Account 100.00

Bought Ledger
A's Account
Purchases BDB4 100.00

B has bought the goods costing £100 and this figure will eventually be posted to the Purchases Account—the credit being entered in A's account. If B has only paid £95 for £100 of goods, he has made a 'profit', or he has 'received' a discount of £5. The entries for discount received will be as follows:

A's Account

Bank		95.00	Purchases	BDB 3	100.00
Discount received	GL D5	5.00			

Discount Received Account

	A's account	BL A1	5.00

Remember: Discount Allowed is a loss and a debit balance on the Discount Allowed Account.

Discount Received is a profit and a credit balance on the Discount Received Account.

(a) Enter the following transactions in the Cash Book, Bank Book, and the Sales Day Book and post the entries to the ledger accounts.   **NA 7.11**

Discounts and credit purchases should be entered directly in the ledger.

Aug. 1   John Taylor started business with £500 borrowed from High Finance Ltd.

1   He opened a current account and paid in £450, keeping £50 for office cash.

3   Cash purchases of £32.00 and purchases by cheque of £140.00.

5   Cash sales of £87.00.
Advertising expenses paid in cash £15.00.

7   Credit sales to P. Barr of £82.00; B. Parr of £65.00.

9   Shop display units bought on credit from Design Fittings Ltd. £460.00.

> Aug. 12   P. Barr paid his account, deducting 5 per cent cash discount, by cheque.
>
> 14   Purchases on credit from H. Milton & Co. £60.00.
>
> 18   Paid stationery expenses in cash £4.50 and motoring expenses £7.80 in cash.
>
> 22   Credit sales to H. Wilson & Partners £45.00.
>
> 23   Paid a cheque to H. Milton & Co. for £57.50 in full settlement of the account.
>
> 24   H. Wilson returned goods and was allowed a credit of £2.50.
>
> 28   Paid advertising expenses in cash £25.00.
>
> 31   Paid all but £10 cash into bank.

(b) Balance the accounts and draw up a list of accounts with a debit balance and a list of accounts with a credit balance.

(c) Total each list.

Cash discounts in a book of original entry

You have seen how the ledger accounts are entered for cash discounts. **Joe's Rule No. 6** was that no ledger account should have an entry made in it unless it is a posting from a book of original entry. Sometimes it is easier to understand how the ledger accounts are entered before trying to understand the original recording in a book, and this is the case regarding cash discounts. In chapter 10 you will learn how cash discounts are recorded *before* being posted to the ledger accounts.

Asset accounts and expense accounts

When an asset is purchased the entries are:

Debit the asset account: Credit Cash or Bank Account or creditor's account.

When an expense is paid the entries are:

Debit the expense account: Credit the Cash or Bank Account.

Therefore an account with a debit balance can be either an *asset account* (something the business owns) or an *expense account*.

How do you know which type of account it is? An asset account will have the name of the asset in its title—for example, Machinery Account, Buildings Account, Motor Vehicles Account. The expense account will also have the description of the expense in its title—Rent Account, Wages Account, and so on. A debtor is also an asset—in this case his name will be the title of the account, and it will have a debit balance.

Liability accounts and income accounts

If cash is received from sales the entries are:

Debit Cash Account: Credit Sales Account.

If cash is received from the person who rents some of our warehouse space:
    Debit Cash Account: Credit Rent Received Account.

If cash is received from someone who lends us money:
    Debit Cash Account: Credit the account of the lender.

If an asset is purchased on credit:
    Debit the asset account: Credit the supplier's account.

If purchases are made on credit:
    Debit the Purchases Account: Credit the supplier's account.

Therefore an account with a credit balance can be either an *income account* or a *liability account* (something the business owes).

A creditor is a liability—his account will have a credit balance.

1   An account can only have either a credit balance or a debit balance.
2   If it has a debit balance, it is either an asset or an expense.
3   If it has a credit balance, it is either an income or a liability.

What you should remember

How can you tell which type of account it is? By its title.

Enter the name of the account to be debited and the account to be credited for these transactions. (Use a sheet of paper for writing your answer.)

NA 7.12

	Account to be debited	credited
(a) Rent received from subletting premises	Cash	Rent
(b) Carpet cutting machine purchased on credit	C C M	Creditor A
(c) Cheque received from a debtor	Bank	Debtor A
(d) Discount received from W. A. Smith Ltd.	W A Smith	Disc
(e) Interest paid on a loan	Int Pd	Loan
(f) Cash withdrawn by the owner	Drawgs	Cash
(g) Insurance payment by credit transfer	Insurce	Bank
(h) Office typewriter paid for by cheque	Typ	Bank
(i) Dividends received by the bank	Bank	Dvs Rec'd
(j) Goods sold on credit to P. Hood	P Hood	Sales

Tick the column whose heading is the correct type of account for the following. (Use a sheet of paper for writing your answer.)

NA 7.13

(a) Motor vehicle
(b) Bank overdraft
(c) Supplier (of a motor vehicle purchased on credit)
(d) Rent paid
(e) Rent received
(f) Commissions received
(g) Sales
(h) Bank charges
(i) Office equipment and fittings
(j) Repairs to office equipment
(k) Cash
(l) Motor repairs
(m) Redecorating the office and
factory
(n) Customer to whom we have sold
goods on credit
(o) Loan-a-lot Ltd., from whom
money has been borrowed
(p) Drawings

	Asset	Liability	Expense	Income
(a)	✓	✓		
(b)		✓		
(c)		✓		
(d)			✓	✓
(e)				✓
(f)				
(g)			✓	✓
(h)			✓	
(i)	✓			
(j)			✓	
(k)	✓		✓	
(l)			✓	
(m)			✓	
(n)	✓			
(o)		✓		
(p)				

8. Capital and Drawings

Capital

When Joe started the business, he must have put some money into the business Bank Account (or Cash Account), otherwise the business could never have bought any stock, fixtures, premises, or other assets such as motor vans. Although it is Joe's business, you must remember that it is the *business records* that we are keeping—not Joe's records. After all, Joe may have several different businesses, and each one would need to have its own separate books and accounts. We need to know how much money Joe has put into *this* business. This is called *capital* and represents the amount that Joe has invested in the business. The *Capital Account* is the personal account of the owner and shows exactly how much the business owes the owner.

A liability

If capital is the amount of money put into the business, how can it be a liability? Capital is a liability of the business, not the owner. The bookkeeping records are those of the business, and the business has received the money (or value of assets) from the owner. Exactly the same position arises if the business borrows money from a bank or other money-lending firm. Our business receives the money—so debit the Cash Account (or Bank Account) and credit the account of the company or person lending the money. That person's account has then a credit balance and a credit balance on a personal account is a liability.

Like anyone who lends money, the owner would hope someday to have it repaid, and therefore an accurate record must be kept of how much the business owes him.

Drawings

If Joe works in his business full-time, he will need to use some money for his own private expenses. Therefore he will take money out of the business, either in cash or from the bank, probably every week. The record of what he takes out is kept in the *Drawings Account*, and the bookkeeping entries are simple:

Credit the Bank (or Cash) Account: Debit the Drawings Account.

Drawings are made by the owner because the business is (one hopes) making a profit. Of course, the business may be making a loss—in which case drawings represent a repayment to the owner of some of his original capital.

Capital Account

The amount originally put into the business was credited to the Capital Account. Any additional amounts subsequently put into the business and any profit owing to the owner are also credited to the Capital Account (increasing his capital). Since drawings reduce the amount owed by the business to the owner, the total amount of drawings during the year are transferred to the Capital Account.

Look at this example of how a Capital Account might appear.

Capital Account

Dec. 31	Drawings	GL D1	3,800	Jan. 1 Dec. 31	Bank Profit	BB 1	10,500
	Balance	c/d	10,900		for year	GL T	4,200
			14,700				14,700
				Jan. 1	Balance	b/d	10,900

This account shows that on 1 January the owner introduced £10,500 into the business by paying it into the business Bank Account.

Dr Bank Account: Cr Capital Account.

During the course of the year, the business made a profit of £4,200 which it now owes to the owner:

Dr Trading and Profit and Loss Account: Cr Capital Account.

Also during the year, the owner withdrew £3,800, and this was recorded in the Drawings Account in the General Ledger (D1) and is now transferred to the Capital Account. The owner has, at the end of the year, capital of £10,900.

Opening capital plus profit less drawings = Closing capital. Why is profit credited to the Capital Account?

The business operates to make a profit on behalf of the owner. He benefits if a profit is made, but he also suffers any loss that arises. The accounts required to calculate profits or losses are explained in chapter 14, but you should remember that since a profit is owed by the business to the owner it increases his capital. Obviously, therefore, a loss decreases his capital. Profit is a liability of the *business*, since the business now owes that profit to the owner.

Example   Look at the example below.

Step 1   Jim Pale starts a business with £50 cash. Therefore Dr Cash: Cr Capital.

Cash Account

(1) Capital	50	(2) Purchases	50
(3) Sales	60		

Capital Account

		(1) Cash	50
		(5) Profit	10

Step 2   Goods costing £50 are bought for cash. Therefore Dr Purchases: Cr Cash.

Purchases Account

(2) Cash	50	(4) Trading A/c.	50

Step 3   All the goods purchased are sold for £60 cash. Therefore Dr Cash: Cr Sales.

Sales Account

(4) Trading	60	(3) Cash	60

Step 4   Compare the costs with the incomes: the £50 cost and £60 income gives a £10 profit. Therefore Dr Trading Account: Cr Purchases Account. Dr Sales Account: Cr Trading Account.

Trading Account

(4) Purchases	50	(4) Sales	60
(5) Capital	10		

Step 5   Income in excess of costs (i.e., profits) is transferred to the owner's Capital Account. Therefore Dr Trading Account: Cr Capital Account.

If you look at the Capital Account, you will see that £60 is owing to the owner. (Original capital £50 + £10 profit.) *Therefore the business has a liability of £60.* If you look at the Cash Account you will see that £60 is in hand. *Therefore the business has an asset of £60.*

So the business assets equal the business liabilities. In fact, the business assets *always* equal the business liabilities.

Look at the example above again. After each bookkeeping step—what were the assets and liabilities?

| Step 1 | Started business. | Asset | = Cash | = £50 |
| | | Liability | = Capital | = £50 |

Step 2	Bought goods.	Assets	= Cash	= Nil
			+ Stock	= 50
			Total	= £50
		Liability	= Capital	= £50

Step 3	Sold goods.	Assets	= Cash	= 60
			+ Stock	= Nil
			Total	= £60
		Liability	= Capital	= 50
			+ Profit	= 10
			Total	= £60

Joe's Rule No. 9
The total of the business assets always equals the total of the business liabilities.

You should also remember that since every debit entry has a credit entry (and vice versa):

| Assets plus Expenses (debit balances on accounts) | *always equals* | Liabilities plus Incomes (credit balances on accounts) |

Assets introduced by the owner

When a person starts a business, he may bring into it assets other than cash. If you, for example, owned a motor car, and then you started business as a freelance photographer, you would use the car to carry your equipment and to go to various appointments. The car is being used in the business. Similarly, tools, equipment, stocks of materials, and even premises can be brought into the business by the owner.

If a person started a business on 15 March with the following assets

Premises	£12,500
Stock	550
Motor van	850
Equipment	400

then his capital at that date would be the total of all the assets he has introduced into the business, i.e., £14,300. The entries in the accounts would be as shown below. If he then paid £200 into the bank on 18 March, his capital is increased to £14,500.

Capital Account

	Mar. 15	Premises	12,500
		Stock	550
		Motor van	850
		Equipment	400
	18	Bank	200

Premises Account

Mar. 15	Capital	12,500

Stock Account

Mar. 15	Capital	550

Motor Van Account

Mar. 15	Capital	850

Equipment Account

Mar. 15	Capital	400

Bank Account

Mar. 18	Capital	200

Drawings by the owner

The value of whatever the owner takes out of the business is debited to his Drawings Account and credited to:

1 Purchases Account in the case of stock.
2 Bank Account if taken out by cheque.
3 Cash Account if taken in cash.
4 The appropriate expense account if the business has paid a private expense.

Perhaps Item 4 needs a little more explanation. Imagine that the owner lives in a flat above his shop. He owns all the premises and pays rates to the local council. He receives a rates bill for £800. This represents £650 for the shop premises and £150 for his flat.

The following could happen:

1 The business pays £650 to the council and the owner withdraws £150 as drawings and pays it to the council.

or

Bookkeeping entries

Cash

| | | Rates | 650 |
| | | Drawings | 150 |

Rates

| Cash | 650 | | |

Drawings

| Cash | 150 | | |

2 The business pays £800 to the council. *But*—since £150 relates to the owner's flat—the business has really paid it on behalf of the owner. Although it has saved the owner from paying it himself, he must be charged with that sum. Therefore: Debit Drawings: Credit Rates.

The result is the same either way.

Cash

| | | Rates | 800 |

Rates

| Cash | 800 | Drawings | 150 |

Drawings

| Rates | 150 | | |

A business may pay many bills on behalf of the owner—electricity, gas, motor expenses, rents, telephone, and so on. Whatever proportion of the bill relates to the owner must be charged to his Drawings Account and credited to the expense account. The effect of this is to leave in the expense account only the amount chargeable to the business.

Try the following exercises:

8.01 T. Taylor started a business by paying £5,000 into the Bank Account of the business on 1 September. On the same date, he also brought into his business a motor car valued at £1,450 and stock worth £500. The following transactions took place in September.

Sept. 2 Cash sales £250; rent paid £55 by cheque.
   3 Credit sales to R. Haskall £42.00; P. Rowler £93.00.
   8 Purchased on credit from London Supply Company, office equipment costing £425.00.
   11 Purchases by cheque £195.00.
      Paid £150 into the bank from office cash.
   12 Paid £3,500 by cheque as a deposit on a shop lease.
   14 Cash sales £231. Cheque received from R. Haskall £39, £3 discount was allowed.

Sept. 18   Sundry expenses paid in cash were: stationery £4.25; postage 85p; packing materials £12.45.

25   Purchases by cheque £442.

28   Owner withdrew stock for his own use £26.

29   A bank loan of £2,500 was agreed by the bank manager and paid into the business Bank Account.

30   Petrol paid by cash £36 (£9 of this was for T. Taylor's own personal use).

(a) Enter the transactions in the books of original entry, and post to the ledger. Balance the accounts at the end of September.

(b) Make up a list of the debit balances and credit balances.

On 1 September Roger Bell had £2,845 in his Capital Account. During the following year he drew out a total of £1,980 in cash and the following transactions also took place.   **8.02**

    Rates paid by business £400   (one-half chargeable to Roger Bell)
    Motor expenses (ditto) £750   (two-thirds chargeable to Roger Bell)
    Heating (ditto)   £240   (one-third chargeable to Roger Bell).

The profit for the year was £3,150 after allowing for the adjustments above. Draw up Roger Bell's Drawings Account and Capital Account at the end of the year. (His Capital Account should show what his capital is at the end of the year.)

The business of Paul Meadowbank has the following assets and liabilities on 1 November. Calculate the owner's capital at that date.   **8.03**

Stock	450	Bank overdraft	390
Cash	25	Owing to credits	850
Premises	9,850	Mortgage	5,000
Debtors	630		
Motor vans	2,800		

The Private Ledger

Where a business employs a number of people recording transactions in the books, the owner may not wish employees to see exactly what he has put into the business in the way of capital. Also, he will probably not wish to disclose just how much profit (or loss) the business is making. Therefore, his Capital Account, Drawings Account, and the business Trading and Profit and Loss Accounts will be kept in a separate ledger which he himself (or his accountant) will maintain. This is the Private Ledger.

The following questions require you to enter the opening balances in the ledger accounts. The total debit balances should equal the total credit balances. Where no Capital Account balance is given, the total of the credit balances, deducted from the total of the debit balances will give you the Capital Account balance. Enter the transactions in the books of original entry, and post to the ledger accounts. Balance the Cash and Bank Books and ledger accounts.

8.04 Feb. 1 *Debit balances*

Cash	£36.25	Fixtures	£290.00
B. Rush	82.50	Motor van	800.00
S. Bade	48.75	Bank	137.00
Stock	285.00	C. Camp—Capital	?

Credit balances

K. Hick	93.00
S. Hoe	33.45

Feb. 2   Cash sales £185.30.
B. Rush paid his account by cheque.

4   C. Camp withdrew £25 stock for his own use.

5   Paid trade expenses in cash £19.50.

8   Sold goods on credit to T. Tymm £98.42.

10   Wages paid in cash £41.75.
Purchases by cheque £438.
Sold goods on credit to F. Fynn £147 and P. Pynn £64.40.

11   A cheque value £50 was sent to K. Hick as payment on account.

18   Dividends of £16.80 received and paid into bank.
The owner drew a cheque value £35 as drawings.
Wages paid in cash £42.50.
Credit sales to P. Pynn £43.25 and M. Minn £57.60.

21   Telephone bill paid by cheque £46.75.
Cash sales to date £288.00.

25   Wages paid in cash £43.95.

28   C. Camp drew stock for his own use £43.
All cash except £25 was paid into bank.
Bank charges were incurred of £5.50.

NA 8.05 Mar. 1 *Credit balances*

C. Toms	£186.00
Bank loan	550.00
T. Twigg—Capital	?

Debit balances

Cash	10.00
Bank	341.00
Plant and machinery	4,250.00
Buildings	10,800.00
A. Short	38.50
G. Rose	76.30
Stock	891.00

Mar. 5   Cash sales to date £436.75.
Trade expenses paid in cash £49.00.
Motor running expenses paid by cheque £77.65.

Mar. 8   Office equipment bought on credit from West End Office Supplies £188.40.

10   Purchases by cheque £350.00.

Amount of £50 paid by standing order towards repayment of loan.

15   Cash sales £295.00, Cash paid to bank £375.00.

17   Cash withdrawn by owner £50.

21   Cheque of £100 paid to West End Office Supplies.

26   Trade expenses paid in cash £34.50.

Insurance premium of £116.00 paid by cheque.

27   Rent received in cash £25.00.

28   Owner withdrew stock value £16.00 at selling price.

30   Cash sales to date £526.85.

31   All cash was paid into the bank.

Cheque paid, in full settlement of his account, to C. Toms for £180.00.

Balance of West End Office Supplies account paid by cheque.

Cheque for £38.00 received from A. Short.

9. The Trial Balance

Proving double entry

The rule that you are using to guide you in making entries in the accounts is that of double entry. It is handy to remember: every debit has a credit and every credit has a debit.

If this rule is properly followed, then all entries made on one side of the accounts will exactly equal all entries made on the other side of the accounts. By now you are using several books—the Cash Book, the Bank Book, the Sales Ledger, and the Nominal Ledger and naturally the more books and accounts that need to be kept, the greater the likelihood of errors arising. If our double entry principle is put into practice correctly, it should be easy to check that the books are correct, by adding up all the debit entries and all the credit entries. If they are not the same, an error has been made. Look at this example.

Transactions

(1) Started business by paying £700 into the bank.
(2) Paid cheque £85 for purchases.
(3) Paid cheque £28 for wages.
(4) Withdrew £90 by cheque for office cash.
(5) Cash sales of £160.
(6) Cash purchases £42.

Bookkeeping entries

Capital Account

		(1) Bank	700

Bank Account

(1) Capital	700	(2) Purch.	85
		(3) Wages	28
		(4) Cash	90

Purchases Account

(2) Bank	85	
(6) Cash	42	

Wages Account

(3) Bank	28	

Sales Account

		(5) Cash	160

Cash Account

(4) Bank	90	(6) Purch.	˙42
(5) Sales	160		

A total of entries would show the following:

	Debit entries £	Credit entries £
Capital		700
Bank	700	203
Purchases	127	
Cash	250	42
Wages	28	
Sales		160
	£1,105	£1,105

However, it is the practice not to show all the entries but merely the *balance* on the accounts, and such a test of balances is called a *trial balance*. The above example then becomes

Trial Balance as at (. . .*)

	Dr £	Cr £
Capital		700
Bank	497	
Purchases	127	
Wages	28	
Cash	208	
Sales		160
	£860	£860

* Always enter date on which the balances are prepared.

The trial balance is always drawn up at the end of a trading period and before the final accounts are prepared. However, in practice the trial balance may be drawn up monthly, quarterly or half yearly, just to check the entries made in the accounts. The final accounts are the Trading Account and the Profit and Loss Account, and obviously if a correct profit or loss is to be calculated, the records must be accurate.

Balancing accounts

The trial balance is *not* an account. It is only a list of accounts which have a balance. The first step in taking out a trial balance is to balance off all the accounts in the ledgers. This is how you should balance the accounts.

1   Cash Account and Bank Account—balance in the normal way and carry down the balances on the accounts.

2 Debtors' accounts in the Sales Ledger—balance as normal and carry down the balances on each account.

3 Expenses and income accounts—since these accounts normally have entries on one side only, it is necessary merely to pencil in the total of that side underneath the last entry, or by its side. See the illustration below.

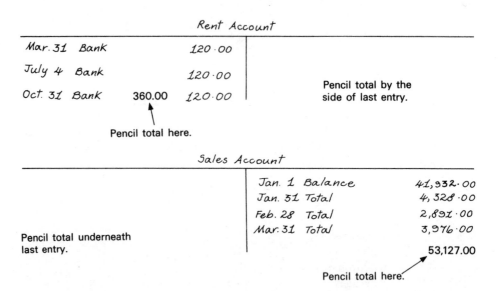

The reasons why pencil totals should be used will be explained in chapter 16, when you start learning about adjustments required at the end of the year. If an account has only one entry then that entry represents the balance, and no further balancing is required.

Difference in totals

If the total debits do not equal the total credits, it could mean that *either* the books and accounts contain an error *or* that you have made an error in preparing the trial balance. This is what you should do.

1 Double check your arithmetic in adding up the debit and credit columns.

2 Check that each item in the trial balance is entered in the correct column. (Remember—assets and expenses are debits, but liabilities and income are credits.)

3 Check from the accounts in the ledger that you have entered the correct balance—and not transposed a figure—and that it is in the correct column.

4 Check that *all* the ledger balances plus the Cash and Bank Accounts are in the trial balance.

5 Check the arithmetical accuracy of the balances in the ledger accounts.

If the totals still do not agree, the books contain an error.

Errors not shown by the trial balance

If the total debits agree with the total credits, then the arithmetical accuracy of the books is proved correct. However, the books and records may still contain errors, since some types of mistakes are not shown up by the trial balance.

These are also called errors of commission. A payment made to A. B. Brown may be debited to A. Brown's account. The entry (debit) is on the correct side—but in the wrong account. Also, for example, rent posted to the Rates Account in error. In both of these examples the wrong account has been entered, but the account wrongly entered is in the same class of account as the correct one.

Errors of mis-posting

If an entry is completely omitted from a book of original entry, then neither a debit nor a credit entry will have been made.

Errors of omission

These are similar to errors of misposting but are more serious since they affect capital and revenue transactions. If assets were debited to the Purchases Account it would result in expenses being overstated and profits understated. If the opposite occurred, and purchases (of goods for resale) were debited to asset accounts, then profits would be overstated.

Errors of principle

These arise where the same arithmetical inaccuracy arises on both the debit and credit sides of two accounts.

Compensating errors

A trial balance, containing balances on *all* accounts, is extracted before preparing the Trading and Profit and Loss Accounts.

Of course, a trial balance can be prepared at any time in order to show that the books are correct.

Joe's Rule No. 10

Use of trial balance in examinations

You have already learned that total debits equal total credits. Often in examination questions you are asked to calculate the *owner's capital*. This can be calculated, since the rules say:

Assets + Expenses = Liabilities + Incomes.
i.e.   Debit balances = Credit balances.

And since capital is a credit balance (a liability of the business) then:

Assets = Capital + Other Liabilities.
or   Assets + Expenses = Capital + Other Liabilities + Income.

65

For example: Tom Bullock's business has the following assets and liabilities on 1 May: Cash at bank £185; Fixtures £250; Stock £4,850; Debtors £592; Loan from Easicome Ltd. £750; and Creditors £670.

Total the assets:	£	Total the liabilities:	£
Bank	185	Loan	750
Fixtures	250	Creditors	670
Stock	4,850		
Debtors	592		
	£5,877		£1,420

Since Assets = Capital + Other Liabilities.
  £5,877 = Capital + £1,420.

Therefore   Capital = £5,877 − £1,420 = £4,457.

9.01   Prepare a trial balance as at 31 December from the following details.

	£
Premises	14,500
Motor vehicles	6,800
Fixtures	975
Wages	7,855
Purchases	14,982
Sales	22,468
Rents received	420
Lighting and heating	370
Telephone	450
Motor expenses	1,420
Creditors	3,400
Debtors	4,805
General expenses	948
Bank overdraft	1,402
Capital	28,000
Drawings	2,585

9.02   The following trial balance has been prepared incorrectly. Draw up a correct trial balance.

Trial Balance as at 28 February

	£	£
Capital		14,000
Plant and machinery		12,000
Wages	3,800	

Purchases	17,400	
Sales		28,650
Rents received	346	
Debtors	3,895	
Creditors	2,450	
Stock		750
Cash in hand	125	
Bank overdraft		361
Drawings	2,118	
Discounts allowed	81	
Discounts received		142
Motor vehicles	3,500	
Motor running expenses		855
Rent and rates	1,425	
	35,140	56,758

Enter the following transactions in the books of account of J.F.K. & Co., balance the accounts, and take out a trial balance at the end of the month.

9.03

Nov.	1	Started business with £4,800 cash.
	2	Put £4,500 of the cash into a bank account.
	3	Purchased shop fixtures by cheque £750.
	5	Bought goods by cheque £650.
	8	Cash sales £92.
	9	Paid rent in cash £20.
	11	Sold goods on credit to A. Hill £145.
	13	Cash sales £130. Paid £100 cash into bank.
	15	Bought a motor van, paying by cheque £1,650.
	16	The owner withdrew cash £45.
		Paid motor expenses: licence £50 and insurance £82, both by cheque.
	17	A. Hill paid his account by cheque £140, having been allowed a £5 discount.
	19	Sold more goods on credit to A. Hill £38.
	20	Purchases by cheque £290.
	21	Advertising bill of £15 paid in cash.
	24	Owner withdrew £55 from the bank.
	29	Cash sales £94.
	30	Banked all cash in hand.

The balances in a trader's account on 1 June 19–7 were as follows: Land and buildings £14,000; Fixtures and fittings £580; Motor van £2,000; Bank balance £1,420; Loan on mortgage of land and buildings £10,000; Creditors £170.

9.04

During the year ending 30 May 19–8 he drew nothing out of the business and paid in no additional capital. On 30 May his position was: Land and buildings £14,000; Fixtures and fittings £650; Motor van £2,000; Bank balance £1,200; Stock £480; Cash in hand £250; Loan on mortgage £9,800; Creditors £245.

You are required to calculate the business profit or loss for the year

(a) Using only the information above.
(b) If the owner had withdrawn £1,715 during the year.
(c) If, in addition to drawing £1,715 he had paid in additional capital of £2,500.

NA 9.05 The following list of balances was taken from the books of Joe Wynn. You are required to draw a trial balance as at 30 September 19–7 and show his capital.

	£
Sales	55,000
Rent	560
Insurance	290
Purchases	40,600
Salaries and wages	4,400
Packing and postage	560
Rates	200
Sundry expenses	390
Carriage inwards	109
Carriage outwards	205
Stock at 30 September 19–6	6,800
Debtors	8,330
Creditors	3,900
Balance at bank	896(Dr)
Cash in hand	80
Buildings	22,000
Machinery	4,000
Motor vehicles	3,900
Drawings	4,580

NA 9.06 The following trial balance has been prepared by C. Baker, a sole trader. The balances failed to agree and he has requested your assistance. You are required to redraft the trial balance as at 31 March 19–6.

Trial Balance as at 31 March 19–6

	Dr	Cr
Capital		20,000
Drawings		2,069
Debtors and creditors	6,600	5,464
Sales		81,740
Purchases	63,190	
Rent and rates	880	
Lighting and heating		246
Salaries and wages	8,268	
Stock in trade, 31 March 19–5	9,274	
Insurance	170	
General expenses	935	
Bank balance	1,582	
Motor vans at cost	8,000	
Provision for depreciation of motor vans, 31 March 19–5	3,600	
Commission received	250	
Motor expenses	861	
Freehold premises at cost		10,000
Rent received	250	
Discount received		771
	£103,860	£120,290

10. The Cash Books

The two-column Cash Book
Now you have learned how to enter both the Cash and Bank Account, Joe is going to explain how and why you are going to use a *two-column Cash Book*. Have a look first of all at the Cash Book you should now have bought and open it to the first double page. The illustration below shows how it is ruled and what the columns are used for.

Dr											Cr
Date	Details	Folio		Cash	Bank	Date	Details	Folio		Cash	Bank

It is the same as your normal Cash Account, but there are *three* columns on each side of the page rather than one. Let Joe explain.

Rather than keeping two accounts apart from each other, the Cash Book enables us to keep both the Cash Account and the Bank Account side by side. This is more convenient and we can quickly see how much cash we have got altogether. In some cases we only need use two of the three columns on each side—hence we have a two-column Cash Book. In the illustration, you can see that the book has three columns on each side. The first column on each side is used, if required, for recording cash discounts. The middle column on both sides is used for cash receipts and payments and the right-hand columns on both sides are used to record receipts into the bank and payments from the bank. For the moment we will use only two columns on each side. Let me show you how it works—look at this illustration.

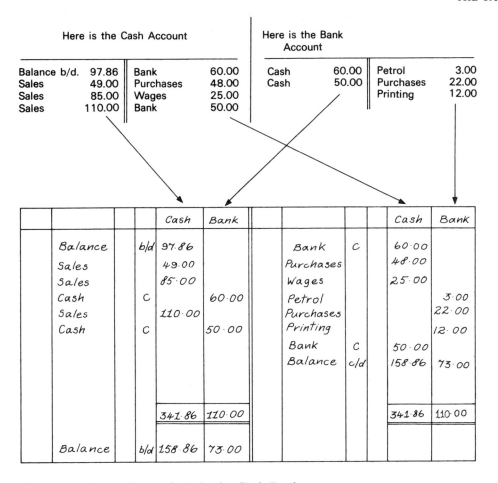

Here is the Cash Account

Balance b/d.	97.86	Bank	60.00
Sales	49.00	Purchases	48.00
Sales	85.00	Wages	25.00
Sales	110.00	Bank	50.00

Here is the Bank Account

Cash	60.00	Petrol	3.00
Cash	50.00	Purchases	22.00
		Printing	12.00

			Cash	Bank			Cash	Bank
Balance	b/d	97.86		Bank	C	60.00	
Sales		49.00		Purchases		48.00	
Sales		85.00		Wages		25.00	
Cash	C		60.00	Petrol			3.00
Sales		110.00		Purchases			22.00
Cash	C		50.00	Printing			12.00
				Bank	C	50.00	
				Balance	c/d	158.86	73.00
		341.86	110.00			341.86	110.00
Balance	b/d	158.86	73.00				

This is how they will now look in the Cash Book.

You can see how the two separate accounts fit into one book. Previously we have had two separate books—one for cash and the other for the bank. When these two accounts are kept in one book, quite separately to the ledger, the book becomes the Cash Book—this is a *two-column* Cash Book.

A *three-column* Cash Book is illustrated later in this chapter, and an analysed Cash Book is shown in chapter 21.

Balancing the Cash Books

This means balancing both the Cash Account and the Bank Account. To balance the Cash Account, imagine the Bank columns do not exist. Then imagine that the Cash columns do not exist when you balance the Bank Account. All you are doing is balancing a Cash Account and a Bank Account as you have already learned. Just remember to leave a line for the balances to be entered when you total the columns (it is the practice to put the totals on the same line).

Contra entries

In the example above, you will see two entries on both sides of the Cash Book that have a C written in the small Folio column. C is the abbreviation for *contra* (Latin for 'opposite'). It is used where an entry in the Cash Book on one side has a corresponding entry in the Cash Book on the other side. Look at the first item on the credit side of the Cash Account. It shows that £60 has gone out of Cash and into Bank. Obviously, the £60 must be recorded as going out of Cash (that is a credit entry) and into Bank (that is a debit entry). Both entries are in the Cash Book—one in the Cash Account and the other in the Bank Account.

Making entries in the Cash Book

The principles used are the same as those you learned in chapters 2 and 3. It will be useful here to summarize the source documents of entries in the Cash Book.

Receipts
1. Copy of receipt note given to the customer.
2. Total of till roll (which should correspond to the total of cash in the till).
3. Cheques received from customers.
4. The bank statement, which shows interest and dividends received and payments made by customers by Bank Giro transfer, should be used to verify the receipts recorded from dividend warrants and credit transfer, and bank giro slips. (The bank statement would be used for entry purposes only if the original documents had been lost in the post.) Bank charges would be entered from this statement.

Payments
1. Records of payments made in cash—e.g., receipt slips, wages sheets.
2. Postal Order counterfoils.
3. Cheque book counterfoils.
4. Bank statement showing bank charges and interest paid to the bank, payments made under standing orders.

Entries should be made in strict date order and no blank lines should be left between entries.

Try these exercises. Enter the transactions in a two-column cash book and balance both the Cash Account and the Bank Account after making all the entries.

10.01

Mar.	1	Cash sales £40.00.
	3	Cheque received from J. Smith £200.00.
	5	Wages paid in cash £25.00.
	7	Cash sales £120.00.
	8	Paid £85.00 cash into bank.
	10	Postages paid by cash £1.50.

Mar. 15   Cash sales £171.00.
     18   Drawings by the owner by cheque £25.00.
     23   Purchases by cheque £48.00.
     31   Cash sales £149.00.

Jan. 1   Balance at bank £400.00.   **10.02**
         Balance in cash £100.00.
     2   Purchased goods with cheque £50.00.
     3   Received cheque from B. Taylor and paid into bank £35.00.
     4   Paid cash—wages £14.00
                —stationery £7.50.
     5   Cash sales to date £44.00.
     6   Banked £30.50.
     7   Paid D. Harvey cheque £35.00.
     8   Cash sales to date £84.

Mar. 1   Balance in cash £2,000.00.   **10.03**
     2   Paid cash into bank £1,500.00.
     3   Bought motor van by cheque £1,250.00.
     4   Paid in cash—wages £125.50
                —rent £114.50.
     5   Cash sales to date £189.00.
     6   Paid cheque to P. White £142.25.
     7   Received a cheque from T. Blake and paid into bank £78.65.
     8   Paid cash for purchases £163.80.
    11   Paid wages in cash £143.45.
         Paid stationery in cash £38.65.
    12   Withdrew cash from bank £90.00.
         Purchased office equipment by cheque £500.00.

Cash discount

Let us recall what we said in chapter 7. When we sell goods to our customers, we state the terms of the sales on the invoice, which may include terms for early settlement of the account. For example, an invoice for sales of £120.00 to Sounds International could show that if they settle the account within 14 days they can deduct 10 per cent from the net invoice price, this 10 per cent deduction being a *cash discount* which we allow them. The idea is to encourage our customers to pay their accounts quickly. If we can get the cash quickly we can use it to buy and sell more goods, or use it to pay our own bills.

Recording the cash discount

Consider the invoice for £120 which we sent on 4 April to Sounds International, and let us suppose that on 11 April they send us a cheque for the amount less the 10 per cent discount. 10 per cent of £120 is £12, so the cheque should be for £108. We will pay this cheque into the bank and debit the Bank Account—see next page.

Cash Book

Dr Date			Disc. Allow.	Cash	Bank	Cr Date			Disc. Recd.	Cash	Bank
Apl. 1	Balance	b/d		13.50	491.00	Apl. 15	John Taylor	BL 72	5.00		45.00
11	Sounds International	SL 5	12.00		108.00	30	Trade Subs s/o	GL 5			12.00
28	Bow Furnishings	SL B			150.00	30	Bank Charges	GL B			3.00
29	Funfare Centre	F	3.00		21.00	30	Motor Van	GL M			800.00
30	Balance	c/d			90.00	30	Balance	c/d		13.50	
			15.00	13.50	860.00				5.00	13.50	860.00
30	Disc. Allowed Dr	GL D3				30	Disc. Received Cr	GL D4			

The corresponding credit entry will be in Sounds International's account in the Sales Ledger—see below.

Date		Folio	£ p	Date		Folio	£ p
Apl. 1	Sales	GL 5..	120.00	Apl. 11	Bank	CB2	108.00
				11	Discount	CB2	12.00

Sounds International Ltd.   SL No.

The cash discount of £12 allowed to Sounds International has been entered in the Discount Allowed column in the Cash Book and is credited to their account as a gain to them. Since it is a gain to them (they owed us £120 but need only pay £108), it is a loss to us, because we have given away the value of £12 which will not be repaid. So it will be recorded in the Discount Allowed Account as a debit.

However, to save making a number of individual entries in the Discount Allowed Account, the column in the Cash Book is added up, when the Cash Book is balanced, and the total is posted as one entry to the account in the ledger. The illustration on page 74 shows the details entered on 30 April against the total of £15 for Discount Allowed.

Similarly, if we receive discounts from our creditors, they will be gains to us and so we shall record them in the Discount Received column. For example, on 15 April we paid John Taylor £45 by cheque in full settlement of £50 owed to him. The entries will be as shown in the Cash Book. You should note that the Discount columns are *not* ledger *accounts*. They are memorandum columns, similar to a day book. So at the end of the month we add up the columns and open ledger accounts in the General Ledger for them as shown below.

Dr	Discount Allowed Account		Cr		Dr	Discount Received Account		Cr
Apl. 30	Total	CB2 12.00				Apl. 30	Total	CB2 5.00

The entries will appear on the same side as in the Cash Book because it is not a double entry, but a posting from a day book to the ledger.

The Cash Book and double entry

The Cash Book is a book of original entry. The first record of cash received or paid is made in this book. Unlike the Sales Day Book or Bought Day Book, the Cash Book is not merely a *memorandum book*. It also contains the account for the cash and bank transactions. The entry made in the Cash Book is one half of the double entry record. Can you remember the double entry rule?

Every debit entry must have a corresponding credit entry.
Every credit entry must have a corresponding debit entry.
Cash received is *debited* in the Cash Account and *credited* to the account which records its origin.

Here are some examples.

Cash is received from a debtor:	*debit* Cash Account and *credit* the debtor's account.
Cash is received from subletting a part of the office:	*debit* Cash Account and *credit* Rent Received Account.
A cheque is paid for insurance:	*debit* Insurance Account and *credit* Bank Account.
Cash is paid to a creditor:	*credit* Cash Account and *debit* the creditor's account.

If you look back at the illustration on page 74 you will see that each entry has a reference number against it in the Folio column. The fact that such a number appears means that the corresponding (double) entry has been made in the account in the ledgers. The first entry shows that a cheque for £45 was paid to John Taylor. The debit has been made to his account in the Bought Ledger—Account No. T2 (BL T2).

Credit transfers, standing orders, bank charges

In chapter 3 the use of standing orders and credit transfers was discussed. Our bank may receive a payment direct from some of our debtors. This is a *credit transfer* (or giro transfer, as it is sometimes called). We may also instruct our bank to pay some of our bills, say, quarterly or yearly. This instruction to our bank is called a *standing order*. When we receive our bank statement it will show any credit transfers, standing orders and bank charges—see below.

Bank charges are the amount the bank deducts for the services they offer us.

J. Wynn   Bank Statement

Date	Details	Dr	Cr	Bal.
Apr. 28	Bow Furnishings Ltd. C.T.		150.00	150.00
30	Sundries: Standing order			
	(Trade subs)	12.00		
	Charges	3.00		135.00

These entries on the bank statement will be recorded in the Cash Book as shown in the illustration on page 74.

Bank overdraft

Joe has arranged with his bank manager so that the business may draw some money from the bank in excess of the amount standing in its account. The limit of the amount we can overdraw is £200. This overdrawn amount is called an *overdraft*.

Enter the balances in the Cash Book and then enter the following transactions and balance the Cash and Bank Accounts. (Do not post the double entry.)

10.04

Apr.	3	Cash balance brought forward £33.50, bank overdraft £90.00.
	3	Cash paid for expenses £28.00.
	4	Cash sales paid direct to bank £114.00.
	6	Cash sales £49.50.
	7	Paid wages in cash £25.40.
	8	Received a cheque from Betta Bake Co. for £80.00 in full settlement of a debt of £88.00.
		Cash sales £51.40.
	10	Received a cheque from Sounds International in payment of their debt of £120.00 less 15 per cent discount.
	15	We paid Wholesale Suppliers by cheque £48.00 after deducting £2.00 discount.
	16	Paid for purchases by cheque £203.00.
		Bought postage stamps by cash £2.13.
	21	Bow Furnishers Ltd. were paid by cheque £48.00 after deducting £6.00 discount.
	25	Dividend received by the bank £315.00.
	28	Cash sales £112.50.

Bank loans and bank overdrafts

While both bank loans and bank overdrafts are liabilities, there is a difference between them. When the loan is received, the amount is debited to the Bank (current) Account and credited to a separate Bank Loan Account in the nominal (or private) ledger. Interest is payable on this loan for the period of the loan and usually is deducted by the bank from the current account, in the same way that interest on an overdraft is deducted. The bookkeeping entry for interest is to credit the Bank Account and debit the Bank Interest Payable Account.

As previously explained, an overdraft (which is another form of loan) appears in the Cash Book as a credit balance on the Bank Account.

Interest is usually charged on a daily basis on the actual amount overdrawn daily.

The importance of the Cash Book

Originally a Cash Account and a Bank Account were kept in the ledger. Due to the number of entries required and the importance of knowing the cash position exactly, a separate Cash Book is usually kept by a cashier, who is held responsible for its accuracy.

Joe's Rule No. 11

The Cash Book is both a book of original entry and a record book, since it contains the Cash and Bank Accounts.

Dishonoured cheques

Cheques received from debtors are paid into our bank and our bank will usually enter the amount immediately as a receipt in our account. Our bank will then proceed to collect the amount stated on the cheque from our customer's bank. If our customer does not have sufficient money in his account to pay this cheque then, naturally, his bank will not pay our bank. The return of a cheque unpaid is referred to as the *dishonouring* of a cheque, and our bank will return it to us and take out of our account the amount originally entered. The cheque will usually have R/D written across it, meaning *Refer to Drawer*. We must now remember to credit the Bank Account and debit the customer, who now owes the sum to us again.

10.05 William Smith records all his cash and bank transactions in a three-column Cash Book. The following are his transactions for the month of May 19–5.

May 1 Cash in hand £19. Cash at bank £427.
  5 Paid by cheque the amount due to F. Gardner (£70) less £4 discount.
  8 Received from H. Evans cash £38 in full settlement of the debt of £40.
  10 Received from W. Bidmead a cheque for £68 in full settlement of his debt of £72. This cheque was placed in Smith's cash box.
  14 Paid into bank the sum of £99—including the cheque received from W. Bidmead on 10 May.
  19 Paid wages in cash £11.
  21 Paid by cheque the amount due to N. Jackson (£55) less £3 discount.
  28 Drew cheque for £25 for office cash.

Required:
Draw up the three-column Cash Book for the month of May 19–5. The two Discount columns should be totalled. You should state to which ledger account these totals should be posted and on which side of the ledger account the entry should be made.

(LCC Elementary)

NA 10.06 Alfred Jackson records all his cash and bank transactions in a three-column Cash Book and the following are his transactions for the month of February 19–6.

Feb. 2 Cash in hand £22. Cash at bank £533.
  4 Paid to T. Robinson by cheque £62, being full settlement of a debt of £65, less £3 discount.

Feb. 6   Paid wages in cash £11.
7   Received from F. Smith £43 in cash, being full settlement of his debt of £47, less £4 discount.
12   Received from H. Williams a cheque for £39, in full settlement of his debt of £44, less £5 discount.
        This cheque was placed in Jackson's cash box.
17   Paid into bank the sum of £60, including the cheque received from H. Williams on 12 February.
23   Paid in cash the amount due to H. Parsons (£25) less £2 discount.
27   Drew cheque for £20 for office cash.

Required:
Draw up the three-column Cash Book for the month of February 19–6, carrying down the balances of cash in hand and cash at bank. The Discount columns should be totalled, and you should state to which ledger accounts the totals should be posted and also on which side of the ledger account the entries should be made.
(LCC Elementary)

(a) Write up a trader's three-column Cash Book for the month of April 19–5, from the following particulars.   **NA 10.07**

Apr. 1   Cash on hand £55, cash at bank £323.
2   Paid cheque to Gossages for £133, after deducting £7 discount for cash.
4   Paid wages in cash £75.
4   Cash takings £600, of which £500 was banked on 7 April.
8   Paid cheque for rent £100.
9   Paid cash to British Road Services £14.
11   Paid wages in cash £86.
11   Cash takings £545, of which £500 was banked on 14 April.
16   Paid cleaner in cash £12.
17   Paid cheque to Thorburn & Son £620, after deduction of £25 for cash discount.
18   Paid wages in cash £82.
19   Cash takings £380.
21   Paid cash for window cleaning £6.
23   Paid cash for rates £120.
25   Paid wages in cash £80.
26   Cash takings £640.
28   Paid electricity account in cash £30.
29   Paid £285 cash to Robinson & Co., after deducting a cash discount of £15.
30   Paid £300 cash into bank account.
30   Cash takings £220, all of which was retained by the trader as drawings to cover his personal expenses.
        Rule off and balance the Cash Book at 30 April 19–5.

(b) Explain how the trader would record in his ledger the total of his Discounts Received column.

(RSA–COS)

NA 10.08 At 1 May 19–7, a retailer has the following balances in his Cash Book: Cash in hand £42; Overdraft at bank £138. During the month of May:

Cheques were issued as follows.
May 2   To Surrey for £95 in full settlement of a debt of £100.
    8   To Hampshire who is owed £80 and who is prepared to allow $2\frac{1}{2}$ per cent cash discount.
    19   To Kent RDC £66 in payment of rates.
    25   Withdrawn from bank for use as change in the till £20.
    31   Proprietor withdrew for private purposes £100.

Cheques were received as follows.
May 17   From Mrs Lancashire £26 in payment of a monthly account.
        On 30 May you are advised by the bank that this cheque has been returned marked R/D.

Cash received during the month:
Shop takings for week ending 5 May £125, of which £100 was paid to the bank.
Shop takings for week ending 12 May £144, of which £120 was paid to the bank.
Shop takings for week ending 19 May £159, of which £150 was paid to the bank.
Shop takings for week ending 26 May £148, of which £105 was paid to the bank.

Cash paid out during month:
Wages 5, 12, 19, and 26 May: £28 on each date.
May 23   Telephone account £15.
    29   Delivery charges £8.

You are required to draw up the Cash Book for the month of May and enter the above transactions in date order. Balance the book as at 31 May and bring down the balances.
(N.B. No ledger accounts are required.)

(RSA–COS)

10.09 The books of C. Baker showed the following balances on 1 July.

Cash	£40.50	*Debtors*	P. Steele	£150.00
Bank	£185.00 (dr)		K. Hoe	£75.00
Stock	£931.00	*Creditors*	SRS Ltd.	£185.00
Fixtures	£1,010.00		J. Dove Ltd.	£96.50

Enter these balances in the ledger accounts. Calculate Baker's opening capital and post also to his account. Enter the following transactions in the books of original entry and post the memorandum totals to the ledger accounts at the month end. Balance all the accounts at the month end and take out a trial balance at that date.

July 1   Credit sales of £90.00 to M. Hart.

2   Cash sales of £72.50; cash purchases of £65.00.

3   Paid rent in cash £25.00; stationery expenses £2.15 in cash.

4   C. Baker withdrew stock value £43.00, at selling price.

5   K. Hoe paid his account, deducting 5 per cent cash discount, by cheque. The cheque was entered in the cash column.

6   A cheque value £180.00 was paid to SRS Ltd. in full settlement of their account.

7   Cash sales to date £532; cash paid to bank £571.25 (this included the cheque from K. Hoe).

8   Credit sales to P. Steele £72.00 and R. Reeves £86.50.

9   Motor expenses paid by cheque £33.00.

10   Paid rent in cash £25.00; cash sales £69.00.

11   Bank advised that P. Steele had paid into the bank account £145 by Bank Giro. Purchases by cheque £325.00.

12   Received a cheque £90.00 from M. Hart and paid direct to bank.

14   Shop display units purchased by cheque £287.65.

15   Credit sales to L. Rodgers £58.00.

16   Bank advised Baker that cheque from M. Hart had been returned with 'No Funds' marked. Cash sales £172.54.

17   Rent paid in cash £25.00.

21   Baker drew £19.00 cash for his own use.

24   Rent paid in cash £25.00.

25   Purchases by cheque £297.00.

26   Motor expenses paid in cash £42.50.

28   Advised by the bank that bank charges of £14.86 had been made. Cash sales £141.00.

29   Standing order payment, for hire charge of equipment, made by bank of £46.00.

30   A customer returned goods previously bought and complained about the quality. £10 cash was refunded to him. (Debit a Sales Returns Account.)

31   The bank agreed to make a loan of £750.00. This was entered into our current account on this date.

31   A cheque for £860.00 was paid for a second-hand motor van.

31   L. Rodgers paid a cheque of £55.00 in settlement of his account. £3.00 discount was allowed. The cheque was entered into the Cash column.

11. Credit Purchases

Whenever goods are bought on credit, the buyer will need to record the value of the goods purchased and the amount now owing to the supplier. The supplier to whom money is owed is called a Creditor. Creditors have accounts in the Bought Ledger (or Creditors Ledger) and, as you would expect, they have credit balances on their accounts. Compare these two illustrations:

Bookkeeping entries for cash purchase

Cash Account

	Apl. 10	Purch	GL P1	85.00

Purchases Account

Apl. 10	Cash	CB 3	85.00

Goods are bought and paid for in cash. A receipt will be obtained by the buyer. The payment is posted to the Purchases Account.

Entries for credit purchase

Supplier's Account

	Apl. 10	Purch.	85.00

Purchases Account

Apl. 10	Suppliers.	85.00

Goods are bought on credit. An invoice will be received showing the amount due to the supplier. The ledger entries are shown above.

In both cases, the Purchases Account is debited because we have received the value of the goods. In the case of the cash purchase, cash was given, therefore credit the Cash Account. In the case of a credit purchase, the supplier has given the goods (until he is paid) and therefore his account is credited.

11.01   If the supplier were to be paid cash of £85.00 on 11 April what two entries would be required to record the payment?

Joe's Rule No. 6 (learned in chapter 5) is that no entry should be made in a ledger unless a record first appears in a book of original entry. Let Joe continue the explanation regarding the credit purchases of carpets and accessories.

Let me draw you a simple diagram. In the middle is a book of original entry (or prime entry) called the Bought Day Book. It is entered from invoices received. Only the date of the invoice, the supplier's name, and the invoice total are entered. Look at the illustration on next page.

Once the invoices are entered in the Bought Day Book, the ledger clerk can post the entries to the creditors' accounts, entering the folio references.

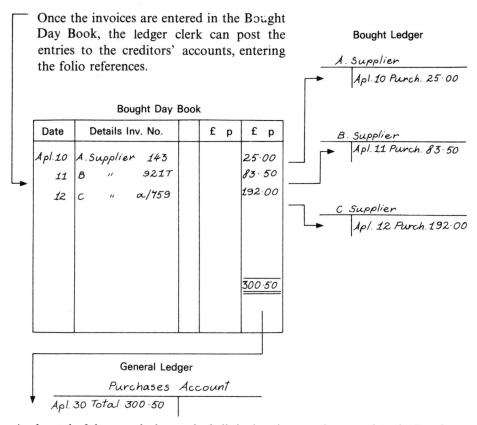

Bought Day Book

Date	Details Inv. No.	£ p	£ p
Apl.10	A.Supplier 143		25.00
11	B " 921T		83.50
12	C " a/759		192.00
			300.50

Bought Ledger

A. Supplier
Apl. 10 Purch. 25.00

B. Supplier
Apl. 11 Purch. 83.50

C Supplier
Apl. 12 Purch. 192.00

General Ledger

Purchases Account
Apl. 30 Total 300.50

At the end of the month the total of all the invoices can be posted to the Purchases Account in the General Ledger.

You can see that the three credit entries in the individual creditors' accounts (totalling £300.50) have a corresponding debit entry in the Purchases Account.

Totalling entries in the Bought Day Book

Instead of copying all the details from the purchase invoices into the Bought Day Book, only the invoice *total* is entered. So the two invoices illustrated on page 84 will appear in the Bought Day Book as follows:

Bought Day Book

Apl. 12	XY Wearing Inv No. B1735			53.25 → Cr XY A/c
Apl. 15	BKW Carpets Inv No. 77/1934			42.00 → Cr BKW A/c
Apl. 30	Dr Purchases A/c			xx

Detailed entries in the Bought Day Book

Look at the invoice below, and see how it may be entered.

Inv. No. B/1735	XY Wearing Co. Ltd.
	21 Farr Drive,
	Greenway.
Invoice to: J. Wynn	

	£
22 yds A1 Tufted @ £3 per yd.	66.00
10 yds B1 Beige @ 50p per yd.	5.00
	71.00
25% trade discount	17.75
Net total	53.25

Bought Day Book

Date	Details Inv. No.	£ p	£ p
Apl. 12	XY Wearing B1735		
	22yds. A1 @ £3 per yard	66·00	
	10yds. B1 @ 50p per yard	5·00	
		71·00	
	Less 25% trade disc	17·75	53·25

Here is another invoice. See how this one is entered.

BKW Carpets	Inv. No. 77/1934		
To: Joe Wynn	Date April 15		
		£ p	£ p
10	metres Broadloom		
	@ £4 per metre	40.00	
	Less 20% trade disc.	8.00	32.00
20	metres Underlay		
	@ £1 per metre	20.00	
	Less 50% trade disc.	10.00	10.00
	Net Invoice Total		42.00

Bought Day Book

		£ p	£ p
Apl. 15	BKW Carpets		
	10 metres of Broad-loom @ £4 per mtr.	40·00	
	Less 20% t. disc.	8·00	
		32·00	
	20 metres Underlay @ £1 per mtr.	20·00	
	Less 50% t.d. 10·00	10·00	42·00

In the above illustration the calculation on the invoice is shown within the details section in order to show the two separate calculations and yet leave in the right-hand column the amount that is to be posted to the Bought Ledger. *Only one figure* should appear in the right-hand column for each invoice. This figure will be added to all the other invoice totals in that column to obtain the weekly or monthly total of credit purchases.

The general rule is that the Bought Day Book is entered with the invoice totals only. If anyone wishes to see the details of the amount owing to each supplier, it is necessary only to refer to the invoice, which will have been filed away. It is because the invoice is usually readily available for reference that the time-consuming job of copying all the invoice details is avoided.

The Bought Day Book records only credit purchases of goods for resale and is not an account.

*Joe's Rule
No. 12*

Remember: only the *net total* is entered in the creditors' account since it is only the *net amount* that is owed.

Enter the following invoices received in the Bought Day Book.

11.02

May 2   Allweather Covers Ltd.
         120 metres narrow plastic sheet @ 75p per metre net.
         100 metres coated gauge @ 50p per metre net.

May 3   Allday Protectors Ltd.
         25 metres heavy duty tarpaulin @ £5.00 per metre less 10 per cent trade discount.

May 5   Allpurpose Sheeting Ltd.
         60 metres printed cotton @ 45p per metre less 40 per cent trade discount.
         150 metres rubbed polythene @ £3.00 per metre less $33\frac{1}{3}$ per cent trade discount.

Total the Bought Day Book.

On 1 May Circular Tracks started business with a bank balance of £2,505 and cash in hand of £143.00. Enter these amounts and also the transactions below in the books of original entry. Post entries to the ledger accounts, and balance the Cash Book. Balance the accounts and take out a trial balance.

11.03

May 2   Cash purchases £48.50.
         Invoice received from Square Way Dealers £73.00.
         Rent paid by cheque £19.50.
     3   Invoice No. 313 issued to Sampson Brothers for goods sold on credit, value £98.00.
     4   Motor repairs paid by cheque £49.50.
         Wages paid in cash £85.40.
         Cash sales £133.45.
         Purchase by cheque £600.00.
     5   Invoice received from Round Wheels Ltd.—net invoice total £256.00.
         Invoice No. 314 issued to Tubular Poles Ltd. for goods totalling £76.00.
         Petrol paid in cash £5.50.
     6   Invoice No. 315 issued to Wheeltappers Institute for goods totalling £100.00.
     8   Cash sales £68.50.
         Invoice received from Rollover Blind Ltd.—total £157.00.
    11   Wages paid in cash £81.45.
    12   Sampson paid his bill by cheque deducting 5 per cent for cash discount.
         All cash was paid into bank.

12. Bought Ledger (or Creditors Ledger)

In chapter 11 the Bought Day Book was demonstrated. That book records credit purchases, showing the totals of suppliers' invoices, the name of the supplier, and the date of the invoice. From this book the postings are made to the accounts of the suppliers which are credited. All suppliers' accounts are kept together in a separate ledger and, since suppliers are people to whom we owe money, the ledger is often called the *Creditors Ledger*. Another common name for it is the *Bought Ledger*. Remember, then, that these two titles refer to the same ledger—the one in which creditors' accounts are kept. Joe needs to know how much he owes to suppliers, so a separate ledger account for each supplier records what we have purchased (on credit), what payments we have made to the supplier, what goods were sent back to him (called 'returns'), and what discounts (if any) Joe was allowed. Each account will have its own Bought Ledger reference number. In a bound ledger each page is numbered consecutively, and BL 3 would be the third account, on the third page of the Bought Ledger. When the number of suppliers is large, the accounts are grouped alphabetically as follows:

Allyn Displays Ltd.	—BL A1	In this case a loose-leaf binder will form
American Pile Carpets	—BL A2	the ledger so that new accounts can be
BKW Carpets	—BL B1	entered in the appropriate place.
Bemrose & Co. Ltd.	—BL B2	
Books Galore	—BL B3	
⋮		
XY Wearing	—BL X1	

Let us look at XY Wearing's account in the Bought Ledger.

XY Wearing Account

			Apr. 12	Purchases	BDB 3	54.00

The credit entry shows that the supplier has 'given' the value of £54.

12.01 Can you remember where we record the value 'received'?

The folio reference is BD B3—showing that the entry has been posted from the Bought Day Book page 3.

Payments to creditors

When we pay XY Wearing, the double entry will be:

Credit . . .

Bank Account

| | | Apr. 19 | XY Wearing | BL X1 | 54.00 |

and debit

XY Wearing Account

| Apr. 19 | Bank | CB 17 | 54.00 | Apr. 12 | Purchases | BDB 3 | 54.00 |

Credit the supplier's account with the value of the goods we have purchased on credit, and debit the supplier's account with amounts paid to him.

Joe's Rule No. 13

Before XY Wearing was paid the amount owing, the account had a credit balance of £54.00. An easy point to remember—a creditor has a credit balance on his account in the Bought Ledger. A credit balance means that we *owe* that sum to the supplier, therefore creditors equal *liabilities*. A liability is an amount owing by our business. The Bought Ledger therefore contains accounts of creditors and shows the liabilities of the business for the credit purchases of goods, the credit purchases of assets, and amounts owing for services (but you will have to wait until chapter 21 to learn more about the last aspect).

Cash discounts received

Paying suppliers' bills promptly may allow a business to deduct a certain percentage from the outstanding amount. As our business would offer a cash discount to our customers (discount allowed) to encourage them to pay us, so we are offered a cash discount (discount received) if we pay our bills within a specified time limit.

Using XY Wearing's account as an example,—let us say that we may deduct $2\frac{1}{2}$ per cent if we pay the bill within seven days. Our cheque will be for only £54 less $2\frac{1}{2}$ per cent = £54 less £1.35 = £52.65. The discount of £1.35 will be shown in the Discount Received column (memorandum only) in the Cash Book—and posted to XY Wearing's account in the ledger at the same time as the payment to them. The total of the entries in the Discount Received column in the Cash Book will be posted to the credit of the Discount Received Account in the General Ledger at the end of the week or month, or whenever the Cash Book is balanced.

12.02   Draw up the statement that Bill Byer will expect to receive at the end of October from his supplier, Syd Cellar, in respect of the following transactions. Make out the statement with the correct headings and names.

Oct. 5   Goods invoiced to Byer at a net value of £36.00 on invoice No. SC/432.

12   Byer sent a cheque in respect of his purchases on 5 October deducting 5 per cent cash discount.

18   Goods invoiced to Byer (Invoice No. SC/443) for a catalogue value of £90 less 30 per cent trade discount.

21   Byer received a debit note from Cellar for £10.00, being a charge for containers used in despatching the goods invoiced on 18 October.

12.03   From the information below prepare the account of F. Lower-Miller as it would appear in the Bought Ledger of B. Baker.

Jan. 1   Balance due to F. Lower-Miller £98.00.

5   Purchases by Baker (catalogue price £120.00) less 20 per cent trade discount.

8   F. Lower-Miller charged Baker £7.50 for containers.

12   F. Lower-Miller received goods returned by Baker and allowed credit of £25 net.

20   Baker paid the amount due on 1 January, by cheque, and returned the containers, receiving full credit.

28   Baker paid the balance of Lower-Miller's account by cheque deducting $2\frac{1}{2}$ per cent cash discount.

12.04   (a) Record the following transactions in the Cash Book and other books of original entry.

(b) Total and post the subsidiary books to the ledger.

(c) Balance all the accounts and extract a trial balance at 30 September.

Sept. 1   L. Hockey started business as a painter and decorator under the name of L. & H. Painters and paid £580 into a newly opened business bank account. He also brought into the business his motor van, valued at £800.

2   The business purchased ladders and brushes by cheque costing £340. Tables and other equipment costing £250 were bought on credit from N. Evans & Co. Ltd.

4   Materials costing £80 were purchased on credit from P. & D. Supplies Ltd. and costing £42 from Allday Services Ltd.

8   A cheque was drawn from the bank for £55, £35 being paid as wages, £7.50 for miscellaneous materials, £2.50 for stationery, and the reminder being kept by L. Hockey.

10   Invoices were sent to T. Hawker for £88 and C. Hat for £59.

Sept. 15   A cheque was sent in payment of P. & D. Suppliers Ltd's account and the Road Fund Licence of £50 was paid by cheque for the motor van.

      18   Materials were purchased on credit from P. & D. Supplies for £166 and a cheque for £65 was drawn for cash. Cash was paid for wages £35 and Hockey took £20 for his own use.

      21   Cash sales of £15.00 were received out of which miscellaneous materials costing £6.50 were purchased.

      22   Invoices were sent to S. Pecker for £185.00 and Mr and Mrs Voyce for £248.00.

      24   Cash withdrawn from bank totalled £106. £38.00 was paid as wages, £4.50 was spent on stationery and postage, and materials cost £33.50. L. Hockey retained £30 for his own use.

      25   Invoices were sent to L. Affter for £175.00, W. Hisper for £70.00 and Cy-lant Receivers Ltd. for £200.00.

      29   Cheque for £88 received from T. Hawker.
              Cash sales totalled £22.00.

      30   Invoice, for petrol and oil used in the month, for £39.50 was received from A. Garage Ltd.
              A cheque for £80.00 was drawn and paid as follows: wages £45.00, drawings £30.00, £5 casual labour.

13. Further Consideration of Debtors/Creditors

Recording sales returns

Sales returns are sometimes called *returns inwards*. Customers may not be satisfied with the goods you have sold them; you may, in error, have dispatched incorrect goods; or the goods may be damaged in transit. Whatever the reason, some record will be kept of goods returned to the business.

From the bookkeeping viewpoint, we must know the value of the returns, otherwise we cannot make any entries in the books. Two situations arise frequently.

1 Customers return goods which have been previously bought for cash. The bookkeeping entries for the actual amount refunded are:
   Credit Cash Account (or Bank Account, if paid by cheque): Debit Sales Returns Account.
2 Customers return goods which have previously been bought on credit; the customer having been invoiced. Since the customer's account has been debited in the Sales Ledger with the original invoice value, any refund needs only to be credited to his account in the ledger (which reduces the amount owing to us). The double entry in the accounts will be:
   Credit the customer's account in the Sales Ledger: Debit the Sales Returns Account.

Before these entries can be made, the ledger clerk will need to know the actual amount to be credited, and this he finds in the Sales Returns Book (or Returns Inwards Book). This is a book of original entry and it is a record of *credit notes* (with an abbreviation of C/N) sent to customers. The procedure is as follows. Goods returned by the customer are noted by the storekeeper, who sends details to the sales manager and the accountant. The sales manager agrees to the 'refund' and authorizes the accountant to 'credit' the customer. The accountant will arrange for a *credit note* to be prepared and sent to the customer. Credit notes are usually printed in red so that they do not become confused with invoices. The credit note is sent to the customer to tell him of the amount which has been credited (in our books) to his account. The copy of the credit note is used to enter our Sales Returns Book with the details of the customer, the goods returned, and the total of the credit note. The total of each credit note is posted to the credit of the customer's account in the Sales Ledger and the total of the Book is posted to the debit of the Sales Return Account in the General Ledger.

Allowances, containers, errors

There are many reasons why we will need to credit customers' accounts even though we do not actually receive goods returned. The customer may wish to keep damaged goods if we reduce the price to him. Such a reduction is called an *allowance*, and if we agree to this we must raise a credit note. Customers previously overcharged will need a reduction equivalent to the overcharge; customers previously invoiced for returnable containers will expect a refund when the containers are returned. In all such cases, a credit note is prepared and sent to the customer.

Example

July 3   B. Baker returned seven rugs that were badly stained. He had previously been charged £3.50 each and was now given full credit on C/N 093.
18   P. Edwards returned a length of carpet which had damage marks and was unsuitable for use. We allowed him a credit of £14.00 on C/N 094.
21   C. Woolerton informed us that we had overcharged him £4.00 on Invoice No. A/1643. This was checked and the error agreed. C/N 095 for £4 was sent to him.
26   C/N 096 was sent to W. Marshall for £15 for containers returned.

Sales Returns Book   16

July 3	B. Baker Rugs returned	C/N 093	SL B3		24.50
18	P. Edwards Damaged carpet	C/N 094	E1		14.00
21	C. Woolerton Overcharge	C/N 095	W2		4.00
28	W. Marshall Containers	C/N 096	M4		15.00
31	Sales Returns Account	Dr	GL S6		£57.50

In the Sales Ledger the accounts would be entered as follows.

B. Baker   B3

| June 21 | Sales | SDB 6 | 48.35 | July 3 | Returns | SRB 16 | 24.50 |

C. Woolerton   W2

| July 16 | Sales | SDB 7 | 84.00 | July 21 | Sales Return A/c (Overcharge) | SRB 16 | 4.00 |

Sales Returns Account   S6

| July 31 | Total | SRB 16 | 57.50 | | | | |

91

BOOKKEEPING: THE BASIS OF ACCOUNTING

Note the following points.

1 The accounts for Edwards and Marshall would be similarly entered to those shown—that is, the reason for the credit is actually written in the Details column; if it is sales returns, that will be entered.
2 The Sales Returns Book is entered in exactly the same way as the Sales Day Book.
3 The double entry is completed when the total is posted at the month end.

Recording purchases returns

Purchases returns (or *returns outwards*) arise when we find that goods supplied to us are faulty, incorrect, or damaged. The goods may be sent back by us to the supplier, or we may wish to retain them if the supplier will give us an allowance. We may also return to him containers with which we have previously been charged. In all these cases we expect him to credit our account in his books with the amount of the allowance or refund. We will receive his *credit note* showing us the amount credited to our account in his Sales Ledger. This document is recorded in our *Purchases Returns Book* (or *Returns Outwards Book*). This book is ruled in the same way as the Purchases Day Book, and it too is a book of original entry. In posting to the ledger, remember that the supplier's account in the Creditors Ledger is *debited* (since we now owe him less), and the total of the Book is posted to the *credit* of the Purchases Returns Account.

Bad debts

A large business will employ a *credit controller*, who has the responsibility of deciding whether or not goods should be sold on credit to new customers. Despite this, some customers may not pay their debts. If it is known that a debtor cannot pay, then it is incorrect for his account to be kept in the Sales Ledger—since the asset is no longer an asset! The amount which cannot be obtained from him is lost and must be considered as a loss. It is transferred from his account in the Sales Ledger to a Bad Debts Account in the General Ledger.

The double entry in the account is:

Credit the customer's account: Debit the Bad Debts Account

with the irrecoverable amount. (The authority to do this will be an entry in the Journal—a book of original entry.)

Dividends in bankruptcy
It often happens that when a business goes into liquidation, or an individual goes bankrupt, all the business debts cannot be paid in full, but there is some money available. This is distributed proportionately among the creditors. For example, if a business owes £10,000 but can only raise £4,000, then the amount each creditor will receive will be a *dividend* of 40p in the £. So if we are owed £120 we will actually receive 120 × 40p = £48. The entry in our Sales Ledger Account will be:

A. Customer Account

Balance	b/d	120.00	Bank		48.00
			Bad Debts Account		72.00
		120.00			120.00

The bookkeeping records for bad debts are made in the Journal; this section is explaining the double entry in the ledger.

Dishonoured cheques

Cheques from customers are paid into the bank account and our bank collects this sum from the customer's bank. Should our bank not be able to collect this, because the customer's account has insufficient money in it, then our bank returns the cheque to us marked R/D (Refer to Drawer). The amount previously entered into our Bank Account has now not in fact been received, so we must take it out of our Bank Account and debit the customer who still owes this sum. This was discussed in chapter 10 on the Cash Book and mentioned here because it can cause a situation to arise which is discussed below (see first section under Disallowed Discounts).

Disallowed discounts

1   Discounts previously allowed to customers. If a discount previously allowed is now *disallowed*, then the original entries have to be reversed. The original double entry was:

Debit Discount Allowed Account: Credit the customer's account.

Obviously, therefore, the reverse is:

Debit the customer's account (since he now owes this sum): Credit Discount Allowed Account.

The point to note here is that the discount disallowed is *not* shown in the Cash Book, because, although the disallowed amount could be entered in the Discount Received column, and posted, correctly, to the debit side of the customer's account, the amount is included in the Discount Received, posted to the Discounts Received Account. This is incorrect. (If a debtor pays his account and deducts discount to which he is not entitled—then the actual amount received posted to his account will leave the amount unpaid as a balance.)

2   Discounts previously received from creditors. Although in theory it should not happen to our business, it may arise that we pay a creditor and deduct a cash discount from his account, when in fact we are not entitled to do so. The original entries for the discount received will need to be reversed:

Credit the supplier's account (we owe this amount to him): Debit the Discount Received Account (to cancel the original credit entry).

Offsetting accounts

We may buy goods from, and sell goods to, the same person. In this case this person will have two accounts in our books—one in the Sales Ledger, and another in our Bought Ledger. This is necessary to show exactly what the position is between us, and the two sets of transactions should preferably be kept quite separate. We pay him for goods bought; he pays us for goods we have sold to him. However, even if we want to do this, he may wish to offset one account against the other. For example, if we owe him £50 and he owes us £60, rather than pay us the £60 (and wait for us to pay him the £50) he may simply pay us £10, which is the difference owing to us. If this happens, it will be necessary to effect what is sometimes called a *contra entry* ('contra' means 'within the same account'), that of transferring £50 from his account in our Bought Ledger to his account in our Sales Ledger.

Note   These last three sections are explaining the double entry postings to the ledger accounts: the book of original entry used to record these details is the Journal.

Debtors and creditors arising from sale and purchase of assets

Assets are normally purchased on credit and the original record of purchase entered from the supplier's invoice will be in either the Journal (see chapter 19) or the analysed Bought Day Book (see chapter 24). It is possible to operate a simple three-column Bought Day Book, which analyses purchases between 'Goods for Resale' and 'Others'. The personal accounts of creditors are entered as normal, and so is the Purchases Account. The column headed 'Others' will need analysing for posting to the nominal accounts.

Example

Bought Day Book

Date	Details		Goods for Resale	Others	Total
Oct. 4	ABC Ltd.		149.00		149.00
5	Sevenways Garage Ltd. (Petrol)			25.00	25.00
10	Office Supplies Ltd. (Desk)			83.00	83.00
18	Printing Company (Stationery)			15.75	15.75
	Dr Purchases A/c		149.00	123.75	272.75
	Dr Motor Running A/c			25.00	
	Dr Office Fixtures A/c			83.00	
	Dr Stationery A/c			15.75	

Similarly, an analysed Sales Day Book can be used to record the sales of goods and other sales, such as assets, containers, scrap materials, etc. It would be ruled in the same way as the example above.

Joe's Rule No. 14   In chapter 5, the rule regarding entries in the ledger was that entries should be made only from the books of original entry. Further to this is Joe's **Rule No. 14**: A record made in a book of original entry must be based on documentary authorization.

At 1 May 19–5, McAllister, a wholesaler, had the following accounts, amongst others, in his ledger.

13.01

Sales Ledger   Debit balances—Thomas £180, Gaddes £245, and Middleditch £83.

Bought Ledger Credit balances—Gibbon £379, Hall £46, and Jackson £91.

Cash Book   Cash in hand amounted to £78, and cash at bank £4,154.

During the month of May:

Invoices were issued in respect of goods supplied on credit to:
Gaddes £155, and Middleditch £92.
Invoices were received in respect of goods purchased on credit from:
Gibbon £201, and Jackson £177.
A credit note was received in respect of goods returned to:
Hall £16 (wrong make supplied).

Cheques were received from:	*Cheques were paid to:*
Thomas, for the balance due, less 5 per cent cash discount.	Gibbon £551 in full settlement of the account.
Gaddes £380 in full settlement of his account.	Hall £30.
Middleditch £100 on account.	Jackson £225 on account.

You are required to open personal accounts for Thomas, Gaddes, Middleditch, Gibbon, Hall, and Jackson and then enter the above transactions into those accounts. Each account should be balanced off at the end of May and a balance carried down, where appropriate. You are also asked to show the necessary entries in the Cash Book, but this need not be balanced.

(N.B. Day Book entries are *not* required, and you should *not* attempt to extract a trial balance.)

(RSA–COS)

Enter the following balances into the ledger of T. Roome as at 1 Jan. 19–8.

13.02

Cash in hand £30.00; Cash at bank £192.50; Stock of goods £889.00; Premises £10,800.00; Fixtures and equipment £1,500.00;
Debtors A. Cowley £49.50; J. Plant £118.00; P. Sharp £94.00.
Creditors Allday Services Ltd. £245.00.

Calculate and post T. Roome's capital to his Capital Account. Enter the following transactions in the books of original entry and post to the ledger, completing the double entry at the end of the month. Balance the three-column Cash Book, rule off the ledger account and take out a trial balance on 31 January.

Jan. 1 Received an invoice from G. Groves for goods at a net price of £166.00.

2 Cash sales £143.50. Paid sundry expenses in cash £15.25.

4 Sold goods on credit to L. Butler £75.00 and R. Rawson £132.00.

5 J. Plant returned goods that had been wrongly supplied and a credit note for £22.00 was sent to him.

8 Wages paid in cash £48.55.

9 T. Roome withdrew goods for his own use valued £18.70 at selling price.

15 Cash sales to date £391.00. Wages paid in cash £46.15.
Paid into bank £300.00.

18 Sold goods on credit to R. Rawson £87.50.
L. Butler returned goods unsuitable and a credit note for £35.00 was sent to him.
J. Plant paid his account at 18 January by cheque.

20 P. Sharp paid his account at 1 January by cheque, deducting £4.00 for discount. This was not allowable.

22 Purchase by cheque £250.00. Wages paid in cash £46.30.
Cash sales to date £272.00.

24 Invoice received from Allday Services Ltd. for goods purchased valued £845.00. A cheque was sent to pay their account at 1 January.

25 T. Roome withdrew cash £25.00 for own use.

27 L. Butler paid his account by cheque deducting $2\frac{1}{2}$ per cent cash discount.

28 Goods valued at £16.50 were returned to Allday Services Ltd. and a credit note received for this sum.

29 Cash sales to date £314.00. Wages paid in cash £46.50.

31 T. Roome drew £35.00 cash for his own use.
All cash except £30.00 was banked.

NA 13.03 The following statement is received by E. Wise from E. Southport Ltd.

E. WISE: North Street Hornford				STATEMENT
To: E. Southport Ltd.			Date	
July 1	Balance			245.00
6	Goods Inv. No. B/164	30.00		275.00
12	Bank		240.00	
	Discount		5.00	30.00
18	Credit–Returns C/N D12		2.00	28.00
19	Goods Inv. No. B/178	95.00		123.00
24	Credit–Containers		10.00	113.00

Explain the purpose of the statement and the meaning of the entries shown on it.

NA 13.04 On 1 May the following balances were in the books of A. King.

Sales Ledger   T. Price £49.00; A. Thomas £313.00; D. Goodall £137.00.
Bought Ledger   C. Carter Ltd. £98.50; M. Nash & Co. £148.60; F. Hulse & Son
                  Ltd. £75.00.
Cash Book   Bank Account £491.50 (Dr).

During the month the following transactions occurred.

Invoices were issued to:
B. Cutts £65.00; T. Jones £36.00; J. Bright £92.00.
Credit notes were sent to:
T. Jones for containers returned £6.00.
A. Thomas for damage allowances £25.00.
Invoices were received from:
D. Spencer £166.00; P. Sharrock £61.00; C. Carter Ltd. £98.50.
Credit notes were received from:
M. Nash & Co. £16.80, for goods returned.
F. Hulse & Son Ltd. £10.00, for container returned.

Cheques were received from:	*Cheques were sent to:*
A. Thomas £288.00.	C. Carter & Co. £94.00 in full settlement
D. Goodall £134.00, being allowed	of the balance on 1 May.
£3.00 discount.	M. Nash & Co. £131.80.
B. Cutts, less 5 per cent cash discount.	D. Spencer—deducting 2½ per cent cash
	discount.

A dividend of 50p in the £ was received from the court on behalf of T. Price. It was decided to write off the balance of his account as a bad debt. You are required to:

(a) Open personal accounts for debtors and creditors and enter the transactions for May.
(b) Open the Cash Book and make the entries required during the month.
(c) Balance the personal accounts and the Bank Account.

Note: Do *not* open the day books.

From the information given below, prepare the account of L. Kent as it would appear in the Sales Ledger of F. Surrey (a wholesaler), balancing the account and bringing down the balance on 1 March.   **NA 13.05**

Feb. 1   Balance due to Surrey £82.50.
      3   Sales to Kent (catalogue price) £75.00 less 20 per cent trade discount.
      3   Surrey charged Kent £1.50 for containers.
      7   Surrey received goods returned by Kent valued at £15.00 (catalogue price) and the containers, allowing credit in full for the latter.
      13   Purchases by Kent valued at £120.00 net.
      23   Kent sent a cheque for the amount due on 1 February, less 5 per cent cash discount.

Feb. 27   £80.00 standing to the credit of L. Lent's account in the Bought Ledger is transferred to this account.

(RSA 1)

NA 13.06   (a) State clearly and fully how you would proceed to check a batch of purchase invoices prior to passing them for payment.
(b) Name the document you would expect to receive from a supplier of goods, i.e. a creditor, in respect of:
   (i) an overcharge
   (ii) an undercharge.

(RSA 1)

NA 13.07   C. Baines, a wholesaler, has, among others, the following personal accounts in his ledger: Epstein & Co., R. Hart Ltd. On 1 July 19–5 these accounts showed the following balances:

	£
Epstein & Co.—debit balance	360
R. Hart Ltd.—credit balance	480

(a) Enter these balances in the personal accounts, make entries in these accounts which record the following transactions, and balance the two accounts at 31 July 19–5.

19–5
July 4   Paid cheque to R. Hart Ltd. for the amount of their account less 5 per cent cash discount.
       9   Sold goods to Epstein & Co. at list price £200 less 20 per cent trade discount.
      14   Received from Epstein & Co. cheque which was paid into the bank for the amount of the balance on their account at 1 July 19–5 less $2\frac{1}{2}$ per cent cash discount.
      17   Purchased 14 crates of goods from R. Hart Ltd. at £40 per crate. These crates are returnable and are charged at an additional 50p each.
      21   Epstein & Co. returned part of the goods sold to them on 9 July list price £30, and a credit note was sent.
      29   8 empty crates at 50p each were returned to R. Hart Ltd. and a credit note was received.

(b) What do the closing balances on each of the two accounts mean to C. Baines?
(c) C. Baines records his cash discounts in the one Cash Discount Account, the debit balance on which at 1 July 19–5 was £80. Open this account, enter the debit balance at 1 July 19–5, and make the additional discount entries to complete the account to 31 July 19–5.

(AEB 'O')

Many small businesses still record transactions using a number of books of original   **NA 13.08**
(prime or first) entry.

Assume you are the bookkeeper with a business of this type; in respect of each of the six transactions which follow:

(a) Name, but do not write up, the book you would use.
(b) Write up the appropriate ledger accounts.

19–4

May	2	Goods for resale, value £320, were purchased from Dawsons Supplies.
	5	£3 cash was paid for the purchase of postage stamps.
	10	Goods to the value £640 were sold on credit to Chatterson Brothers.
	14	A credit note for £40 was sent to Chatterson Brothers for an agreed allowance on the goods sold 10 May.
	20	A cheque for £310 was sent to Dawsons Supplies in full payment of the goods bought from them on 2 May.
	30	An office desk was purchased for business use for which a cheque of £50 in payment was immediately issued.

(RSA–COS)

14. Trading and Profit and Loss Accounts

When Joe has traded for a period of time he would like to know how the business is doing—whether it is making profits or losses. Apart from Joe, there are other interested parties who would like to know whether or not the business is profitable—for example, the Inland Revenue (Tax Office) would like to know, so that they can work out how much tax Joe will have to pay. Also the bank manager of the business would like to know the results of trading, should Joe want a loan or overdraft. The Trading and Profit and Loss Accounts are usually referred to as 'the final accounts'. We can prepare final accounts for any period of time—for example, every six months. However, it is usual to prepare final accounts for a twelve-month period.

Before preparing the final accounts

If any results of trading are to be prepared then they must be correct. The results can only be based on the accounts and records maintained by the business, and obviously these accounts must be accurate. To check the accuracy of the accounts, a trial balance is always taken out before preparing the Trading and Profit and Loss Accounts. The trial balance should be balanced before proceeding further.

Finding the profit

Now, let Joe explain.

We buy a roll of carpet for £800 and sell the same carpet for £1,000—we have £200 more than what we paid for it (selling price minus cost price) and if we do not incur any other expense on the carpet before selling it then we say our profit is £200 (£1,000 − £800 = £200). You do remember that when the carpet was bought we debited our purchases account as shown in the illustration on page 101. As we have sold the whole carpet, we credit sales and there will be no stock of carpets left in the warehouse.

If these were the only transactions in that period we would transfer the total of the entries to the Trading Account.

Debit Trading Account: Credit Purchases Account.
Debit Sales Account: Credit Trading Account.

Purchases Account				Sales Account			
Cash	800	Trading A/c	800	Trading A/c	1000	Cash	1000

Trading Account			
Purchases	800	Sales	1000
Gross profit	200		
	1000		1000

When the Trading Account is balanced, the 'balance' is the gross profit. Remember that if the sales income is less than the cost of purchase the result is a gross loss. A profit results in a credit balance on the account, and a loss in a debit balance. Often it happens that all the carpets will not be sold at the end of the year when we prepare the Trading Account. For example, let us say that during the period from 1 January to 31 December Joe's total purchases of carpets came to £3,500 and his total sales came to £3,000. If you compare these two figures it appears that he has made a loss. However, the stock of carpets left in the warehouse is worth £1,800, so we can say that Joe has sold £1,700 of the carpets (£3,500 − £1,800 = £1,700) for £3,000. So the cost of the carpets he has sold for £3,000 is £1,700. Look at it again.

Cost of the whole stock of carpets	=	£3,500
Cost of stocks left over on 31 Dec.	=	1,800
Therefore, cost of the carpets sold	=	1,700

The stocks left will be transferred to the Stock Account by debiting the Stock Account and crediting the Trading Account. This will be shown in the accounts as follows:

Purchases Account				Sales Account			
Cash	3500	Trading A/c	3500	Trading A/c	3000	Cash	3000

Trading Account for the year ended 31 Dec. 19–0				Stock Account		
				Trading A/c	1800	
Purchases	3500	Sales	3000			
(Balance) Profit	1300	Stock	1800			
	4800		4800			

101

The 'balance' on the Trading Account is the profit and it is called *gross profit* because it is the profit made on the trading transaction *before* any deduction of expenses in connection with running the business. The heading of the Trading Account shows that the account is for a one-year period of trading: 'Trading Account for the year ended 31 December 19–0'.

Closing stocks

All the goods purchased for resale are recorded in the Purchases Account at cost prices. All the goods sold are recorded in the Sales Account at selling prices. Nowhere in our accounts do we have any record of the actual stock that is still held in the business. How can Joe find out exactly what stocks of carpets there are in the warehouse—and what value should be put upon these carpets? The only way to do this is to have a *stocktake*. This means an actual count of the stock and recording the quantities on stock sheets. When it has all been checked, reference can be made to the original invoices from the suppliers and the cost price applied to the quantity in stock to give a stock value. This value is the closing stock entered in the Trading Account.

The double entry for closing stock

Having counted and valued the stock at the year end, that value is the actual asset value at that time. Assets are recorded as debit balances and therefore the value must be debited into a Stock Account. Since every debit has a credit, the corresponding credit is usually made in the Trading Account. The reason for this is as follows: the purpose of the Trading Account is to determine the gross profit, which is the difference between the selling price and the cost price *of the goods sold*. So far you have transferred the sales value of the goods sold to the Trading Account, but the Purchase Account, also transferred, shows the value of the goods *bought*, and since some of them are left in stock the purchases figure does not show the cost price of the goods sold. If you look at these two entries in the Trading Account—

Trading Account for the . . .

Purchases	3,500	Closing stock	1,800

you will see how the balance between the two figures represents the purchase cost of the goods that have been sold. To show this more clearly the Trading Account is usually laid out as follows:

Trading Account for the . . .

Purchases	3,500	
less Closing stock	1,800	
Cost of goods sold	1,700	

Trading expenses

Joe may have incurred some expenses directly connected with buying the goods for resale—i.e., in connection with the purchases—such as the amount paid to bring the goods to Joe's warehouse (carriage inwards or freight and insurance charges, and wages of the warehouseman). Such expenses can also be deducted from the sale proceeds to arrive at the gross profit.

Let us use the following figures to prepare the Trading Account for the year ended 31 December 19–0.

Purchases £3,500; Sales £3,000; Carriage charges on purchases £145; Warehouse wages £782; Closing stock £1,800.

Trading Account for the year ended 31 December 19–0

Purchases	3,500	Sales	3,000
Carriage charges	145	Closing stock	1,800
Wages	782		
Gross profit	473		
	4,800		4,800

The Trading Account shows the profit made by the business on the goods bought and the expenses directly connected with the goods. Since the Trading Account is usually prepared so as to show the 'cost of goods sold', as previously explained, the layout above is not preferred and so you are recommended to prepare the Trading Account in the form shown below. You will see that wages have not been included— these are always considered to be a Profit and Loss Account item. This approach is preferred by examiners and so students should prepare the Trading Account in this way.

Continuing from the above illustration, let us suppose that in the following year, ended 31 December 19–1, the following trading transactions took place:

Purchases £4,200; Sales £7,300; Carriage charges on purchases (carriage inwards) £150; Stock at the end of the year £2,000.

The Trading Account will be prepared as below.

Trading Account for the year ended 31 December 19–1

Opening stock (see note below)	1,800	Sales	7,300
Purchases	4,200		
Carriage inwards	150		
	6,150		
less Closing stock	2,000		
Cost of goods sold	4,150		
Gross profit	3,150		
	7,300		7,300

Note   The closing stock of the previous year ended 19–0 becomes the opening stock of year 19–1. The value of the closing stock on 31 December 19–0 was £1,800 and this was the value after the close of trading on the last day of the financial year. When the business opened on 1 January 19–1 (the following day) the stock already in hand to begin that year was, of course, the same stock valued at £1,800. The stock account would then look like this.

		Stock Account		
19–0		19–1		
Dec. 31 Trading A/c (1)	1,800	Dec. 31 Trading A/c (2)		1,800
19–1				
Dec. 31 Trading A/c (3)	2,000			

1   Debit the closing stock value: Credit the Trading Account.
2   Transfer the closing stock of the previous year to the Trading Account for the current year. Entries Dr Trading Account: Cr Stock Account
3   Debit closing stock value on 31 December 19–1: Credit the Trading Account.

The arithmetic calculation of the cost of goods sold for 19–1 is as follows.

	£
Value of stock held on 1 Jan. 19–1	= 1,800
Cost of purchases made during 19–1	= 4,200
Cost of carriage on purchases	= 150
	6,150
Value of stock held on 31 Dec. 19–1	= 2,000
Cost of the purchases sold during year	= 4,150

Sales returns and purchases returns

Look at the following trial balance extract (i.e., some of the items that appear in the trial balance).

Trial balance (extract) as at 31 Dec. 19–3

	£	£
Sales		28,950
Purchases	16,940	
Opening stock 1 Jan. 19–3	2,800	
Sales returns	600	
Purchases returns		185

We also know that the stock value on 31 December was £3,750.

On double entry principles, the Trading Account will look as follows.

Trading Account . . .

Purchases	16,940	Sales	28,950
Sales returns	600	Purchases returns	185
Opening stock (1 Jan.)	2,800	Closing stock	3,750
Gross profit c/d	12,545		
	32,885		32,885
		Gross profit b/d	12,545

This layout does not show cost of goods sold, net sales, or net purchases. The layout below is the one that you should adopt.

Trading Account . . .

Opening stock		2,800	Sales	28,950	
Purchases	16,940		less Sales returns	600	
less Purchases returns	185				28,350
		16,755			
		19,555			
less Closing stock		3,750			
		15,805			
Gross profit c/d		12,545			
		28,350			28,350
			Gross profit b/d	12,545	

Profit and Loss Account

If Joe wants to know the 'true' profit (or loss) made by the business he would have to deduct from the gross profit all the other revenue expenses incurred in running the business—for example, light and heat, telephone, stationery, and salaries.

Suppose in addition to the information given in the illustration on page 103 you knew the following figures.   **Example**

	£
Wages	850
Light and heat	120
Telephone charges	175
Stationery and printing	42
Salary—office clerk	720
Interest received	32

We can find the 'true' profit, called the *net profit* for the year, by preparing a Profit and Loss Account. The Profit and Loss Account is a continuation of the Trading Account. We bring down the gross profit to the credit side of the Profit and Loss

Account and transfer the expenses to the debit side of the account, as shown below.

Transfer of expenses to Trading and Profit and Loss Account

Trading and Profit and Loss Account for the year ended 31 December 19–1

Opening stock	1,800	Sales	7,300
Purchases	4,200		
Carriage inwards	150		
	6,150		
less Closing stock	2,000		
Cost of goods sold	4,150		
Gross profit c/d	3,150		
	7,300		7,300
Wages	850	Gross profit b/d	3,150
Salary	720	Interest received	32
Light and heat	120		
Telephone	175		
Stationery and printing	42		
Net profit c/d	1,275		
	2,332		2,332
		Net profit b/d	1,275

Carriage Inwards A/c

Balance	150	Trading A/c	150

Wages A/c

Balance	850	Profit & Loss A/c	850

Salary A/c

Balance	720	Profit & Loss	720

Light and Heat A/c

Balance	120	Profit & Loss	120

Telephone A/c

Balance	175	Profit & Loss	175

Stationery and Printing A/c

Balance	42	Profit & Loss	42

Interest Received A/c

Profit & Loss	32	Balance	32

The net profit of £1,275 made by the business belongs to the owner of the business and so it will be transferred to his Capital Account (or current account, if there is one) as below.

Profit and Loss (extracts)

Capital Account	1,275	Net profit b/d	1,275

Capital Account

		Balance 1 Jan.	8,000
		Net profit for year	1,275

This will be shown in the Balance Sheet (see chapter 15).

Closing nominal accounts in the ledger

When entries are made for expenses and incomes in the nominal accounts, the rule is:

Debit expenses: Credit incomes.

Each account in the nominal ledger is totalled at the end of the trading period and transferred to either the Trading Account or the Profit and Loss Account. The result of this is that expenses and losses which appear as *debits* in their respective accounts are shown as *debits* in the final accounts. Also, incomes and gains that appear in the nominal ledger as *credits* are shown as *credits* in the final accounts. The final accounts summarize to total activities of the business, but the entries in these accounts must correspond to the rules of double entry.

Transfers to the final accounts are made by closing each nominal account. To close an account means making an entry on the side *opposite* to the existing balance—if you refer to the example on page 106 you will see that in the case of the expense accounts which contain debit balances, they have been closed by credit entries. Following the rules of double entry, these credit entries must have corresponding debit entries—which are those in the Trading and Profit and Loss Accounts.

As an example, this is how the Advertising Account will appear in the ledger.

		Advertising Account				
Mar. 31	Bank	48.00	Dec. 31	Profit and Loss A/c	175.00
July 4	Bank	51.00			
Sept. 25	Bank	31.00			
Dec. 31	Bank	44.00			
		175.00			175.00

The effect of all this is that all income and expense accounts are *closed* (no balances appear on these accounts in the ledger) and the totals of each account are shown in the final accounts. The final accounts are in turn 'closed' as follows: any gross profit or loss is transferred (carried down) to the Profit and Loss Account: any net profit or loss is transferred to the owner's Capital Account.

Procedure for preparing final accounts

1 Balance all accounts and prepare a trial balance, which must be balanced before proceeding further.
2 Conduct a stocktake and calculate the value of closing stock—Debit the Stock Account: Credit the Trading Account.
3 Close off all nominal accounts by transfer to the Trading and Profit and Loss Accounts.

4   Calculate the gross and net profits (or losses) and close the final accounts by transfer to the owner's Capital Account.
5   Verify that the remaining balances in the ledgers are correct by preparing a Balance Sheet. These balances consist of personal accounts—i.e., debtors and creditors—and real accounts—i.e., assets.
6   Transfer drawings to Capital Account.

Example

Step 1 results in the following. Trial balance as at 31 Dec. 19–2

Step 3 affects the nominal accounts as follows.

	Dr	Cr	
Capital		9,275	
Machinery	6,600		
Purchases	16,800		
Sales		24,650	Transfer to Trading A/c
Returns inwards	150		
Carriage inwards	78		
Salaries	3,600		
Advertising	165		
Rent and rates	985		Transfer to Profit and Loss A/c
Interest received		240	
General expenses	698		
Debtors	1,500		
Creditors		2,800	
Vehicles	3,500		
Stock 1 Jan. 19–2	2,000		Transfer to Trading A/c
Bank		911	
Drawings	1,800		
	37,876	37,876	

Stock 31 Dec. 19–2	3,800		*Step 2* affects the Stock and Trading
Trading Account		3,800	Accounts.

Step 4

Trading and Profit and Loss Account for the year ended 31 December 19–2

Opening stock	2,000	Sales	24,650	
Purchases	16,800	less Returns inwards	150	24,500
Carriage	78			
	18,878			
less Closing stock	3,800			

Trading and Profit and Loss Account—*continued*

Cost of goods sold	15,078			
Gross profit c/d	9,422			
	24,500			24,500
Salaries	3,600	Gross profit b/d		9,422
Advertising	165	Interest received		240
Rent and rates	985			
General expenses	698			
Net profit to capital A/c	4,214			
	£9,662			£9,662

Step 5 You will have to see chapter 15 to learn about the Balance Sheet, but the position regarding the accounts in the ledgers after *Step 4* above will be as shown by the trial balance *after* preparing the final accounts.

Trial Balance as at 31 December 19–2
(after preparation of the final accounts)

Capital		13,489 ⎫ See *Step 6*
Drawings	1,800	⎭
Machinery	6,600	
Debtors	1,500	
Creditors		2,800
Vehicles	3,500	
Stock	3,800	
Bank		911
	£17,200	£17,200

Step 6 Transfer Drawings Account to the owner's Capital Account. (Note that the balance of £13,489 consists of opening capital and net profit—i.e., £9,275 + £4,214.)

Profits Due to Owner

You have had to learn many bookkeeping rules in this chapter concerned with the preparation of the final accounts. Always remember the *purpose* of preparing such accounts—to determine the profit or loss of the business. The business operates to make profits for the owner and when the profit is determined it appears as a liability of the business (credit balance on the Profit and Loss Account)—since the business now *owes* that profit to the owner. Should the business suffer a loss, then the owner must bear that loss. The bookkeeping rule that summarizes the position is **Joe's Rule No. 15**.

The owner of a business receives the profits, but also has to bear the losses. Therefore *profits* are *credited* to the owner's Capital Account, and *losses* are *debited* to the owner's Capital Account.

Joe's Rule No. 15

109

14.01   At the beginning of the year, Herbie Jones had stock valued at £2,100. During the year he purchased goods costing £14,690. If the closing stock was valued at £3,050, calculate.

(a) Cost of goods sold.
(b) Cost of goods sold if returns outwards had totalled £380.
(c) Cost of goods sold if returns inwards had totalled £150 (ignore (b)).
(d) Gross profit if sales had been £18,260 (ignore (b) and (c)).
(e) Gross profit if sales had been £18,260 and returns inwards had totalled £150 (ignore (b) and (c)).

You may do the calculation arithmetically or draw up the Trading Account in each case.

14.02   Calculate gross profit in each case below.

(a) Stock at 1 April   1,000 units @ £5 each
    Purchased during April 3,000 units @ £5 each
    Sold during April   2,500 units @ £6.50 each

(b) Stock at 1 May   1,500 units at £5 each
    Purchased during May   4,000 units at £6 each
    Returned to supplier   200 units at £6 each
    Sold during May   4,100 units at £8 each
                    and   250 units at £4 each

14.03   The following balances are taken from the books of a sole trader at 30 April 19–8.

Trial Balance as at 30 April 19–8

	Dr £	Cr £
Capital (at 1 May 19–7)		2,231
Drawings	1,200	
Purchases and sales	8,406	12,909
Stock (at 1 May 19–7)	352	
Debtors and creditors	390	184
Discounts received		24
Rent, rates and insurance	664	
Wages and salaries	1,773	
Sundry expenses	125	
Fixtures and fittings	1,500	
Motor vans	410	
Cash at bank and in hand	528	
	£15,348	£15,348

Stock at 30 April 19–8 was valued at £433. You are required to prepare the Trading and Profit and Loss Account for the year ended 30 April 19–8, and a Balance Sheet as at that date.

(RSA–COS)

Author's note In this question, do not prepare the Balance Sheet at this stage, since this work has not yet been dealt with in the text.

Prepare the Trading and Profit and Loss Account from the following trial balance. **NA 14.04**

Trial Balance as at 31 May 19–8

	£	£
Opening stock 1 June 19–7	1,240	
Capital		5,873
Purchases and sales	10,260	16,840
Returns	190	210
Discounts allowed	45	
Commission received		82
Rent received		364
Wages and salaries	3,675	
General expenses	942	
Carriage inwards	156	
Debtors and creditors	3,455	1,862
Motor vans	3,010	
Cash at bank	383	
Drawings	1,875	
	£25,231	£25,231

Closing stock is valued at £2,845

(a) (i) Give reasons why stocktaking is carried out.   **14.05**
   (ii) What would be the effect of an undervaluation of stock on gross and net profit?
(b) On 1 May a business commenced trading with a stock of 1,000 articles which cost £8 each. In the same month, a further 2,000 similar articles were purchased at a cost of £7 each. 2,500 of the articles were sold for £10 each, of which 10 articles were returned by the customers because the articles were substandard. These 10 articles were immediately disposed of to a trade customer for £4 each. You are required to record the above transactions as they would appear in a Trading Account. This account should record both stock and financial transactions. The quantity and value of the closing stock must be clearly shown.

(RSA–COS)

NA 14.06   J. Jones had a stock consisting of 500 articles of £5 each on 1 September 19–6. He purchased during September: 1,000 articles at £5.25 each on 9 September, and 2,500 articles at £4.55 each on 20 September. On 25 September he sold 3,000 articles at £6.25 each. On 28 September 50 of the latter were returned to Jones in perfect condition.

You are required to:

(a) Calculate the quantity in stock at 30 September 19–6.
(b) Value the stock at this date.
(c) Prepare the Trading Account for the month of September 19–6.

(RSA)

14.07   From the following list of balances prepare:

(a) a trial balance, and (b) the Trading and Profit and Loss Account for the year ended 31 December 19–4.

Stock 1 January 19–4 £1,800; Shop fittings £750; Capital £2,360; Sales £6,850; Purchases £4,100; Wages £2,865; Commission received £255; Discounts received £168; Sales returns £42; Debtors £1,008; Creditors £1,400; Bank £92 (overdrawn); General expenses £560.

Stock on 31 December was valued at £875.

NA 14.08   From the following list of balances prepare the trial balance and the Trading and Profit and Loss Account for the year ended 31 May 19–5.

Capital 1 June 19–4 £10,865; Stock 1 June 19–4 £3,800; Plant and equipment £6,500; Vehicles £2,850; Sales £38,672; Purchases £20,431; Carriage inwards £640; Wages and salaries £8,760; Sales returns £98; Discounts allowed £140; Interest received £16; Debtors £2,219; Creditors £2,477; Drawings £3,540; Bank £1,104; Advertising £550; General expenses £1,398.

One-third of the wages and salaries should be charged to the Profit and Loss Account. Closing stock was £2,650.

NA 14.09   You have prepared the accounts of a grocer for the year ending 31 December 19–5. The sales for the year amounted to £15,000. The grocer explains that during the year a small quantity of stock, which cost £60, deteriorated and was thrown away, and he points out that there appears to be no charge against the profits in respect of this amount.

(a) Give your explanation of the position, and
(b) state how the treatment of stock deterioration would have differed if the amount involved had been £1,000.

(AEB '0')

15. The Balance Sheet

The Balance Sheet is a summary of the balances of the accounts remaining open in the ledgers after the Trading and Profit and Loss Accounts have been prepared. It seeks to show the financial state of affairs of a business at one point in time. The Balance Sheet does not relate to a period, but sets out the book values of the assets, liabilities, and capital *as at a particular date*. The heading for a Balance Sheet should therefore be 'Balance Sheet as at . . . (the date)' and *not* 'Balance Sheet for the year ended . . .', which is used in the heading of the final accounts. The Balance Sheet shows on the one hand the amount of capital put (invested) into the business by the owner (and sources of borrowed money), and on the other hand the form in which such capital is employed. So the liabilities side of the Balance Sheet will show, for example:

1   The capital put into the business by the owner.
2   Loans from other people.
3   The amount of money the business owes to other people (creditors).

The other side of the Balance Sheet will show the assets divided into *fixed* assets and *current* assets.

Balance Sheet layout
On one sheet of paper the assets are compared with the liabilities. Often the assets are shown on the right-hand side and the liabilities on the left-hand side. This layout is in contrast with the entries in the accounts and the Trading and Profit and Loss Account. However, it is not surprising, because the Balance Sheet is not a part of the double entry system and so it does not have to comply with the double entry rules. *It is not an account.* Entries are *not* posted to the Balance Sheet. It is a *list* of the assets and liabilities of the business (*not* the owner) at one particular date.

The different forms of layout are illustrated on pages 115 to 116.

Accounts in the ledgers at the year end
When the net profit or loss has been calculated, the nominal accounts have all been closed. The only accounts remaining 'open'—i.e., containing balances—are those

113

for assets and liabilities, plus the owner's Drawings and Capital Accounts. So this is what we can say.

1 Every debit entry has a credit entry.
2 Therefore the total debits must equal the total credits (which is proved by the trial balance).
3 However, after calculating the profit or loss, the only debits are assets and the only credits are liabilities.
4 Therefore the assets of the business *must* equal the liabilities of the business.

All we need to do to prove this is to make a list of the assets, and make a list of the liabilities—and see that they agree. If they do, your Balance Sheet is correct. That is what a Balance Sheet is: a list (often called a statement).

Assets

Fixed assets are the assets which the owner of the business buys to use in the business for more than one accounting period and which he does not intend to sell as part of his stocks or turn into cash.

Current assets are those assets which are bought with the intention of turning them into cash, and they include debtors and cash.

Examples of fixed assets	*Examples of current assets*
Land	Stock of raw materials
Buildings (premises)	Stock of goods being processed
Plant and machinery	Stock of finished goods
Fixtures and fittings	Debts owed to the business (debtors)
Motor vehicles	Cash in bank
	Cash in hand

Although there is no statutory order for arranging the items in the Balance Sheet, they should be grouped under the heading of fixed and current assets to show the financial position to people who know little about accounts. Remember that these assets would appear in the asset accounts in the ledgers.

Liabilities

On the liabilities side, the capital shown first is the balance of capital at the beginning of the year. Added to this is the net profit which the business owes to the owner (but take away any loss), and then the total drawings are subtracted, leaving the figure representing the owner's capital at the date of the Balance Sheet. This figure corresponds to the balance in the Capital Account in the ledger. In preparing accounts for small businessmen, it is usual to show the transactions on Capital Account in the Balance Sheet as shown in the illustration on page 115. The figure of £2,700 is the liability to the owner—but he can see how that has been determined.

Below the capital appear the other business liabilities.

Horizontal presentation

Joe Wynn
Balance Sheet as at 31 December 19–7

	£	£		£	£
Capital					
			Fixed assets		
Balance Jan. 1		2,000	Shop premises	3,000	
Add Net profit for year	1,500		Fixtures and fittings	700	
					3,700
			Current assets		
Less Drawings	800	700	Stock	600	
		2,700	Debtors	780	
Long-term liability					
Loan from Betty Wynn		2,000	Cash at bank	900	
			Cash in hand	20	2,300
Current liabilities					
Creditors		1,300			
		6,000			6,000

Note The increase in capital arises from retained profits.

In horizontal presentation, the assets are on the right-hand side and the liabilities on the left-hand side.

As mentioned earlier, there is no statutory order about how particular items in a Balance Sheet should be arranged. Usually the assets are arranged in descending order of liquidity. In other words, they are arranged in order of how quickly the asset can be turned into cash, with the most liquid asset at the bottom and the most fixed asset at the top. So you see from the above illustration that cash comes last and premises are listed on top. We do the same for the liabilities. Current liabilities are shown at the bottom, to match the current assets. They are current because they will have to be settled fairly soon—usually within six months.

The current liabilities are followed by the long-term liabilities in ascending order, because long-term liabilities (such as loans) are normally taken out for several years. Finally, the amount due to the owner of the business (capital plus net profit less drawings) is put on top of the liabilities because, unless the business is being discontinued, this amount of money will not be repaid.

Vertical presentation
The assets and liabilities can also be arranged with one group on top of the other instead of one beside the other. This is what is called vertical presentation.

Vertical layout (a)

Joe Wynn
Balance Sheet as at 31 December 19–7

	£	£
Funds Invested		
Capital:		
Balance January 1	2,000	
Add Net profit	1,500	
	3,500	
Less Drawings	800	
		2,700
Loan		2,000
Current liabilities		
Trade creditors		1,300
		6,000
Represented by:		
Fixed assets		
Shop premises	3,000	
Fixtures and fittings	700	
		3,700
Current assets		
Stock	600	
Debtors	780	
Cash in bank	900	
Cash in hand	20	
		2,300
		6,000

This vertical presentation is acceptable but the layout shown next is preferable.

Vertical layout (b)

Joe Wynn
Balance Sheet as at 31 December 19–7

	£	£
Fixed assets		
Shop premises	3,000	
Fixtures and fittings	700	
		3,700
Current assets		
Stock	600	
Debtors	780	
Cash in bank	900	
Cash in hand	20	
	2,300	
Less *Current liabilities*		
Creditors	1,300	
Working capital		1,000
		4,700

Balance Sheet—*continued*

Represented by		
Capital:		
Balance January 1	2,000	
Add Net profit for year	1,500	
	3,500	
Less Drawings	800	
		2,700
Long-term liability		
Loan from Betty Wynn		2,000
		4,700

Of the two layouts shown, layout (b) is the more usual. We may start with the assets, grouping them under fixed assets and current assets as usual, in subtotals. These are followed by the current liabilities, which are deducted from the total current assets. This will show the net amount of the working capital available to the business. Working capital is the fund available to the owner for running the business. It does not include funds which have been used on fixed assets. Therefore working capital is current assets less current liabilities.

Summary of Balance Sheet purposes

By the proper grouping of assets and liabilities, the owner can see the exact financial state of affairs of the business at the year end. Where repayments have to be made to creditors, the effect on working capital can be seen. Also the fact that the Balance Sheet balances is good evidence that all the bookkeeping has been correctly carried out.

Other uses of a Balance Sheet

1. To determine the owner's capital where double entry records have not been kept. The assets and external liabilities (that is, creditors, bank overdrafts/loans, and loans from other sources) can usually be established fairly easily. Since Assets = Liabilities, the owner's capital can be calculated. (Remember that Liabilities = External liabilities + Capital.)

Total assets arc valued at £3,975 and liabilities to external creditors amount to £1,015.   **Example**

Assets   = External liabilities + Capital.
Therefore £3,975 = £1,015 + Capital.
Therefore Capital = £2,960.

2. To calculate the business profit or loss where double entry records have not been kept. When goods are bought and sold at a profit, the assets of the business must increase. Conversely, if the business is making a loss, the assets will decrease. The profit or loss for a trading period can be calculated by reference to the increase or

decrease in net assets over that trading period. (Note that net assets are total assets less external liabilities.)

Example

On 1 January 19–2 the assets of Henry Pells totalled £8,963 and on that date his capital was £6,850.

On 31 December 19–2 the assets totalled £10,801 and the only liabilities were to trade creditors for £2,075.

A balance sheet drawn up in the normal way will show:

Balance Sheet of H. Pells as at 31 Dec. 19–2

Capital Jan. 1	6,850		Assets	10,801
Profit for year	1,876			
	*8,726			
Trade creditors	2,075			
	10,801			10,801

* Assets (£10,801) = Liabilities (£2,075) + Capital (£8,726).

The figure of £8,726 is calculated first. Since capital on 1 January was £6,850, the profit added must be £1,876.

The effect of drawings

It is unlikely that Henry Pells has drawn nothing at all from his business during the year. If it can be established that he drew £2,125 during the year, then the Balance Sheet would appear as follows.

Balance Sheet of H. Pells as at 31 Dec. 19–2

Capital Jan. 1		6,850	Total assets	10,801
Add Profit	(3)	4,001		
	(2)	10,851		
Less Drawings		2,125		
	(1)	8,726		
Trade creditors		2,075		
		10,801		10,801

1. The capital at the year end is calculated as before.
2. Since £8,726 is the capital *after* deducting the drawings of £2,125, the capital *before* deducting the drawings must be the total of the two, i.e., £10,851.

3. £10,851 is the capital *after* adding the profit, and since the capital before adding the profit was £6,850, then the difference must equal the profit, i.e., £4,001.

All assets and *all* liabilities, together with *capital* must be shown in the Balance Sheet. It is called a Balance Sheet because assets of the business should balance with the capital plus liabilities.

Joe's Rule No. 16

In all answers lay the Balance Sheet out in the horizontal method, unless the question specifically states otherwise.

Note

The following balances remained in the books of P. Jarvis after the preparation of the Trading and Loss Account for the year ended 31 December 19–5.

15.01

	£
Sundry debtors	1,965
Stock	2,412
Balance at bank	900
Freehold premises (at cost)	5,460
Mortgage (repayable over 30 years)	5,000
Drawings	2,360
Profit for year 19–5	4,670
Trade creditors	1,520
Expense creditors	340
Furniture and equipment (cost £3,000)	2,620
Rates in advance	150
Capital 1 January 19–5	4,337

Prepare the Balance Sheet of P. Jarvis at 31 December 19–5.

(RSA 1)

(*Author's note* Rates in advance should be treated as a current asset.)

(a) What is the difference between fixed assets and current assets?

NA 15.02

(b) You are required to list as 'fixed' or 'current' these assets of a building firm:
   (i) Stocks of bricks and timber.
  (ii) Tools used by the craftsmen.
 (iii) Workshop machinery used by the craftsmen.
 (iv) Stocks of sand and cement.
  (v) A cement-mixer.
 (vi) Building land.
(vii) The firm's own premises.

(RSA–COS)

119

15.03   A sole trader has prepared the following 'Balance Sheet'.

Balance Sheet for the year ended 31 May 19–5

	£		£
Net profit	870	Bad debts written off	80
Creditors	1,470	Fixtures and fittings	560
Provision for bad and		Cash	30
doubtful debts	70	Drawings	800
Bank overdraft	190	Discount allowed	110
Capital 1 June 19–4	1,900	Debtors	1,380
		Stock	1,540
	£4,500		£4,500

Required:
Redraft the above statement to conform with modern commercial practice. If you consider the net profit figure of £870 to be incorrect, you should correct the figure but show your calculation.

(LCC Elementary)

Note The Provision for bad debts should be shown in the Balance Sheet as a deduction from the debtors, so that debtors will appear as 1,380 − 70 = £1,310.

NA 15.04   The following balances appeared in the books of A. Roberts after transfers of revenue accounts had been made to Trading and Profit and Loss Account for the year to 31 December 19–9.

	£
Profit and Loss Account—net profit	3,500
Capital—1 January 19–9	14,250
Loan from A.B. (repayable in 19–5)	3,000
Trade debtors	3,200
Trade creditors	4,200
Motor vehicles	4,000
Stock in trade	2,500
Drawings of A. Roberts	2,500
Fixtures and fittings	2,000
Bank overdraft	1,500
Cash in hand	250
Freehold premises	12,000

You are required to prepare the Balance Sheet at 31 December 19–9, drawn up in such a way as to show:
    total of fixed assets,
    total of current assets,
    total of current liabilities,
    the capital of A. Roberts.
In addition, you are required to calculate the working capital at 31 December 19–9.

(EMEU 01)

On 1 July 19–5 D. Loss commenced business with £6,000 in his Bank Account. After trading for a full year, he ascertained that his position on 30 June 19–6 was as follows.   **15.05**

Plant	£3,600	Fixtures	£360
Creditors	£720	Bank balance	£600
Debtors	£930	Stock in trade	£1,350
Cash in hand	£135	Drawings	£1,600

You are required to:
(a) Calculate D. Loss's capital at 30 June 19–6.
(b) Prepare D. Loss's Balance Sheet at 30 June 19–6 (assuming a profit of £1,855), set out in such a manner as to show clearly the totals normally shown in a Balance Sheet.

(RSA 1)

Re-draft the following Balance Sheet of Kandy Stores in its correct form.   **15.06**

Balance Sheet for the year ended 31 December 19–5

	£		£
Capital	20,000	Cash	248
Trade debtors	6,420	Bank overdraft	1,500
Prepaid expenses	460	Trade creditors	5,140
Net profit for the year	7,364	Stock in trade	4,656
		Drawings	3,000
		Freehold premises	12,000
		Furniture and fittings	2,500
		Motor vehicles	4,960
		Accrued expenses	240
	£34,244		£34,244

(RSA 1)

Note Accrued expenses should be treated as a current liability.

A sole trader, whose knowledge of bookkeeping is very poor, prepared the following document from his records.   **NA 15.07**

Dr   Balance Sheet for the year ending 31 October 19–6   Cr

	£		£
Capital 1 November 19–5	1,980	Cash in hand	40
Bank balance	480	Debtors	1,670
Net profit for year	1,380	Office furniture	300
Creditors	930	Drawings	1,160
Discount received	80	Bad debts	90
		Discount allowed	120
		Stock	1,470
	£4,850		£4,850

121

The items shown in the above document have been correctly extracted from the ledger—i.e., those on the left-hand side are credit balances whereas those on the right-hand side are debit balances.

Required:
(a) Commencing with the incorrect net profit figure of £1,380, calculate the correct net profit.
(b) Redraft the above document so that it conforms with modern practice.

(LCC Elementary)

NA **15.08** From the following trial balance prepare the Trading and Profit and Loss Account for the year and the Balance Sheet as at 30 November 19–4.

Trial Balance as at 30 November 19–4

	£	£
Capital 1 December 19–3		11,650
Purchases/sales	26,841	35,492
Debtors/creditors	4,815	3,076
Returns inwards	149	
Discounts		36
Wages and salaries	6,941	
Advertising	562	
Postage and stationery	79	
Rent and rates	1,436	
General expenses	849	
Premises	5,600	
Vehicles	1,500	
Stock 1 December 19–3	2,300	
Drawings	1,300	
Bank and cash		2,118
	52,372	52,372

The closing stock on 30 November 19–4 was valued at £2,150.

16. End of Year Adjustments

The accrual principle

This is a simple principle, which says that all expenses relevant to a trading period should be compared with the incomes (called revenues) for that period when calculating the profit.

Payments and expenses

Cash payments do not always correspond exactly with expenses. Take a simple example with which you are already familiar. In May, cash purchases are £492.00 and credit purchases (for which payment has not yet been made) are £768.00. All the goods have been sold for £1,582.00 cash.

The accounts look like this.

Cash Account					Supplier's Account		
May	Sales	1,582.00	May	Purchases	492.00		May	Purchases	768.00

Purchases Account			Sales Account		
May	Bank	492.00		May	Cash	1,582.00
	Suppliers	768.00				

If you were asked to calculate the profit, you would say:

$$
\begin{array}{lll}
\text{Sales} & = & 1,582.00 \\
\text{Purchases} & = & 1,260.00 \\
\hline
\text{Therefore Profit} & = & 322.00 \\
\end{array}
$$

You would *not* say that, because the cash is now £1,090.00 more at the end of the month, your profit is £1,090.00. What has actually been paid during the month is not what the total expenses are for the month.

But you already know this and practise it with regard also to credit sales and stocks when you prepare the Trading and Profit and Loss Accounts. What Joe now expects you to learn is how this rule of matching expenses with revenues is applied to all expenses and revenues in addition to sales and purchases. Joe is going to tell you the rule now so that you can apply it to all transactions.

Joe's Rule No. 17 When preparing the accounts for a trading period, the expenses and revenues to be included are those expenses that should be charged to the period and those revenues that should have been received in the period.

Adjustments after the Trial Balance is extracted

In applying this rule you must always ask yourself the question: What *should* be charged into the accounts for this expense, and what *should* have been received as income?

Example 1 If the local council charges £475.00 rates for the year, what should be charged into the Profit and Loss Account for rates? Answer: £475.00. If however, only one-half of the rates bill has been paid, the Rates Account in the ledger will show only £237.50. Only this amount will appear in the trial balance. Obviously, therefore, some adjustments are needed *after* the trial balance has been taken out.

Example 2 Another example will help to explain this point. Let us say that a business rents a factory and pays £1,000.00 per quarter, at the end of each quarter. While payments ought to be made promptly, a few days difference at the end of each quarter may arise because of holidays, illness, or weekends. The Rent Account at the end of the year may appear as follows:

Rent Account

Mar. 30	Bank	1,000.00
July 2	Bank	1,000.00
Oct. 3	Bank	1,000.00

Obviously, the last quarterly payment due on 31 December has been missed. The Rent Account in the trial balance will appear with a total of £3,000—after all, only £3,000 has actually been paid at 31 December. When preparing the Profit and Loss Account, it is important that £4,000 is included therein, because that is what the expenses for the year *should* be—and indeed *will* be, since the £1,000 due on 31 December will no doubt be paid on 1 January or thereafter. The position on 31 December is that we have paid £3,000 and owe £1,000.

Book-keeping entries The trial balance, once taken out and balanced, will not itself require alteration. But adjustments will need to be entered in the ledgers as a double entry. You have already learned how to deal with closing stock—that is an adjustment after the trial balance has been proved. Remember that it is credited to the Trading Account and debited to a Stock Account. Take the example of rent above. What double entry is required to record the fact that £1,000 is owed for rent on 31 December?

There are two ways of recording this.

Method 1

Rent Account

(1,000 × 3 qrts. as above)		3,000	Dec. 31 Profit and Loss A/c		4,000
Dec. 31 Bal. c/d		1,000			
		4,000			4,000
			Jan. 1 Balance c/d		1,000

Method 2

Rent Account

Mar. 30	Bank	1,000	Dec. 31 Profit and Loss A/c 4,000			
July 2	Bank	1,000				
Oct. 30	Bank	1,000				
Dec. 31	Landlord's A/c	1,000		Landlord's Account		
				Dec. 31 Rent A/c 1,000		
		4,000	4,000			

Both methods are correct and can be used. In the second method, what is owed at the end of the year is debited in the Rent Account and credited to the personal account of the person to whom it is owed. The balance on the Rent Account is then the sum that should be taken to the Profit and Loss Account.

You might believe that the second method is preferable—after all, you do owe the landlord £1,000 on 31 December and the double entry is easy to understand. When you pay the rent due at the year end, the debit will be made to the landlord's account—which will then be cleared.

The first method may not appear so simple, but it is used because it saves opening a landlord's account, and in other cases saves opening many accounts. The thought process to use is as follows: How much *should* be charged to the Profit and Loss Account for the year? Answer = £4,000. Therefore credit the Rent Account and debit the Profit and Loss Account with this amount. The result of the credit entry in the Rent Account will be that a balance arises of £1,000 (N.B. a *credit* balance). You have already learned that a credit balance is either an income or a liability. Since rent (that you pay) cannot be income, the balance must be a liability. £1,000 of rent is *owed*. This liability will appear in the Balance Sheet under current liabilities. Expenses underpaid are called *amounts owing* or *accruals*, and, while they can be shown separately, are usually called *sundry creditors*.

Expenses prepaid

While some expenses may not have been paid, others may have been paid in advance. This is the reverse of the above situation. Instead of owing expenses, someone owes us the money that we have paid to them before the due time. Therefore an asset will appear in the books.

125

Example Rent is paid quarterly in advance (i.e., at the beginning of each quarter) at the rate of £500 per quarter. You would expect four payments in the year. Again due to dates of holidays, amounts available in the bank, and so on, it may be that the Rent Account appears as follows.

Rent Account

Jan. 1	Bank	500	Dec. 31	Profit and Loss A/c	2,000
Mar. 30	Bank	500		Balance c/d	500
July 4	Bank	500			
Oct. 2	Bank	500			
Dec. 30	Bank	500			
		2,500			2,500
Dec. 31	Balance b/d	500			

Note the following points.

1 The actual Rent payable for the year of £2,000 is transferred to the Profit and Loss Account.
2 Since £2,500 has actually been paid during the year, a balance of £500 appears as a debit balance.
3 A debit balance is either an expense or an asset. In this case on 31 December, the balance is an asset, since the landlord has received the sum in advance of the actual date.
4 Prepayments appear in the Balance Sheet under the heading *Current assets*, as prepaid expenses, or payments in advance, or simply prepayments. Very often the various prepayments are added together and shown under the title Sundry debtors.

Revenue adjustments

Just as expenses can be prepaid or owing, so can income be outstanding (i.e., owing to us) or paid to us in advance (and thereby owing by us). You are already familiar with the fact that debtors' accounts enable the business to record sales on credit— the revenue earned is in the Sales Account (which is transferred to the Trading Account) although the money has not been received. Debtors are assets and appear in the Balance Sheet. The same type of treatment is required at the year end when we are owed rent by persons to whom we have sublet premises, commissions by persons for whom we have worked, interest by persons to whom we have lent money, dividends on investments made, and similar revenues.

Remember the rule regarding those items that need adjustment: the amount to be taken to the Profit and Loss Account is the amount that *should* have been received in the year, not the actual amount that appears in the account and in the trial balance.

Example Interest is receivable on a loan made by our business. The Interest Received Account has only the following entry: 4 September 19–8 (for the half year to 30 August) £120.

On 28 February 19–9 the business received £120 interest for the half year ended 28 February 19–9. If our business makes its accounts up to 31 December, this is how the Interest Receivable Account will appear.

Interest Receivable Account

Dec. 31	Profit and Loss A/c	200.00	Sept. 4	Bank	120.00
			Dec. 31	Balance c/d	80.00
		200.00			200.00
Jan. 1	Balance b/d	80.00			

Up to 31 December our business earned £200 in interest—£120 up to 30 August and 4 months up to 31 December, i.e., $4/6 \times £120 = £80$.

The borrower owed us £80 on 31 December and this item will appear as an asset in the Balance Sheet under Current assets. These amounts are shown as Sundry debtors.

Revenues in advance

We may receive income in advance of its due date. Rents receivable, for example, may be paid to us before the end of one year, for the following year. In this case, we owe this money to the person renting the property. The Rent Receivable Account will have a credit balance after transferring the correct sum for the trading period to the Profit and Loss Account. This balance is a liability and will be shown in the Balance Sheet under the title Sundry creditors.

A Balance Sheet summary

Balance Sheet as at . . . . . .

Current liabilities		*Current assets*	
Trade creditors	(4)	Stock	
Sundry creditors	(5)	Trade debtors	(1)
Accrued expenses	(6)	Sundry debtors	(2)
		Payments in advance	(3)
		Bank	

Notes

(1) Debtors for goods sold on credit.
(2) Amounts due to us from transactions other than goods sold on credit—e.g., dividends due, interest receivable or yet to be received, commissions owing to us.
(3) Expenses that we have paid in advance of when they should have been paid.
(4) Creditors for goods and services purchased.
(5) Amounts due by us for transactions other than specifically connected with buying and selling—e.g., amounts owing for VAT, amounts due to the Inland

Revenue, amounts paid to us in advance of the due date (such as rent from subletting premises).

(6) Expenses that were owing at the Balance Sheet date—for wages, rent, telephones, electricity, and so on.

The effect of adjustments

Always remember to account for the two effects of end of year adjustments. One effect is on the Trading or Profit and Loss Account, the other is on the Balance Sheet. The adjustment, since it is made *after* the Trial Balance is prepared, will obviously affect the amount of that item to be charged to the Profit and Loss Account.

Example   The Trial Balance below shows that rent actually paid totals £490.

Trial Balance as at . . . . . .

	£	£
	.	.
	.	.
	.	.
Rent	490	.

If we owe £50 for rent, then the bookkeeping entries will be:

Debit Rent Account £50: Credit Landlord's Account £50.

Therefore additional to the accounts already in the Trial Balance.

we now have . . .	Rent	50	
and . . .	Landlord's A/c		
	(or Rent A/c)		50

The Profit and Loss Account will show a total of £540 for rent and £50 liability will appear in the Balance Sheet.

Depreciation

The actual methods of providing for depreciation are dealt with in detail in chapter 17. The important point to remember is that the actual adjustments for depreciation are usually made after the trial balance has been prepared. Considering only the ledger accounts involved, any loss in the value of assets due to depreciation will need to be taken into a separate Depreciation Account.

Example   If a motor van is purchased during a trading period, the record will be made in a Motor Van Account.

At the year end, the trial balance will show the cost price as a debit balance.

Trial Balance . . .

	Dr	Cr
Motor van	2,800	

Depreciation will reduce its value, so the motor van at the end of the year may be worth only £2,450. The value of the asset must be reduced and the loss shown as:

	Dr	Cr
Motor van		350
Depreciation	350	

Since the trial balance and adjustments are used as the basis of the Trading and Profit and Loss Account, you can see that the loss of £350 will be shown in the Profit and Loss Account and the motor van shown in the Balance Sheet at its true value of £2,450 (2,800 − 350).

Provision for bad and doubtful debts

When it is finally decided that a debtor will not be paying his debt, the amount owing is written off as a *bad debt*. This reduces the assets (of debtors) and increases the expenses (losses). Therefore, at the end of a trading period, the Bad Debts Account will show the bad debts actually written off. Consequently the debtors' accounts, if totalled, will give you the asset of debtors to show in the Balance Sheet. Suppose for a moment that some of those debtors do not pay in the future. The value of debtors shown in the Balance Sheet is then not correct.

Also—since the sales were made to them during the current year, losses arising from their non-payment should be charged against this year's profits, and shown in this year's Profit and Loss Account (the matching concept). But if we do not know how many of them will not pay, how do we allow for this type of loss? Obviously, we cannot be exact. What we can do, though, is to examine closely all the debtors' accounts and decide whether or not each debtor is likely to pay the sum he owes. This is a serious matter. We do not sell goods to people in the expectation that they will not pay. We sell them and expect to receive the money. Occasionally, however, individuals go bankrupt and companies go into liquidation, and this means that we do not get paid. What guidance do we have to indicate that we may not receive payment?

There are many questions we can ask ourselves. Is the amount overdue? If so, by how long? Have we received any replies to our requests for payment? Is the person still in business and at the same address? Have we received only a part payment?

What we are trying to do is to assess just how much money we may lose by non-payment. It is this sum that should be used to reduce the debtors to an agreed, realistic, figure.

Definition of a provision

A *provision* is an amount of money set aside out of profit for a known future loss, the amount of which cannot be exactly determined. If we believe that, out of the total debtors at the end of the year of £8,975, the amount of £460 will be lost through non-payment, then the Balance Sheet should show only £8,515 as the asset. The double entry bookkeeping for this is as follows:

Debit £460 to the Profit and Loss Account: Credit £460 to a Provision for Bad and Doubtful Debts Account.

Why does a Provision Account have a credit balance? The provision is created by setting aside some of the profit made (remember that profits appear as credits—a liability of the business since it owes profits to the owner) in case the loss arises. If the loss does not arise then the amount set aside is still owed to the owner.

Bad debts and provisions for bad debts

Do not confuse the two. They are quite separate.

1 Bad Debts are *actual* losses which are written off to the Profit and Loss Account. When the loss arises, it is taken out of the debtor's account and into a Bad Debts Account. Do not enter these *actual* losses in the Provision Account.

2 A provision for bad debts is made *only* at the year end, based on what is believed to be a *future* loss that will arise. The debtors' accounts are in no way altered.

Example 1

On 31 December 19–6, the debtors totalled £6,241.00, the balance on the Bad Debts Account was £146.00, and it was considered that £171.00 should be provided for future possible bad debts.

This is how the accounts will look

Debtors Account

Dec. 31	Balance	6,241.00			

Bad Debts Account

Dec. 31	Balance	146.00	Dec. 31	Profit and Loss A/c	146.00

Profit and Loss Account (Extract) 19–6

Dec. 31	Bad debts	146.00		
Dec. 31	Provision for bad debts	171.00		

Provision for Bad and Doubtful Debts Account

	Dec. 31 Profit and Loss A/c	171.00

Balance Sheet (Extract) 19–6

Asset side Debtors		6,241.00
Less provision for bad debts		171.00
		6,070.00

Note the following points.

(a) The expected loss of £171.00 is put into the Profit and Loss Account.
(b) The real value of debtors is shown in the Balance Sheet. (See how the provision reduces the debtors, rather than being entered under the liabilities on the Balance Sheet.)

Continuing from the above, on 31 December 19–7 the bad debts provision is required to be £260. Since a provision already exists of £171.00, it needs only to be increased by £89.00. Therefore the entries will be: **Example 2**

Profit and Loss Account (Extract) 19–7

Increase in Provision for bad and doubtful debts	89.00

Provision for Bad and Doubtful Debts Account

	Dec. 31 19–6 Profit and Loss	171.00
	Dec. 31 19–7 Profit and Loss	89.00

Balance Sheet Extract 19–7

Asset side Debtors (actual balances)		8,672.00
Less provision for bad and doubtful debts		260.00
		8,412.00

Of course, in 19–7 there will, no doubt, have been some actual bad debts. These will already have been taken out of the debtors' accounts and written off to the Profit and Loss Account.

In 19–8, the provision required may be only £235. Consequently, since the account already has a credit balance of £260 brought forward from 19–7, some of the profit previously set aside can now be written back into the Profit and Loss Account. The entries will appear as follows. **Example 3**

Profit and Loss Account (Extract) 19–8

	Decrease in Provision for bad and doubtful debts	25.00

131

Provision for Bad and Doubtful Debts Account

Dec. 31 19–8	Profit and Loss		25.00	Dec. 31 19–6	Profit and Loss	171.00
Dec. 31 19–8	Balance c/d		235.00	Dec. 31 19–7	Profit and Loss	89.00
			260.00			260.00
				Jan. 1 19–9	Balance b/d	235.00

Balance Sheet (Extract) 19–8

Asset side	Debtors (actual amount)		5,968.00
	Less Provision for bad and doubtful debts		235.00
			5,733.00

16.01   A Trial Balance has the following accounts included.

Insurance	£141.00 (Dr)
Commission	£75.00 (Cr)
Telephones	£293.00 (Dr)
Carriage	£77.00 (Dr)

The following adjustments are required in respect of these items.

Insurance is prepaid by £39.00
Commission receivable, due, amounts to £25.00
Telephone bill outstanding £76.00
Carriage expenses outstanding £15.00

Show the ledger account for each item above after the adjustment has been made and the transfer effected to the Profit and Loss Account.

16.02   On 1 January 19–9 the Wages Account had a credit balance brought forward of £87.55. During the year £9,174.62 was paid in cash for wages. On 31 December 19–9, £110.76 was outstanding for wages due but unpaid. Show the Wages Account after adjustment.

NA 16.03   Losses are written off to the Profit and Loss Account. How is a future loss dealt with at the financial year end; explain the double entry required.

16.04   A professional association publishes a monthly journal which brings in considerable advertising revenue. During the year to 30 May 19–8, the following information is available.

Amount due from advertisers 1 June 19–7 £885.00
Monies received from advertisers during the year £9,742.00

Discounts allowed to advertisers during the year £376.00
Amounts due from advertisers 31 May 19–8 £651.00

Show the Advertising Revenue Account for the year, showing the amount to be transferred to the Revenue Account for the year ended 30 May 19–8.

16.05

S. White leased a shop on 1 January 19–7 at a rental of £1,200 per annum, payable in arrears as follows.

£200 on 28 February 19–7.
£300 on 31 May 19–7 and £300 at the end of each quarterly period thereafter, until 31 May 19–8 when quarterly rent is increased to £360 payable on this date.

Rates were paid as follows:

	£
20 March for period to 31 March 19–7	60
29 April for period to 30 September 19–7	200
18 November for period to 31 March 19–8	200
3 April for period to 30 September 19–8	210
25 November for period to 31 March 19–9	210

You are required to prepare separate Rent and Rates Accounts for the financial years ended 31 December 19–7 and 19–8.

(EMEU 01)

NA 16.06

From the following information, write up separate ledger accounts for (a) rent received, (b) rent paid, and (c) rates, for the year ended 31 December 19–6.

19–6			£
Jan.	1	Three months rent outstanding	150
	1	Three months rates paid in advance	20
	2	Paid the rent due	150
Mar.	31	Paid rates	20

Rent £150, and rates £20, are both paid at quarterly intervals thereafter.

On 1 June, part of the premises were sub-let at £25 for six months. This amount was received on 1 June.

Three-quarters of the rent and rates is to be charged to Trading Account and one-quarter to Profit and Loss Account. The whole of the rent received is to be transferred to Profit and Loss Account.

(EMEU–COS 2)

Author's Note. The rent outstanding on 1 Jan. is that rent payable by the firm.

NA 16.07   (a) Why is it necessary to make adjustments for prepayments and accruals when preparing final accounts?

(b) The following balances are included in the balance sheet of A. Green at 31 December 19–8.

Prepayments		*Accruals*	
	£		£
Insurance	18	Electricity	60
Rent payable	100		
Rates	30		

You are required to write up these accounts as they would appear in the ledger at 1 January 19–9 and to record the following transactions for the year 19–9, showing in each case the amount to be transferred to Profit and Loss Account for the year ended 31 December 19–9.

(i) Electricity bills paid:

	£
14 February	253
16 May	205
10 August	178
18 November	184

Estimated consumption accrued to 31 December 19–9, £85.

(ii) Insurance paid on 31 October amounted to £98, of which £16 was for the period after 31 December 19–9.

(iii) Rent was paid quarterly in advance:

	£
31 March	100
30 June	110
30 September	110
31 December 19–0	110 for quarter to 31 March, 19–0

(iv) Rates for year to 31 March 19–0 amounted to £132 and were paid in two equal half-yearly instalments on 20 April and 1 July.

(EMEU 01)

16.08   The following trial balance was taken from the books of Smart's, a store, at the end of the financial year on 31 March 19–9.

	Dr	Cr
Capital Account, 1 April 19–8		2,000
Cash in hand and bank overdraft	50	2,500

Premises	2,400	
Fixtures and fittings	600	
Debtors and creditors	1,800	1,200
Rates and taxes	200	
General expenses	150	
Wages	1,200	
Discounts allowed and received	90	10
Drawings	600	
Stock on 1 April 19–8	1,000	
Purchases and sales	4,910	7,290
	£13,000	£13,000

Prepare the Trading and Profit and Loss Account for the year ending on 31 March 19–9, and a Balance Sheet at that date, taking into account the following additional information.

(a) Stock on 31 March 19–9, £1,500.
(b) Rates owing on 31 March 19–9, £50.
(c) Wages owing on 31 March 19–9, £70.

(RSA–COS)

From the following Trial Balance of a *sole trader* at 31 December 19–5, you are to prepare a Trading and Profit and Loss Account for the financial year ended 31 December 19–5, and a Balance Sheet as at 31 December 19–5. **NA 16.09**

Trial Balance—31 December 19–5

	Dr £	Cr £
Capital, 1 Jan. 19–5		36,000
Drawings	6,000	
Premises	17,000	
Fittings and equipment	4,200	
Stock, 1 Jan. 19–5	15,000	
Sundry debtors	12,400	
Sundry creditors		5,800
Rates	750	
Insurance	250	
Cash in hand	120	
Cash at bank	5,300	
Wages and salaries	15,000	
Mortgage on premises		12,000
14% mortgage interest (6 months)	840	

135

Discounts allowed	620	
Discounts received		130
Carriage inwards	380	
Carriage outwards	950	
Purchases	30,700	
Sales		56,660
Sales returns	590	
Purchases returns		410
Lighting and heating	900	
	111,000	111,000

In preparing the accounts you are to allow for the following matters.

(a) £250 rates were paid in advance. £150 was still owing for electricity.
(b) Provide for the six months' mortage interest owing.
(c) Depreciate the fittings and equipment by 15 per cent.
(d) Make provision for bad debts of £400.
(e) The value of the stock on 31 December 19–5 was £13,600.

(RSA–COS)

NA 16.10 Explain what you understand by any three of the following bookkeeping expressions.

(a) 'The Bank Account is in credit.'
(b) 'Accrued expenses totalled £100.'
(c) 'A compensating error was found.'
(d) 'There is a debit balance on our Rent Account of £200.'
(e) 'Cost of goods sold amounted to £20,000.'

(RSA–COS)

16.11 A. Kemp owns a small restaurant and the following balances appeared in his books at 30 June 19–5.

	£
Revenue received from restaurant	11,750
Stocks (1 July 19–4):	
Food and drinks	120
China, glass and cutlery	584
Purchases	
Food and drinks	5,169
China, glass and cutlery	172
Kitchen equipment	826

Wages:	
Kitchen	1,040
Restaurant	1,000
Rates and insurances	420
Heat and light	300
General expenses	180
Trade creditors	700
Cash in hand and balance at bank	463
Loan from bank as at 1 July 19–4	3,000
Freehold premises	4,000
Furniture and fittings	1,560
Proprietor's drawings	2,500

Required:

From the above list of balances, compile a trial balance at 30 June 19–5, calculate the capital of the business, and prepare A. Kemp's Trading and Profit and Loss Account for the year ended 30 June 19–5 and a Balance Sheet as at at that date, taking into account the following.

On 30 June 19–5:

(a) stocks of food and drinks were valued at £160 and of china, glass and cutlery at £580,

(b) a full year's interest at 12 per cent per annum on the bank loan was due but had not been paid,

(c) depreciate kitchen equipment by £40 and furniture and fittings by £78,

(d) A. Kemp had taken £150 (at cost) of stock for his own use.

Note Prepare the Trading Account in such a way as to show clearly the cost of food and drinks sold and the china, glass and cutlery lost or broken.

(AEB 'O')

Weatherstone's Balance Sheet at 31 March 19–2 included among the list of current **NA 16.12** assets the following entry:

	£	
Debtors	10,000	
Less Provision for bad debts	250	9,750

At the end of the two following financial years, the amounts of debtors before deducting any provision for bad debts were:

	19–3	19–4
At 31 March	£9,600	£10,400

On each of these dates a provision for bad debts was calculated on the same percentage basis as at 31 March 19–2.

The actual amounts of bad debts written off were:

	19–3	19–4
During the year to 31 March	£630	£580

Required:
To prepare accounts for bad debts and provision for bad debts for the years ending 31 March 19–3, and 31 March 19–4.

(AEB 'O')

NA 16.13 Frederick Layton, a sole trader, extracted the following trial balance from his books as at the close of business on 29 February 19–6.

	Dr £	Cr £
Purchases and sales	3,190	6,620
Drawings	1,320	
Capital Account 1 March 19–5		2,700
Stock 1 March 19–5	760	
Debtors and creditors	1,450	820
Wages and salaries	1,280	
Bank	860	
Cash	40	
Rent and rates	430	
Office furniture	660	
General office expenses	120	
Discounts	220	190
	£10,330	£10,330

Notes
(a) Stock 29 February 19–6—£830.
(b) Provide for depreciation of office furniture—£60.
(c) Wages and salaries accrued due at 29 February 19–6 amounted to £80.

Required:
Draw up the Trading and Profit and Loss Accounts for the year ending 29 February 19–6 together with a Balance Sheet as at that date.

(LCC Elementary)

17. Purchase of Fixed Assets, Depreciation and Disposals

So far, Joe Wynn has been hiring a van to bring the carpets he has bought to his warehouse. He wants to buy a motor van so that he can bring the carpets to the warehouse himself and also deliver the carpets which his customers have bought.

When a business acquires a motor van, the van is called a *fixed asset*. Fixed assets are those which are acquired and retained in the business and not turned into cash. Such assets are normally used for more than one year. Other examples of fixed assets are plant and machinery, fixtures and fittings in the shop, and land and buildings. You may remember that Joe Wynn said to you once that goods which he has bought to resell, such as carpets, paints, and polish, are *stocks*. These stocks are assets which we turn into cash by selling them. So we buy the goods in bulk with the intention of selling them for cash. They are called *current assets*. Other current assets are cash in the till, cash in the bank, and amounts owed by debtors.

Capital and revenue expenditure

When Joe Wynn incurs expenditure on a fixed asset, such expenditure is called *capital expenditure*. The fixed asset has a benefit in the future. So we may say that capital expenditure is that which is incurred in order to acquire, improve, or manufacture assets to be used solely for the purpose of earning income. For example, purchase of a motor car is a capital expenditure because, as we have said before, we intend to use the motor car in the business and not for resale.

After purchasing the motor car, we buy petrol and incur insurance, tax, and maintenance expenses. These expenses are not capital expenditure because the expenditure has no benefit in the future. The petrol may have been used up and the maintenance is a thing of the past. However, the expenditure on such items helps Joe to run the business and to earn some income. Therefore, the expenditure is called *revenue expenditure*. We may define revenue expenditure as expenditure incurred in the maintenance of fixed assets, in acquiring assets which we convert into cash, in

139

selling and distributing goods, and in running the business. The benefit from revenue expenditure is used up during the period of the expenditure.

We can think of many examples of revenue expenditure: wages, gas, telephone, rent and rates, repairs to machinery, and many more.

Joe's Rule No. 18
Assets bought for use in the business to earn income represent *capital expenditure*, while the expenditure incurred in the daily operating of the business is *revenue expenditure*.

You have already learned of the importance of this distinction, but to remind you:
Capital expenditure is recorded in an asset account.
Revenue expenditure is recorded in an expense account—which is then transferred to the Profit and Loss Account at the end of the year.

17.01
Give four examples of (a) fixed assets, (b) capital expenditure, and (c) revenue expenditure.

17.02
Ledger accounts are classified as real, nominal, and personal. Distinguish between these types of accounts and state what effect the debiting of a nominal account with £400 for the purchase of a second-hand delivery van would have on the Profit and Loss Account and the Balance Sheet of a business.

Depreciation of fixed assets

A fixed asset may have a number of years of useful life. A machine may be used for four years, at the end of which we will sell it or give it away. During each of the four years, the value of the machine goes down and this decrease in value is said to be the cost of the use of the machine. Depreciation, therefore, is the permanent reduction in the value of an asset. Depreciation may be due to the following factors.

1   Wear and tear—i.e., usage of plant and machinery.
2   Passage of time.
3   Obsolescence—e.g., due to a new invention.

The actual loss does not arise until the asset is sold or destroyed but it is one of the principles of accounting that allowances should be made for all possible losses. We must also try to show as accurate a profit (or loss) as possible.

Since depreciation is a loss, it is transferred at the year end (or on the sale of an asset) to the Profit and Loss Account. To find the precise amount of depreciation of an asset is difficult, if not impossible. The amount of depreciation is determined by the owner of the business or the accountant using one of the main methods in common use. These are listed below.

This method suggests that we can determine for how long we are going to use the asset. The charge is then calculated by dividing the asset cost, less any estimated scrap value, by the estimated working life of the asset. For example, if we take a machine for which we have paid £84, and we know it is going to be used for four years at the end of which we can sell it for £4, the depreciation we charge at the end of each year for the use of the machine will be £20. We arrived at £20 by using the following formula. **Straight line (or fixed instal- ment) method**

$$\frac{\text{Cost of the machine less the scrap value}}{\text{Number of years of its useful life}} = \frac{£84 - £4}{4} = £20$$

This method is suitable for plant and machinery and leasehold property.

In this method we do not have to find the number of years the asset will be used. Instead, a fixed percentage of the *diminishing balance* is written off annually. The asset can never be completely written off by this method (that is why the method is also called the diminishing balance method). For example, a motor van cost Joe Wynn £700, and he has decided to write off 10 per cent of the balance at the end of each year as depreciation. In year one, the depreciation will be £70, and the balance is now £630. In year two, the depreciation will be 10 per cent of £630, which comes to £63. **Reducing balance (or reducing instal- ment) method**

Again, this method is suitable for plant and machinery, and motor vehicles, but is more commonly used by those firms which have plant and equipment that may quickly lose value through obsolescence—such as chemical and similar processing plant.

The asset is revalued annually and any decrease in value is the depreciation for the year. We use this method where the other methods may not be appropriate or practicable. The method is used for livestock, loose tools, and stock in trade. **Revalu- ation method**

Use the straight line method to work out the annual depreciation in these examples. **17.03**

(a) Plant and machinery, bought in 19–1 for £8,000, which will be used for 5 years and will have no sale value at the end of the 5 years.
(b) Motor car, cost £1200, has 8 years' useful life and sale value £40.
(c) Fixtures and fittings, cost £2,800, have 20 years useful life and no sale value.
(d) Calculating machine, cost £750, with 15 years' useful life, and no sale value.

Use the reducing balance method to work out the annual provision for depreciation in the following examples for the first two years. **17.04**

(a) Motor van, cost £2,000, depreciation at 15 per cent per annum.
(b) Plant and machinery, cost £8,000, depreciation at 20 per cent per annum.
(c) Office machinery, cost £600, depreciation at 10 per cent per annum.
(d) Fixtures, cost £500, depreciation at 8 per cent per annum.

17.05   Use the revaluation method to work out the annual provision for depreciation in the following examples.

(a) Cost of tools on 1 January 19–1 £250, cost of tools on 31 December 19–1 £215. Find the depreciation for the year.

(b) Cost of tools on 30 June 19–2 £780, cost of tools on 1 January 19–2 £800. Find the depreciation for the period.

(c) At the beginning of the year the cost of loose tools was £170; during the year Joe Wynn bought a set of tools for £120; at the end of the year the tools were valued at £250. Find the depreciation for tools.

(d) Jim Springtime farms in a big way. The value of livestock shown in his books at the beginning of the year was £70,000. During the year there was an outbreak of foot and mouth disease which affected his trade appreciably. He bought some stock costing £25,000 and his net cost of disposals was £35,500. His livestock was valued at £56,000. Show his depreciation for the year.

Bookkeeping entries

No matter which method of providing for depreciation is adopted, the bookkeeping entries are the same.

> *Debit* a *Depreciation Account* with the depreciation provided (this is then transferred at the financial year end to the Profit and Loss Account or Manufacturing Account, as appropriate, depending on the nature of the asset).

> *Credit*   either the *asset account* or a *Provision for Depreciation Account.*

Generally, and particularly in the case of limited companies, the asset is shown in the Balance Sheet at cost less the total depreciation to date, and therefore the Provision for Depreciation Account is used. Let Joe show you how to make the entries in the accounts.

Joe bought some office machinery for £400 on 1 January, and decided to provide for a depreciation of 10 per cent per annum using the reducing balance method. Joe prepares his accounts on 31 December each year.

Procedure 1

Depreciation Account

19–1			£				£
Dec. 31	Office machinery		40				

Office Machinery Account

19–1			£	19–1			£
Jan. 1	Bank		400	Dec. 31	Depreciation A/c		40
				Dec. 31	Balance	c/d	360
			400				400
19–2							
Jan. 1	Balance	b/d	360				

In Procedure 1 we have written off the depreciation against the asset (office machinery) and the account shows a balance of £360.

Joe will deduct the £40 from his trading profit at the end of the year, by crediting the Depreciation Account and debiting the Profit and Loss Account.

In this case, the Depreciation Account will be the same. You will debit the account with £40. However, the credit entry will be in the Provision for Depreciation Account instead of the credit side of the asset account. **Procedure 2**

Provision for Depreciation on Office Machinery Account

			19–1			£
			Dec. 31	Depreciation A/c		40

Office Machinery Account

19–1			£				
Jan. 1	Bank		400				

You will notice that the office machinery remains at cost in the ledger account. In the previous illustration it is shown at its written down value (WDV).

In some textbooks, and also in examinations, you will find that the amount of depreciation is charged to the Profit and Loss or Manufacturing Account, whichever is appropriate. The fact is that they have ignored the Depreciation Account, which is in any case a temporary account. You must note that the depreciation is charged to the Profit and Loss Account via the Depreciation Account.

Balance Sheet layout

Fixed assets are shown as the first item on the asset side of the Balance Sheet. Whatever depreciation method is used, or however the bookkeeping entries are made, it is the reduced value of the asset that is shown in the Balance Sheet.

Since limited companies are required to show both the original cost and the total depreciation provided, it is usual for companies to use a Provision for Depreciation Account. Using the example above, look at the Provision for Depreciation Account at the end of the second year.

Provision for Depreciation on Office Machinery Account

		19–1		£
		Dec. 31	Depreciation A/c	40
		19–2		
		Dec. 31	Depreciation A/c	36

143

This is how the Asset may appear in the Balance Sheet.

Balance Sheet (Extract) as at 31 December 19–2

		£
Asset side		
Fixed assets		
Office machinery		324

1 Layout usually expected in elementary examinations. (See **Note** below.)

Fixed assets

Office machinery at cost	400	
Less Depreciation	76	324

2 Layout expected in post-elementary examinations.

Fixed assets

	Cost	*Depn.*	*WDV*
Plant and equipt.	10,800	5,800	5,000
Office machinery	400	76	324
Motor vehicles	5,600	4,000	1,600
	16,800	9,876	6,924

3 Layout where a number of different types of fixed assets exist.

Note

At the elementary stage of bookkeeping it is not usual to require knowledge of the use of a Provision for Depreciation Account. Depreciation is usually credited directly to the asset account. The Balance Sheet figure shows simply the balance on the asset account.

Purchase of assets

The practice of providing depreciation on a new asset varies. The following practices may be followed.

1 Depreciation is charged on a *time* basis—that is, from the date of purchase of the asset to the end of the accounting year or to the date of sale.
   In Joe Wynn's case, if the office machinery had been purchased on 1 July, a half year's depreciation (of £20) would have been provided.
2 A full year's depreciation is charged in the year of purchase and none in the year of disposal. Taking the example immediately above, Joe Wynn will charge a full year's depreciation of £40. However, if the asset is disposed of, say, on 30 September in a certain year, although it would have been used for nine months no provision for depreciation will be provided in that year.

144

3   Depreciation is ignored in the year of purchase but a full year's charge is made in the year of disposal.

In answering examination questions, the instructions should be followed exactly. If no instructions are given but dates of sales and purchases are indicated then method 1 should be adopted, otherwise you should use method 2 and state that you have done so.   **Note**

Thomas Jones, a sole trader, purchases new office furniture for £500. He decides to write off depreciation at 10 per cent per annum but cannot decide whether this would be on the straight line method or the diminishing balance method.   **17.06**

Required:
To demonstrate to Jones the difference between the two methods, draw up the Office Furniture Account for the first three years, as it would appear:
(a) for the 'straight line' method, and
(b) for the 'diminishing balance' method.

(LCC Elementary)

Disposal of assets

After using an asset for a number of years, Joe Wynn may decide to dispose of the asset. The procedure for recording the disposal is as follows.

1   Where the provision for depreciation had been written off against the asset, the sale proceeds will be credited to the asset account and any resulting balance (which may be a profit or a loss) is transferred to the Profit and Loss Account.
2   Where the provision for depreciation is recorded separately and the asset is shown at cost, the recording of the disposal of the asset should be as follows.
   (a) Open an Assets Disposal Account and debit this account with the cost of the asset disposed. The corresponding entry will be on the credit side of the asset account, thereby removing the value of the asset from the asset account.
   (b) Debit the Provision for Depreciation Account and credit the Assets Disposal Account with the total depreciation provided on the asset disposed. Since we no longer have the asset, we cannot have a depreciation provision for it.
   (c) Finally, credit the Assets Disposal Account with the proceeds of sale and debit Cash or Bank Account.
   If the asset were given in part-exchange for another asset, the value received for the old asset would be debited to the supplier's account and credited to the Asset Disposal Account.

Joe Wynn sold for £250 some shop furniture which he had used for three years. The cost originally was £450, and annual depreciation had been provided at the rate of 20 per cent per annum on cost. Show the ledger accounts to record these events.   **Example**

145

(a) *With a Provision for Depreciation Account*

1 Asset Account remains at cost until the asset is sold.

Shop Furniture Account

Year 1	Bank	450	Year 4	Assets Disposal A/c	450

2 Provision for Depreciation Account—accumulates depreciation charged to Depreciation Account (and the Profit and Loss Account) at the end of each financial year.

Provision for Depreciation

Year 4	Asset Disposals	270	Year 1	Depreciation	90
			Year 2	Depreciation	90
			Year 3	Depreciation	90
		270			270

3

Assets Disposal Account

Year 4	Furniture Account	450	Provision for Depreciation		270
	Profit and Loss Account	70	Bank Account		250
		520			520

To record the transfer from the asset account.

To record the depreciation provision (for the three years) transferred from the Depreciation Provision Account.

(b) *Without a Provision for Depreciation Account*

1 Asset Account—written down value is shown each year until . . .

Asset Account

Year 1	Bank	450	End Year 1	Depn	90
				Bal. c/d	360
		450			450
Year 2	Bal. b/d	360	End Year 2	Depn	90
				Bal. c/d	270
		360			360

Asset Account—*continued*

Year 3 Bal. b/d	270	End Year 3	Depn	90
			Bal. c/d	180
	270			270
Year 4 Bal. b/d	180	Year 4	Bank	250
End Year 4 P/L	70			
	250			250

2 . . . asset is sold when the amount received is credited.

The profit of £70 is the result of selling an asset that is standing in the books at a value of £180 (also called the Book Value or WDV) for a sum of £250. The profit is really caused by over-providing depreciation. The amount over-provided is now being taken back to the Profit and Loss Account.

Posting the ledger from a book of original entry

You should know **Joe's Rule No. 6** off by heart. Yet in this chapter entries have been made in asset accounts, depreciation accounts, disposals accounts, and so on, without any mention of being recorded first in a book of original entry. In fact, disposal of assets on credit can be first recorded in a three-column Sales Day Book (chapter 13), or the Journal (chapter 19) or, in a large firm, an analysed Sales Day Book, and this is explained in chapter 21.

Depreciation transfers are recorded first in the Journal.

John Jones, a sole trader, purchases a new delivery van for £1,000. He cannot decide whether to write off depreciation of the van on the straight line method or the diminishing balance method.   **NA 17.07**

Required:
To illustrate how the two methods work, draw up the Delivery Van Account for the first three years as it would appear
(a) for the straight line method, and
(b) for the diminishing balance method.

Note
 (i) You must indicate clearly the method used.
(ii) The rate of depreciation in both cases is to be 20 per cent per annum.

(LCC Elementary)

NA 17.08   (a) What is meant by the term 'depreciation'?

(b) Machinery is purchased by a business at a cost of £5,500. It has an estimated life of 10 years and a residual value of £500. You are to explain clearly, by referring to one well-known method, how you would deal with the annual depreciation in the books of a business.

(RSA–COS)

NA 17.09   G. Dixon starts in business at Dock Green on 1 January 19–6, and for his financial years ending 31 December 19–6, 19–7, and 19–8, you are to show:

(a) The machinery account.

(b) The Provision for Depreciation Account.

(c) The Balance Sheet extracts for each of the years 19–6, 19–7, 19–8.

The machinery bought was:

19–6 1 Jan.	1 machine costing £1,000.
19–7 1 July	2 machines costing £750 each.
1 Oct.	1 machine costing £400.
19–8 1 Apr.	1 machine costing £200.

Depreciation is at the rate of 10 per cent per annum, using the straight line method, machines being depreciated for each proportion of a year.

NA 17.10   The following is the trial balance of the business of a sole trader at 31 December 19–3

	Dr £	Cr £
Capital Account 1.1.–3		7,000
Cash in hand	100	
Bank balance	4,400	
Premises	27,000	
10% mortgage loan		20,000
Mortgage interest 30.6.–3	1,000	
Stock on hand 1.1.–3	8,000	
Drawings	3,000	
Sundry creditors		9,000
Sundry debtors	3,100	
Sales (net) for the year		72,000
Rent and rates	3,000	
Lighting and heating	2,600	
Purchases (net) for the year	31,250	
Advertising	590	
Salaries	17,000	

148

Sundry expenses	360	
Furniture and fixtures	5,300	
Repairs and maintenance	1,300	
	108,000	108,000

Prepare a Trading and Profit and Loss Account and a Balance Sheet for the year and take into account the following adjustments.

(a) Closing stock £6,250.
(b) Six months' interest on mortgage due on 31.12.–3.
(c) Depreciate furniture and fixtures by 8 per cent.

(RSA–COS)

Charles Steptoe and his son have been in business as rag and bone merchants for many years. They maintain their fixed assets at cost and have Depreciation Provision Accounts, one for each type of asset. The motor van is to be depreciated at the rate of $12\frac{1}{2}$ per cent per annum, and fixtures at the rate of 10 per cent per annum, using the reducing balance method.

NA 17.11

The following transactions in assets have taken place in recent years:

19–6 1 Jan.	Bought motor van £840, fixtures £200.
1 July	Bought fixtures £400.
19–7 1 Oct.	Bought motor van £720.
1 Dec.	Bought fixtures £150.

The financial year end of the business is 31 December.

Depreciation is to be calculated on assets in existence at the end of each year, giving a full year's depreciation even though the asset was bought part of the way through the year.

You are to show:

(a) The Motor Van Account.
(b) The Fixtures Account.
(c) The two separate Provision for Depreciation Accounts.
(d) The Fixed Assets section of the Balance Sheet at the end of each year, for the years ended 31 December 19–6 and 19–7.

(a) What do you understand by 'Depreciation of fixed assets'? Give two methods of depreciation with which you are familiar and state circumstances under which they may be used.

17.12

(b) R. May is a transport contractor and owns a fleet of vans. He provides for depreciation on these vehicles by the fixed instalment (straight line) method at 25 per cent on cost. Depreciation is provided for the full year on the acquisition of a vehicle, irrespective of the actual date of acquisition. His financial year ends on 31 March. On 31 March 19–3 his ledger contains the following accounts.

Motor Vans Account

19–3		£
Mar. 31	Balance (at cost) b/d	15,000

Provision for Depreciation (Motor Vans) Account

	19–3		£
	Mar. 31	Balance b/d	6,000

On 1 April 19–3 one of his vans, bought on 1 April 19–1 for £1,200, was so badly damaged that it was considered as 'scrap'. His insurance company offered £650 as compensation and R. May accepted this, payment being made on 16 May 19–3, on which date he bought a new van, paying £1,400 cash for it.

Required: The entries necessary
(i) To record in the accounts of R. May the transactions given above.
(ii) To provide for depreciation for the year from 1 April 19–3 to 31 March 19–4.
(iii) To balance the accounts on 31 March 19–4.

(AEB 'O')

NA 17.13   On 1 December 19–2 the following accounts appeared in A.B.'s ledger.

		£
Advertising	debit balance	64
Rates	debit balance	80
Motor vehicles	debit balance	1,400

You are required:
(a) To enter these balances in the ledger accounts.
(b) Make the entries in these accounts which arise from the following transactions during December.

19–2
Dec. 13   Paid cheque for advertising £400.
Dec. 18   Sold an old delivery van, book value £250, for cheque £290 and purchased a new van for cheque £860.

Note A Bank Account is not required.
(c) Close the accounts for the financial year ended 31 December 19–2, taking into consideration the following additional information.

(i) Write off the old balance brought forward of £64 on Advertising Account and carry forward three-quarters of the £400 payment made on 13 December 19–2.

(ii) The rate demand of £60 for the half year 1 October 19–2 to 31 March 19–3 has been received but not paid or entered in the books.

(iii) Depreciation at the rate of 20 per cent is to be written off old motor vehicles, and 5 per cent off the new vehicle.

(AEB 'O')

18. Looking at the Results

Measuring success

Joe, the owner of the business, will want to know how much profit he has made (or loss suffered), and this shown in the Trading and Profit and Loss Account. The gross profit and the net profit, while showing the actual results for the year, do not give any indication to the owner of how well the business is performing in comparison with similar businesses—or whether or not his business is improving in comparison with the previous year. You might think that a comparison between profits will quickly show whether or not a business is improving. If, for example, in year 1 a business made £6,000 profit and in year 2 it made £7,000, it appears that year 2 was the better year. Indeed, year 2 did make more profit—but if in year 2 the owner sold twice as many goods, employed twice as many staff, and worked himself twice as hard—was year 2 really a better year than year 1? Let us compare the results of two years of trading.

Trading and Profit and Loss Accounts

	19–7	19–8		19–7	19–8
Opening stock	4,000	6,000	Sales	20,000	30,000
Purchases	18,000	29,000			
	22,000	35,000			
Closing stock	6,000	10,000			
	16,000	25,000			
Gross profit	4,000	5,000			
	20,000	30,000		20,000	30,000
Admin. expenses	500	1,000	Gross profits	4,000	5,000
Selling expenses	1,000	1,000			
Net profit	2,500	3,000			
	4,000	5,000		4,000	5,000

		19–7	19–8
Gross profit			
1	Actual gross profit	4,000	5,000
2	Gross profit as % of cost of goods sold	25%	20%

3	Gross profit as % of sale price	20%	$16\frac{2}{3}\%$

Stocks

4	Average stocks	4,000	6,000
		+ 6,000	+ 10,000
		$= 10,000 \div 2 = 5,000$	$= 16,000 \div 2 = 8,000$
5	Rate of stock turnover	$\dfrac{16,000}{5,000} = 3\frac{1}{5}$	$\dfrac{25,000}{8,000} = 3\frac{1}{8}$

Net profit

6	Actual net profit	2,500	3,000
7	Net profit as % of sales	$12\frac{1}{2}\%$	10%
8	Net profit as % of gross profit	$\dfrac{2,500}{4,000} \times 100$	$\dfrac{3,000}{5,000} \times 100$
		$= 62\frac{1}{2}\%$	$= 60\%$

Expenses

9	Administration expenses as % of gross profit	$\dfrac{500}{4,000} \times 100 = 12\frac{1}{2}\%$	$\dfrac{1,000}{5,000} \times 100 = 20\%$
10	Selling expenses as % of gross profit	$\dfrac{1,000}{4,000} \times 100 = 25\%$	$\dfrac{1,000}{5,000} \times 100 = 20\%$
11	Turnover for each year	£20,000	£30,000

1 19–8 seems to be the better year of the two.

2 Gross profit as a percentage of the cost price of the goods sold is called the **Notes** *mark-up* percentage. In 19–7 the mark-up was 25 per cent. This means that, on average, for every £1 of goods sold (at cost price), 25p was added to profit. In 19–8 the mark-up was only 20 per cent—i.e., 20p on every £1. Therefore 19–7 was the better year.

3 This is another way of showing the gross profit as a percentage of the total sales. This measure is called the *gross margin*. It shows, on average, how much of each £1 of sales represents profit. In 19–8, of every £1 of sales, $16\frac{2}{3}$p was profit. In 19–7, the figure was 20p. Therefore (as in 2 above) 19–7 is the better year

4 The average stock can be calculated by adding the opening to the closing stock and dividing by 2. 19–8 had more stock, on average, than 19–7. Does this mean 19–8 is the better year? The answer is NO! Since stock represents money that is tied up and not available for anything else, the year with the *lower* stock figure is the better year—i.e., 19–7.

5 In 19–7 the cost of goods sold was £16,000. Since the average stock held at any one time was £5,000, it means the the average stock was sold 3 times. The figure is called the *rate of stock turnover*. It was very marginally better than 19–8.

6 It seems 19–8 was the better of the two years.

7   If the net profit is calculated as a percentage of the sales for each year, 19–7 is the better year. Of the sales, 12½ per cent was net profit in 19–7. In 19–8 it was only 10 per cent.

8   More of the gross profit in 19–7 is available as net profit than in 19–8.

9   In 19–8 the administration expenses doubled in total. Measured as a percentage of the gross profit, 19–7 was clearly the better year.

10 Selling expenses remained the same in both years. As a percentage of the 19–8 gross profit, it was lower than in 19–7. It seems here that 19–8 was the better year. This calculation is of doubtful use: after all, it was perhaps because less was spent on selling expenses that profit margins fell so much in 19–8.

11 *Turnover* is equal to *net sales*. Do not confuse this with the rate of stock turnover.

Overall result

In 19–8 sales were 50 per cent more than in 19–7. Gross profit, however, increased by only 25 per cent. Net profit increased by only 20 per cent.

Stocks increased. Expenses increased.

Perhaps 19–8 was not so good after all.

The owner's investment

In measuring the success or otherwise of the business, some consideration should be given to the capital that the owner has invested in his business. He ought also to compare his profits with what he could earn by working for someone else.

Let us look first at his capital position.

Balance Sheet as at . . .

	. . . 31 December 19–7		. . . 31 December 19–8	
	Capital 1 Jan. 19–7	10,000	Capital 1 Jan. 19–8	9,000
	Profit for year	2,500	Profit for year	3,000
		12,500		12,000
	Drawings	3,500	Drawings	4,000
1		9,000		8,000
2	Current liabilities	4,000	Current liabilities	9,000
3		13,000		17,000
	Represented by:		Represented by:	
	Fixed assets	4,500	Fixed assets	4,000
4	Current assets:		Current assets:	
5	Stock	6,000	Stock	10,000
	Debtors	2,000	Debtors	3,000
	Cash	500		
		13,000		17,000

154

		19–7	19–8
1	Average owner's capital	9,000 + 10,000	9,000 + 8,000
		$= 19,000 \div 2 = 9,500$	$= 17,000 \div 2 = 8,500$
	Therefore: Return on owner's capital	$= \dfrac{2,500}{9,500} \times 100 = 26\%$	$\dfrac{3,000}{8,000} \times 100 = 37.5\%$
2 and 4	Working capital (Current assets − Current liabilities)	£4,500	£4,000
	Working capital ratio (Current assets: Current liabilities)	$= 2.1 : 1$	$1.44 : 1$
3	Total (or gross) Capital employed	£13,000	£17,000
	Therefore: Return on total capital employed	$= \dfrac{2,500}{13,000} \times 100$ $= 19\%$	$\dfrac{3,000}{17,000} \times 100$ $= 17.6\%$
5	Liquid ratio (Quick assets: Current liabilities)	$= 2,500 : 4,000$ $= 0.6 : 1$	$3,000 : 9,000$ $0.33 : 1$

Notes

1 The owner's investment is decreasing, because he is drawing more money than the profit being made. The profit, measured as a percentage of his average investment, will naturally increase. This is beneficial to the owner, since less of his own money is committed to the business. However, if he has less committed, in order for the business to continue, capital will need to be supplied by someone else. In this case, current liabilities, representing trade creditors, bank loan/overdraft, etc., have increased considerably.

3 The total capital employed is, in 19–8, £17,000. The profit of £3,000 represents a return of 17.6 per cent, a decrease from the 19 per cent in 19–7.

2 The *working capital* is the difference between current assets and current
and liabilities. It represents the value of assets available for use now in the
4 operation of the business.

Take 19–7: £4,500 is committed to fixed assets.
            4,000 is committed to paying current liabilities.
Only   4,500 is available for use in buying extra stocks, paying wages
                   and other expenses.

            _____
            13,000
            ========

But in 19–8: 4,000 is committed to fixed assets.
9,000 is committed to paying current liabilities.
and only 4,000 is available for use.

17,000

Measured by itself, the fall in working capital does not appear too serious. That is why it is useful to measure the current assets as a ratio to the current liabilities. In 19–7 the ratio was 2.1:1. In 19–8 the ratio is 1.44:1—a much worse position. The reason it is worse is because current liabilities (liabilities requiring repayment in the near future) take up a much greater proportion, in 19–8, of those assets which will be used to pay them.

5 In 19–7, each £1 of current liabilities has 60p currently 'available' for payment. In 19–8 this has fallen to 33p. The liquid ratio is a more critical analysis of the position of the business in relation to its creditors than the working capital ratio. The latter ratio assumes that creditors will be paid out of the available cash, money collected from debtors, and stock sold. However, if all the creditors wanted immediate payment, only cash and what can be *quickly* collected from debtors is available

18.01 A fire in the accounts section of G. Illington had destroyed all the records for the year ended 31 May 19–6. However, you are asked to (a) prepare a Trading Account from the information which is available.

Stock in trade: 1 June 19–5, £8,500; 31 May 19–6, £7,900.
Purchases during year: £29,000.
Gross profit is always 25 per cent of the cost of goods sold.
G. Illington's Balance Sheet on 31 May 19 5 showed debtors £3,400.
Cash received for credit sales during the year amounted to £36,000.

(b) What should be the figure for debtors in the Balance Sheet on 31 May 19–6?

(RSA 1)

18.02 (a) During the year ended 31 December 19–4, R. Taylor had a turnover of £36,000. His gross profit was at the rate of $33\frac{1}{3}$ per cent on turnover and his net profit 15 per cent on turnover. His rate of turnover of stock was 12.

Required:
Copy the following skeleton accounts on to your answer paper and, from the information already given, insert the missing figures.

R. Taylor
Trading and Profit and Loss Account for the
year ending 31 December 19–4

	Dr £	Cr £
Sales		36,000
Cost of goods sold		
Gross profit c/d		
	36,000	36,000
Gross profit b/d		
Expenses		
Net profit		

(b) Calculate the cost price of the average stock held for the period.

(AEB '0')

The figures that follow refer to the business of a small retail trader.   **NA 18.03**

	June 19–2 £	June 19–3 £		June 19–2 £	June 19–3 £
Stock 1 July	2,500	2,000	Sales	5,000	8,000
Purchases	4,000	12,000	Stock 30 June	2,000	7,000
Gross profit	500	1,000			
	7,000	15,000		7,000	15,000

Required:
(a) Calculate for each of the years ending June 19–2 and June 19–3:
   (i) the average stock,
   (ii) the cost of goods sold,
   (iii) the gross profit as a percentage of sales,
   (iv) the rate of stock turnover.
(b) Which of the two years' trading do you think is the more successful? Give reasons.

(AEB '0')

NA 18.04   (a) What is meant by the 'rate of turnover'? How is it calculated?

     .   (b) What conclusion could be drawn from the following rates of turnover of a business for its first, fourth, and fifth financial years. Give reasons for your conclusions.

Year 1   ...   4.90
Year 4   ...   3.46
Year 5   ...   2.32

(AEB '0')

Where has all the cash gone?

If you look back at the Balance Sheets on page 154 you will see that at the end of 19–7 there was £500 cash in hand. At the end of 19–8 there was no cash. In fact, the current liabilities, when analysed, may show trade creditors £8,000, bank overdraft £1,000. If the owner wanted to know why this was so, you could draw up a *cash flow statement* as follows, by comparing the two Balance Sheets.

		£
Cash/bank balance 1 Jan. 19–8		500
Deduct those items that reduce the cash:		
1 Drawings	4,000	
2 Increase in stock		
(this requires more cash)	4,000	
3 Increase in debtors		
(the business must be providing the		
extra cash to pay for the goods)	1,000	−9,000
		−8,500
Add those items that increase the cash:		
4 Profit	3,000	
5 Decrease in fixed assets	500	
6 Increase in creditors	4,000	+7,500
Bank overdraft		1,000

Imagine a simple Balance Sheet.

Notes on cash flow statements   If stock goes up, then cash goes down (you have had to buy it).
If debtors go down, cash goes up (they have paid you).
If fixed assets go up, cash goes down (you have bought them).
If creditors go up, stock goes up—but when the stock is sold, cash goes up.
If a loan is made to you, the liabilities go up, and cash goes up.
If creditors go down, cash goes down (you have paid them).

The difficult move to work out is that relating to the decrease in fixed assets. The decrease in fixed assets increases cash. The reason may be twofold.

1 The asset is actually *sold*, so cash is received.
2 The asset is *depreciated*. Depreciation is an expense that appears in the Profit and Loss Account. Unlike other expenses, cash is not paid to anyone. This expense reduces the profit but does not reduce cash. Profit represents an increase in cash. Therefore the cash increase is made up of net profit *plus* depreciation.

The Balance Sheets of B. Butler on 31 December 19–8 and 19–9 were: **18.05**

	19–8	19–9		19–8	19–9
Capital 1 Jan.	7,000	7,500	Fixed assets	4,050	4,650
Profit	3,000	4,500	Current assets:		
			Stock	2,840	2,990
	10,000	12,000	Debtors	3,265	3,375
Drawings	2,500	5,000	Bank and		
			cash	1,840	30
	7,500	7,000			
Creditors	4,495	4,045			
	11,995	11,045		11,995	11,045

Draw up a statement for Butler, to show how the cash balance has reduced in 19–9.

On 31 December 19–7, the following balances appeared in the books of T. Sinclair, a   **NA 18.06**
trader:

	£
Capital, 1 January 19–7	2,000
Profit and Loss Account (Cr balance)	2,000
Drawings	1,600
Loan (Cr balance)	3,000
Stock at 31 December 19–7	1,400
Debtors	1,550
Premises	3,000
Fixtures and fittings	1,000
Bank overdraft	900
Cash in hand	50
Trade creditors	700

Prepare a Balance Sheet in such a way as to show clearly within the Balance Sheet:
(a) The total of fixed assets.
(b) The total of current assets.
(c) The total of current liabilities.

In addition you are required to state:
(d) The working capital.
(e) The capital used or employed by Sinclair.
(f) The capital owned by Sinclair.

(EMEU 01)

NA 18.07   You, as an accountant, receive a letter from A. Dunton, a trader, who writes as follows.

'I enclose my Balance Sheets showing comparative figures for the years 19–3 and 19–4. I am perplexed, as my bank balance in these Balance Sheets shows a considerable increase for 19–4 over 19–3, yet I have incurred a loss in 19–4 against a profit in 19–3, and my personal drawings in 19–4 are higher than in the previous year. I shall be obliged if you will explain these points.'

A. Dunton's Balance Sheets are as followed.

19–3 £		19–4 £	19–3 £		19–4 £
12,000	Capital	12,100	5,000	Fixed assets at cost	6,500
1,600	Profit/loss	700	1,500	Additions during years	2,800
13,600		11,400	6,500		9,300
1,500	Drawings	1,700	1,300	less Depreciation	1,800
12,100		9,700	5,200		7,500
1,000	Bank loan	2,300			
	Current liabilities:			Current assets:	
1,650	Creditors	4,000	5,000	Stock	4,200
500	Bank overdraft	—	5,050	Debtors	3,300
			—	Balance at Bank	1,000
15,250		16,000	15,250		16,000

Required:
Write a reply to Mr Dunton explaining the points which he has raised.

(AEB '0')

19. The Journal

A book of original entry

This book has been mentioned before but not yet explained. It is a book used to record, first, those transactions which do not have their own book of original entry. Credit sales, for example, are recorded in the Sales Day Book. Bank transactions are recorded in the Cash Book. But where are the following recorded?

1 Credit purchases/sales of assets.
2 Details of bad debts written off.
3 The correction of errors by entries/transfers.
4 The introduction of assets into the business by the owner.
5 Transfers at the year end—e.g., depreciation.
6 Opening entries upon purchase of a business (including goodwill) or at the commencement of a trading period.

The Journal proper (to distinguish it from the Sales Journal, Purchases Journal, and Returns Journal) is a very useful book, since it can be used for recording all transactions that are not entered in the other books of prime entry. It provides a written record of the details of the transaction and enables an explanation to be noted. It acts as an instruction to the ledger clerk to make entries in the ledger.

The layout is different to other books of original entry but the illustration below should make entries clear.

<table>
<tr><td colspan="5" align="center">Journal</td><td align="right">Page 6</td></tr>
<tr><td>Date</td><td align="center">Details</td><td>Folio Ref.</td><td>£   p</td><td>£   p</td></tr>
<tr><td></td><td>Account to be debited   Dr
    Account to be credited
Narration (explanation of the entries being made)</td><td></td><td></td><td></td></tr>
</table>

The Journal is very often completed by the accountant, who, dealing with the unusual and difficult items, can show the ledger clerk exactly what entries are required in the ledgers. Remember that this book is *not* an account. It is a memorandum book; it shows the accounts that are to be entered. When the ledger clerk has made the ledger entries then the folio reference of the ledger account will be entered in the Folio column.

Narration

The narration is most important: it explains the ledger entries, and reference should always be made to the document authorizing the entry. It may be the invoice from the supplier, or the schedule of bad debts prepared by the accountant. No entries should be made in the Journal without the narration.

1 Purchases and sales of assets on credit

(a) Handytruck Ltd. supplies a forklift truck on credit, at a cost of £2,850, on 3 September.

(b) Two old electric typewriters are sold on credit to S. C. Rapman for £35, on 4 September.

(c) On 5 September a milling machine, standing in the books at £150, was traded in on a part-exchange deal with Machine Tool Supplies Ltd. for a new machine costing £6,800. £100 was allowed for the old machine.

Journal

Sept. 3	Motor Vehicles A/c	Dr	2,850	
	Handytruck Ltd.			2,850
	Purchase of truck No. 1234 per Invoice Number HT/142 dated 3/9/19–7			
Sept. 4	S. C. Rapman	Dr	35	
	Furniture and Equipt. A/c			35
	Sale of typewriters Nos. 131 and 142 per Invoice No. C1831 dated 4/9/19–7			
Sept. 5	Machinery A/c	Dr	6,800	
	Machine Tool Supp. Ltd.			6,800
	Purchase of machine No. 925 per Invoice No. MTS/47 dated 5/9/19–7			
Sept. 5	Machine Tool Supp. Ltd.	Dr	100	
	Machine Disposal A/c			100
	Part exchange value of machine No. 97, per agreement and Invoice MTS/47 dated 5/9/19–7			
Sept. 5	Machine Disposal A/c	Dr	150	
	Machinery A/c			150
	Written down value of machine part-exchanged transferred to Disposal A/c			
Sept. 5	Profit and Loss A/c	Dr	50	
	Machine Disposal A/c			50
	Loss on part-exchange of machine No. 97 [Under depreciation]			

2 Bad debts written off and provisions created

(a) Syd Jones owes the business £45, but, having gone bankrupt, pays us only £15. The balance is to be written off.

(b) At the year end, the provision for bad debts is required to be increased by £88.

(a)	Bad Debts A/c Dr	30	
	Syd Jones's A/c		30
	Balance of account being written off–per court notice of bankruptcy dated 30/11/19–7		
(b)	Profit and Loss A/c Dr	88	
	Provision for bad debts		88
	Increase required per schedule dated 31/12/19–7		

3 Correction of errors

Errors should always be corrected by making an adjusting entry. It may seem simpler to cross out the incorrect item and enter the correct item. This is unsatisfactory. Since entries should always be in ink, crossings out are unsightly, and often become indecipherable.

(a) Salaries of £266 were incorrectly debited to the Factory Wages Account.

(b) A payment by cheque of £145 to A. Evans was wrongly posted to A. Evans' account in the Sales Ledger.

(c) The total of the Sales Day Book for November was incorrectly totalled, and posted to the ledger, as £3,846. The correct total was £3,956.

(a)	Salaries Dr	266	
	Factory wages		266
	Correction of the error of posting salaries to the Wages Account.		
(b)	A. Evans A/c (Bought Ledger) Dr	145	
	A. Evans's A/c (Sales Ledger)		145
	Transfer of payment by cheque from the Sales Ledger Account		
(c)	— Dr	110	
	Sales A/c		110
	Correction for the miscasting of the Sales Day Book for November		

Only one account requires to be entered to complete an otherwise incorrect double entry. The correct sums have been debited to debtors' accounts. [Item (c)]

4 Introduction (and withdrawal) of assets by owner

If the owner introduces cash, the prime entry is in the Cash Book. The owner's Capital Account is then entered. However, should the owner introduce other assets,

BOOKKEEPING: THE BASIS OF ACCOUNTING

such as stock, vehicles, plant and machinery, tools, etc., then some entry must be made to record what has happened. Equally, should the owner take assets other than cash, it is necessary to make a Journal entry.

(a) The owner brings into the business the following assets on 15 August: Stock £845, fixtures and fittings £195.
(b) On 19 September the owner of the business takes for his own use stock valued at £75, and a machine that is standing in the books at a written down value of £130.

(a)	Aug. 15	Stock A/c Dr Fixtures and Fittings A/c Capital A/c Assets brought into the business by the owner	845 195	 1,040
(b)	Sept. 19	Drawings A/c Dr Purchases A/c Machinery A/c Items taken by the owner	205	 75 130

5 Year end transfers (and closing entries)

At the end of a trading period, certain adjustments have to be made in the accounts to allow for depreciation, interest due on loans, amounts to be set aside to provisions, and many others. You will remember that to provide for depreciation the two entries in the accounts are:

Debit Depreciation Account: Credit Provision for Depreciation Account (or the asset account).

(a) Depreciation on motor lorries is to be provided at £1,200.
(b) Interest on loan from Fast Funds Ltd. is due at the year end, amounting to £80.
(c) An amount of £2,500 is to be set aside out of profits as a provision for possible stock losses.

(a)	Dec. 31	Depreciation A/c Dr Provision for depreciation on motor lorries Year end provision calculated as 20% on cost	1200	 1,200
(b)	Dec. 31	Profit and Loss A/c Dr Loan Interest A/c Amount due to Fast Funds Ltd. at year end	80	 80
(c)	Dec. 31	Profit and Loss A/c Dr Provision for stock losses Amount estimated at the year end of possible losses due to lower sales prices	2,500	 2,500

At the year end, the income and expense accounts are transferred to the Trading and Profit and Loss Account. In theory, all such transfers should be made through the Journal, but this is rarely done in practice.

164

6 Purchase of a business

When a business is bought, not only does the purchaser obtain actual physical assets, such as stock, buildings, vehicles, and so on, he also purchases an existing 'trade'. Customers exist, and the value of their trade is measured by the term *goodwill*. This goodwill, in financial terms, is the amount paid for the business in excess of the current value of the physical assets taken over. Imagine Joe was going to buy the business of a competitor in a near-by town.

If I bought the business of Jarvis Carpets what would I be getting?

Carpet stocks valued at	£14,800
Warehouse and showroom valued at	28,400
Fixtures, fittings, display stands, etc., valued at	6,850
Total	£50,050

I would expect to pay at least £50,050 because that is what I would have to pay if I bought all the items separately. Now, Jarvis Carpets obviously hopes to receive as much as possible—and certainly in excess of this sum. I would look at the latest set of accounts to see how much profit the business is making. If it was making £4,500 profit a year—that is what I am buying. Jarvis Carpets may believe the goodwill to be worth £13,500 (three times profit) or £18,000 (four times profit), while I may be willing to give only £10,000. Jarvis Carpets would want to sell their business to the highest bidder. If I bid £62,000 and it was accepted, this is how I would journalize the transaction.

Date	Stock	Dr	14,800	
	Warehouse and Showroom	Dr	28,400	
	Fixtures, fittings, etc.	Dr	6,850	
	Goodwill	Dr	11,950	
	Capital A/c–Joe Wynn			62,000
	Assets acquired from Jarvis Carpets			

Since I have paid £11,950 more than the tangible (i.e., physical) assets acquired are worth, I have bought another asset, called *goodwill*. This is known as an *intangible asset*. It exists, but you can't see it.

This does not happen very often in practice—only when a business is transferred to a partnership (or a limited company) and and a new set of books and accounts are started. The opening assets and liabilities of the new business need to be entered in the Journal for posting to ledger accounts. Examinations often ask for the opening debit and credit balances to be journalized and posted to the appropriate accounts in the ledgers. Frequently, these balances are not equal, and the difference is usually the owner's capital at that date—which you will need to enter.

165

Example 1 T. Browne acquired the business of J. William on 18 December and paid £28,500 as the purchase price. The assets and liabilities acquired were valued as follows:

Leasehold premises	£10,500
Stock	8,750
Debtors	6,500
Fixtures, fittings, etc.	4,250
Creditors	3,700

In journalizing the opening entries, it will be possible to calculate the value of goodwill.

Dec. 18	Leasehold premises	Dr	10,500	
	Stock	Dr	8,750	
	Debtors	Dr	6,500	
	Fixtures	Dr	4,250	
	Goodwill	Dr	2,200	
	Creditors			3,700
	Capital–T. Browne			28,500
			32,200	32,200
	Being assets and liabilities acquired per agreement dated 18/11/19–7			

Example 2 On 1 January 19–8 the assets and liabilities of E. Evans were:

	£
Cash	150
Bank overdraft	640
Stock	970
Leasehold shop	1,000
Debtors	550
Creditors	430
Fixtures	185

Enter these balances in the appropriate books and calculate E. Evans's capital.

Jan. 1	Cash	Dr	150	
	Stock	Dr	970	
	Leasehold shop	Dr	1,000	
	Debtors	Dr	550	
	Fixtures	Dr	185	
	Bank overdraft			640
	Creditors			430
	Capital			1,785
			2,855	2,855
	Being opening balances on Jan. 1			

Note the following points.

1 From the Journal the accounts in the ledger will be posted.
2 The capital is the balancing figure.
3 Strictly speaking, the entry for cash should not appear in the Journal, since that entry will be in the Cash Book—itself a book of original entry. In examinations you will be told whether or not to journalize cash.

Journalize all transactions that cannot be recorded in any other book of original entry.

Joe's Rule No. 19

Show, by means of Journal entries, how the following items should be entered in the ledger of B. Waltham.

19.01

(a) Purchase of office equipment on credit from B. Kirkland & Co., £75.
(b) The Safeway Insurance Co. agreed a claim for £750, being the loss incurred on a motor vehicle due to an accident.
(c) Interest on the bank deposit account had been credited to that account by the bank, £23.
(d) Discount allowed to P. Carter of £4.50 now disallowed on the receipt of his cheque returned by the bank marked 'R/D—No Funds'.
(e) B. Waltham took stock for his own use valued at £18.50.

S. Trader has never kept any books and has decided to set up a double entry system. Draft an opening Journal entry using the following valuations on 1 June 19–6.

19.02

	£
Premises	10,000
Stock	1,500
Motor van	700
Creditors	250
Cash in hand	70
Cash in bank	150

S. Trader informs you that, in addition to the above, he has a mortgage of £2,000 on the premises, and that the rates are paid for the six months April to September 19–6 (inclusive), £120.

(RSA 1)

Prepare the Journal entries and brief narrations in the books of C. Shell, a boat builder, to correct the following errors.

19.03

(a) £560 had been included in the Wages Account and £240 in the Materials Account, which amounts represented expenditure on C. Shell's private sailing yacht.

(b) A cheque payment of £84 to A. H. Clark had been debited to H. Clarkson's account.

(c) The purchase of a calculating machine for the office, value £300, had been posted to the Purchases Account.

(RSA 1)

NA 19.04   T. Thomson is in business as a saw-miller and he has kept his books on a single entry basis. He was not happy with this situation and decided to change his present method of bookkeeping to a double entry system on 1 February 19–3. His position at that date was:

	£
Cash in hand	69
Fixtures and fittings (at cost)	1,800
Bank overdraft	1,500
Investments	3,000
Stock in trade	4,350
Sundry debtors	312
Sundry creditors	750

On 31 July 19–3, Thomson's net assets amounted to £10,800 and during the half year his drawings amounted to £750.

You are required to:

(a) Set out the Journal entry required for the opening of the books under the double entry system.

(b) Show your calculation of the net profit of the business for the six months ended 31 July 19–3.

(RSA 1)

NA 19.05   William Reeve, a sole trader, had the following transactions during May 19–5.

(a) Reeve took goods costing £42 for his personal use.

(b) Harold Jones, a debtor of Reeve to the extent of £59, offers to settle the debt by giving Reeve an office desk valued at £55. This is accepted by Reeve in full settlement.

(c) Simon Mills owes Reeve £32. The debt has been outstanding for a considerable time and there is no hope of the amount being paid. Reeve decides to treat this as a bad debt.

(d) Goods sold on credit to Alfred King—£19—had been correctly entered in the Sales Day Book but had been incorrectly posted to the ledger account of Herbert King.

Required:
Draw up Journal entries to record entries (a), (b), and (c) and to adjust entry (d).

(LCC Elementary)

William Jones, a sole trader, had the following transactions during May 19–6.　　**NA 19.06**

(a) Jones purchased on credit new office furniture costing £96 from Office Suppliers Ltd.
(b) Goods £46 were sold on credit to Alfred Shipley. The entries made in both the Sales Day Book and the personal account in the ledger gave the figure as £64.
(c) Jones purchased a new delivery van for £1,160. In payment for this he trades in his old van at an agreed figure of £420 and issues a cheque for £740. The book value of the old van was £460.
(d) Jones received cash £71 from a debtor named Richard Jackson. This was correctly entered in the Cash Book but in the ledger the entry was made in the account of Robert Jackson.

Required:
Draw up Journal entries to record transactions (a) and (c), and to correct the original entries for (b) and (d).

Note You should journalize the cash entries.

(LCC Elementary)

On 1 June 19–7, T. Brown's Balance Sheet was as follows.　　**19.07**

	£			£
Capital	6,290	*Fixed assets*		
		Motor van	1,000	
Current liabilities		Fixtures	700	
Bank overdraft	1,010		——	1,700
Creditors	2,750	*Current assets*		
	——	Stock	4,950	
	3,760	Debtors	3,400	
			——	8,350
	———			———
	10,050			10,050

On this date he sold the business for £8,300 to J. Parker, who took over the motor van at an agreed valuation of £850 and debtors subject to a provision for bad debts of £150. Brown agreed to pay off the bank overdraft. The rest of the assets and liabilities were taken over at the Balance Sheet values.

On 1 June Parker paid £8,750 into a business bank account and paid Brown a cheque in settlement of the business purchase.

(a) Show the Journal entries, including cash, in the books of J. Parker.
(b) Show Parker's Balance Sheet at the commencement of the business.

20. The Bank Reconciliation Statement

It is important for the owner of a business to know at all times the balance on the business bank (current) account. Cash is needed to keep the business going—to pay wages, expenses, creditors, to repay loans, to pay taxes, and so on. If it appears that insufficient cash is available at particular times, he may need to see the bank manager either to obtain overdraft facilities or to arrange a loan. The business Cash Book should give an up-to-date picture of the position regarding cash in hand and at the bank. The cash balance is verified by physical checking and the balance at the bank is verified by reference to the bank statement that is prepared by the bank and sent to its clients.

Bank statement

1 You must remember that this shows the account of the business in the books of the bank: the statement is a copy of the account entries. Therefore debits in the business Cash Book (amounts paid into the bank), which represent the asset, are shown on the bank statement as credits (being credits in our account in the bank's books), which represent, in the bank's books, a liability.

2 Bank statements usually show the client's account in columnar form. You should refer to the illustration on page 19 in chapter 3.

Differences in the two balances

Unless very few entries appear in the Cash Book, it is unlikely that the balance shown in the Cash Book agrees with the balance shown on the bank statement. There are several reasons why differences arise.

1 Cheques paid and entered in our Cash Book have not yet been presented to the bank for payment.

2 Payments made by the bank on our behalf under standing orders may not be entered in our Cash Book.

3 Receipts by the bank of dividends, interest, and credit transfer payments will be shown on the statement but will not yet be entered into our Cash Book.

4 Charges made by the bank (debited to our account) will be shown on the bank statement but are not yet entered into our Cash Book.

5 Amounts paid into our bank account may not yet be credited on the statement.

In addition, errors that may have arisen in making entries in the Cash Book will be discovered, since, when adjustments have been made for the differences above, the balances in the Cash Book and the statement should agree.

Example

Cash Book

Balance	72.00	Rent	15.00
Sales	+196.00	Cash	25.00+
Sales	100.00	A. Taylor	39.00+
		GPO	22.00+
		Balance c/d	267.00
	368.00		368.00
Balance b/d	267.00		

Bank Statement

	Dr	Cr	Bal
Balance			72.00
Credits		+196.00	268.00
Chq	+39.00		229.00
Chq	+22.00		207.00
Charges	5.00		202.00
Credit transfer–Wm. Wood		44.00	246.00
Cash	+25.00		221.00

Which balance in the example above is correct? The £267 or the £221? The following procedure will disclose the answer.

Verifying the bank balance

Step 1   Mark those items that appear both in the Cash Book and on the bank statement. This will disclose the items that, not being marked, cause the differences in the two totals. (Note that the + sign is used in the example to denote items that agree.)

Step 2   Enter in the Cash Book those items that need to be entered from the bank statement and mark, both on the statement and in the Cash Book, to show that the item now appears on both records. The Cash Book will now appear as follows:

Balance b/d	267.00	Bank charges	5.00
Wm. Wood	44.00	Balance c/d	306.00
	311.00		311.00
Balance b/d	306.00		

All the items on the statement should now be marked.

Step 3   Prepare the Bank reconciliation statement as follows.

Bank Reconciliation Statement as at . . .

	£
Balance per bank statement	221.00
add Item not credited	100.00
	321.00
less Cheques unpresented	15.00
Corrected Cash Book balance	306.00

The Bank Reconciliation Statement can also be prepared by starting with the 'corrected' Cash Book balance, as shown below. (Examination questions will often specify what is required.)

Bank Reconciliation Statement as at . . .

	£
Balance per Cash Book	306.00
add Cheques unpresented	15.00
	321.00
less Item not credited	100.00
Balance per bank statement	221.00

Balance Sheet item

The bank balance shown in the Balance Sheet must be correct. The amount to be shown, therefore, as an asset in the trial balance and the balance sheet is £306. This is the figure disclosed after 'correcting' the Cash Book. By 'correcting' is meant the entering of those additional items required to bring the Bank Account balance in the Cash Book to the correct figure. This figure now discloses the exact position regarding the bank balance.

In practice always 'correct' the Cash Book before preparing the Bank Reconciliation Statement. (Some examination questions presuppose that the Cash Book has been balanced before reconciliation, and therefore cannot be altered. The reconciliation statement will require adjustments for all differences, before these are then posted into the Cash Book at the commencement of the next month.)   *Joe's Rule No. 20*

Briefly, but clearly, explain the differences between each of the following pairs.   **N 20.01**

(a) A *bank statement* and a *Bank Reconciliation Statement.*
(b) A *bank deposit account* and a *bank current account.*

(RSA–COS)

20.02 The following extract is from the bank columns of the Cash Book of J. Coral.

19–6			£	19–6			£
Apr. 26	Balance	b/f	260	Apr. 27	M. Turner		53
27	L. Brown		84	30	K. Jones		21
29	Cash		100	30	S. Cooper		42
30	H. Cane		62		Balance	c/f	390
			£506				£506

On 30 April, he received the following bank statement from the bank.

19–6		Payments £	Receipts £	Balance £
Apr. 26	Balance (credit)			260
28	Brown		84	
28	Credit transfer—S. King		48	392
29	Cash		100	492
30	Turner	53		
30	Charges	25		414

You are required to:

(a) Bring the Cash Book up to date, and carry down the new balance at 30 April 19–6.

(b) Prepare a statement under its proper title to reconcile the difference between the revised balance in the Cash Book and the balance in the bank statement on 30 April 19–6.

(RSA 1)

NA 20.03 (a) Smith receives his bank statement showing a balance in bank of £1,340 on 31 May 19–6. Cheques totalling £130 paid to creditors have not yet been presented for payment, and a sum of £75 credit transfer received by the bank has not been entered in his Cash Book. Calculate the balance which Smith's Cash Book should show before any corrections are made.

(b) Smith receives a statement of account from one of his suppliers. It shows a balance due of £180. The account in Smith's ledger indicates that the amount due is only £50. Explain how this difference could arise without any mistakes being made.

(RSA 1)

20.04 On the 30 June 19–6, B. Back's Cash Book showed a balance of £40.00 overdrawn on his Bank Account. After checking his Cash Book with his bank statement, Back located the following errors and omissions.

(a) Cheques drawn and entered in the Cash Book on 29 June for £35.00 in favour of C. White and £25 in favour of J. Green had not been passed through the bank for payment.
(b) Interest charges of £15 shown in the bank statement had not been entered in the Cash Book.
(c) £80 cash banked by B. Back on the 30 June was not credited by the bank until 1 July although it had been entered in the Cash Book.

You are required to:

(a) Make the necessary entries to amend the Cash Book balance.
(b) Prepare a Bank Reconciliation between the bank statement balance of £75 (overdrawn) and the revised Cash Book balance.
(c) Briefly describe the reason for preparing a Bank Reconciliation Statement.

(RSA 1)

Explain briefly the difference between: **NA 20.05**

(a) Bank statement and Bank Reconciliation Statement.
(b) Fixed assets and current assets.
(c) Trade discount and cash discount.
(d) Personal and impersonal accounts.

Note You should give examples in (b) and (d).

(LCC Elementary)

A business receives a bank statement at the close of business on 31 January 19–4, **20.06** which shows that he has a credit balance of £1,512. This figure does not agree with the balance at the bank according to his Cash Book, for the following reasons.

(a) Cheques for £83, £95, and £162 issued by the businessman in payment of accounts before 31 January had not yet been presented to the bank for payment.
(b) On 31 January the bank paid a premium of £120 for fire insurance under the provisions of a standing order in their possession. This entry had not been made in the Cash Book.
(c) £86 for bank interest to 31 January was charged on the bank statement but was not entered in the Cash Book.
(d) The business 'takings' of £422 for 31 January were recorded in the Cash Book as banked on that date but were, in fact, not paid into the bank until the following day.

Prepare a Bank Reconciliation Statement which commences with the £1,512 as shown on the bank statement and end the Reconciliation Statement with the balance according to the Cash Book.

(RSA–COS)

NA 20.07 Prepare a Bank Reconciliation Statement from the following particulars.

	£
Balance overdrawn per bank statement 31 March 19–8	572
Cheques received and paid into the bank but not yet entered on the bank statement	996
Cheques drawn and entered in the Cash Book but not presented to the bank for payment	314
Bank charges made by the bank but not entered in the Cash Book	28
Balance at bank per Cash Book 31 March 19–8	138

20.08 From the extracts below prepare the Reconciliation Account after correcting the Cash Book.

Cash Book

Dec.				Dec.			
1	Balance	146.00		10	Rent		25.00
2	T. Tolley	98.00		14	B. Brown & Co.		193.00
3	F. Formby	226.00		21	Wages		432.50
14	Cash sales	948.00		23	Petty cash		40.00
18	Cash sales	321.00		31	Telephones		96.25
22	J. Symons	94.00		31	Customs and Excise		148.25
30	Cash sales	435.00		31	Balance	c/d	1,371.75
31	P. Paul	38.75					
		2,306.75					2,306.75

Bank Statement

		Dr	Cr	Balance
Dec. 1	Balance			169.20
3	Credits		324.00	493.20
15	012	25.00		468.20
15	Credits		948.00	1,416.20
16	011	23.20		1,393.00
18	013	193.00		1,200.00
18	Credits		321.00	1,521.00
22	014	432.50		1,088.50
23	Credits		94.00	1,182.50
24	015	40.00		1,142.50
31	Chgs	8.50		1,134.00

Note the following information.

The Bank Reconciliation Statement 30 Nov. 19 . . .

Balance as per bank statement	169.20
less Cheques unpresented	23.20
Balance as per cash book	£146.00

21. Analysed Books

The Petty Cash Book

So far you have been keeping the record of cash payments and receipts in a three-column Cash Book. Joe is now going to give you some more responsibility. You are going to have to keep the Petty Cash Book and also keep the petty cash box in order to pay out sums of money to those employees who have incurred expenses. This means that you will no longer keep a detailed record of cash payments in the Cash Book. (Look at the Cash Book shown on page 71 and see how *all* cash payments are shown.) Now you will have:

1   The Cash Book for recording bank payments by cheque and receipts into bank.
2   The Petty Cash Book for recording *every* detail of cash payments.

The system is simple. Joe is going to give you a sum of cash, called the float. He has got to take this out of the Bank Account so when he draws the cheque it will appear in the Cash Book, on the Credit Side, as follows.

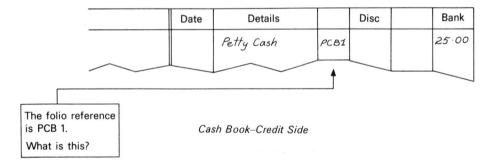

	Date	Details		Disc		Bank
		Petty Cash	PCB1			25·00

The folio reference is PCB 1.
What is this?

Cash Book–Credit Side

The corresponding debit entry is in the Petty Cash Account, which is kept in . . . which book? Yes, of course: the Petty Cash Book. Joe has already got a suitably ruled Petty Cash Book (see page 178) and you can see how he has made the entry into the Petty Cash Account.

From now on you are going to keep the Petty Cash Book and the Petty Cash box containing the £25. You can pay money out to the following people only, and no more than £3 at any one time: to Joe himself; to Tom Brown, the warehouse foreman; to Billy Fury, the senior salesman; to Barney Coalman, the delivery driver; and to yourself.

Petty Cash Book Ruling

DATE	Details	FOLIO	£ p.	DATE	Details	VOUCHER	FOLIO	Total	£ p	£ p	£ p	£ p	VAT
	Bank	CB 38	25·00										

Is this folio reference correct?

Debit column

Credit column

Your Petty Cash Book can be ruled with as many analysis columns as required

Remember that this book is a record of the Petty Cash Account

When you pay out, *you must obtain a receipt from each person* and also *make sure that the person signs a petty cash voucher*—like the one below. (In practice, an authorization signature is often required.)

Petty Cash Voucher		001
Date...............		
Details	£	p
Signature....................		

This is your proof that the expense is a real one. If you do not obtain the signature, how does Joe know that it is a genuine expense?

During the next three days you pay out the following sums.   **Example**

To Barney Coalman	Petrol £2.50	Voucher No. 1
To Barney Coalman	Spares £1.25	Voucher No. 2
To Billy Fury	Postage £0.38 ⎱	
To Billy Fury	Travelling £3.20 ⎰	Voucher No. 3
To Tom Brown	Tea and coffee £1.20	Voucher No. 4
To the milkman	Milk £1.68	Voucher No. 5
To the office cleaner	Cleaning £1.00	Voucher No. 6
To James Brown	A creditor £2.50	—
To Billy Fury	Travelling £1.15 ⎱	
To Billy Fury	Stationery £0.85 ⎰	Voucher No. 7

You did remember to sign Voucher Nos. 5 and 6 yourself? You drew out the money to pay these expenses and should have signed the vouchers yourself. Joe now explains how you should record these in the Petty Cash Book (illustration below).

Petty Cash Book

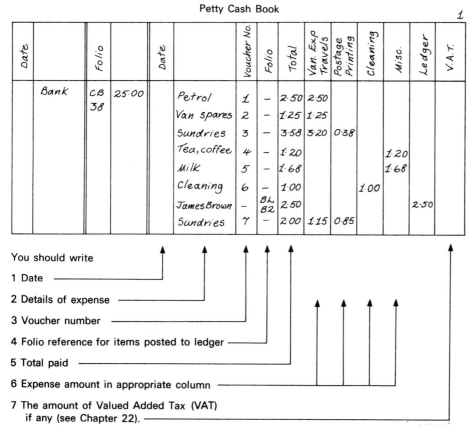

Date		Folio		Date		Voucher No.	Folio	Total	Van Exp Travels	Postage Printing	Cleaning	Misc.	Ledger	V.A.T.
	Bank	CB 38	25·00		Petrol	1	—	2·50	2·50					
					Van spares	2	—	1·25	1·25					
					Sundries	3	—	3·58	3·20	0·38				
					Tea, coffee	4	—	1·20				1·20		
					Milk	5	—	1·68				1·68		
					Cleaning	6	—	1·00			1·00			
					James Brown	—	BL 82	2·50					2·50	
					Sundries	7	—	2·00	1·15	0·85				

You should write

1 Date

2 Details of expense

3 Voucher number

4 Folio reference for items posted to ledger

5 Total paid

6 Expense amount in appropriate column

7 The amount of Valued Added Tax (VAT)
  if any (see Chapter 22).

(Note that vouchers Nos. 3 and 7 each have two different items.)

Joe asks you to total up the payments and work out the amount left. Do that now. The answer should correspond to what you have in the petty cash box. If it does not—beware of trouble. You may or may not spend all of the £25 within the week— as Joe explains in laying down the following rule.

Bring your vouchers to me every Friday morning and I will reimburse you with the amount you have spent. I call this the *imprest system* of Petty Cash Recording. The effect is that you will always have your 'float' made up to the agreed figure at the end of every week. So this means that you now receive £15.71 and should record this in the Petty Cash Book.

The only thing that Joe now needs to explain is how to post the items of expense to the ledger accounts.

Remembering the rule that every debit has a credit, you have not so far entered any debits in the ledger for the credits (payments) in the Petty Cash Book.

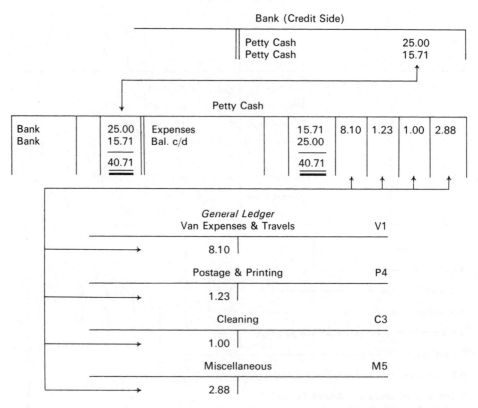

You will notice that the Petty Cash Book has a column headed 'Ledger'. That column will be used to record payments made to persons to whom we owe small amounts of money, and whose accounts appear in the Bought Ledger. (These suppliers would normally be paid by cheque but they may visit your business and expect cash payment.) When the payment is made, the Petty Cash Account will be credited and the corresponding debit entry made in the personal account in the Bought Ledger.

When the posting is made, the ledger folio reference is entered in the Folio column. Having now made the double entry you must remember that when the Petty Cash Book is totalled, the column headed 'Ledger' will not need to be posted again.

It is possible to balance the Petty Cash Book as follows.

Bank	25.00	Expenses	15.71
		Balance c/d	9.29
	25.00		25.00
Balance b/d	9.29		
Bank	15.71		

Look at how Joe rules off the Petty Cash Book and the references he has written in order to show that the expenses and payments have been posted.

Petty Cash Book

Date		Folio	£ p	Date		Voucher No.	Folio	Total Payments	Van Expenses & Travels	Postage & Printing	Cleaning	Miscellaneous	Ledger
	Bank	CB 38	25.00		Petrol	1	—	2.50	2.50				
					Van spares	2	—	1.25	1.25				
					Sundries	3	—	3.58	3.20	0.38			
					Tea and Coffee	4	—	1.20				1.20	
					Milk	5	—	1.68				1.68	
	Bank	CB 42	15.71		Cleaning	6	—	1.00			1.00		
					James Brown	—	BL 82	2.50					
					Sundries	7	—	2.00	1.15	0.85			2.50
					Balance c/d			15.71 25.00	8.10	1.23	1.00	2.88	2.50
			40.71					40.71	GLV1	GLP4	GLC3	GLM5	—
	Balance b/d		25.00										

Note If you cross cast the analysis columns you can agree the total expenditure of £15.71.

21.01   Simon Hunt is a sole trader who keeps his petty cash on the imprest system—the imprest amount being £35. His petty cash transactions for the month of March 19–6 were as follows.

Mar. 1   Petty cash in hand £4.73.

            Petty cash restored to imprest amount.

      4   Paid wages £5.45.

      8   Cost of telegrams £2.19.

    10   Bought foolscap paper £2.48.

    11   Paid wages £5.60.

    15   Cost of postage stamps £2.25.

    18   Paid wages £5.30.

    23   Paid to W. Smith, a creditor, £2.80.

    25   Paid wages £5.70.

    29   Bought envelopes £1.37.

Required:

Draw up the Petty Cash Book for the month of March 19–6 giving also the entry on 1 April 19–6 restoring the petty cash to the imprest amount.

Note   Your analysis columns should be for: (a) wages, (b) postage and telegrams, (c) stationery, and (d) ledger.

(LCC Elementary)

NA 21.02   Alfred Thomas, a sole trader, keeps his petty cash on the imprest system—the imprest amount being £35. The petty cash transactions for the month of May 19–5 are as follows.

May 1   Petty cash in hand £3.72.

            Petty cash restored to imprest amount.

      6   Paid wages £4.76.

      8   Cost of postage stamps £2.15.

    10   Cost of stationery £3.05.

    13   Paid wages £4.42.

    17   Cost of telegrams £1.93.

    20   Paid wages £4.51.

    23   Cost of envelopes £2.20.

    25   Paid to F. Johnson, a creditor, £3.24.

    27   Paid wages £4.48.

Required:

Draw up the Petty Cash Book for the month of May 19–5 and show, on 1 June 19–5, the restoration of the petty cash to the imprest amount. The analysis columns should be for wages, postage and telegrams, stationery, and ledger.

(LCC Elementary)

(a) Write up the Petty Cash Book of J. Stone from the following information. **NA 21.03**

  (i) The book is to be kept on the imprest system.

  (ii) The 'float' amounts to £20.

  (iii) You are to provide analysis columns to record (a) postage, (b) travelling expenses, (c) stationery, (d) miscellaneous items.

  (iv) Record the following transactions for the two-week period.

			£
Sept.	1	Balance of imprest	6.20
		Payment received from the main cashier to make up imprest	
	4	Travelling expenses paid	3.00
	5	Parcels	0.75
	6	Taxi fares	0.65
	7	Sundries for office	1.35
	8	Postage stamps	3.00
	8	Carbon paper and paper clips	0.95
	12	Packet of pencils	0.96
	13	Parcels	1.55
	14	Travelling expenses	4.00
	15	Received payment from main cashier to make up imprest float.	

(b) Explain how the Petty Cash Book is 'posted' to the ledger.

The Bank Cash Book

Because all cash transactions are now recorded in the Petty Cash Book, the Cash Book proper reverts to being purely a Bank Book, recording the transactions on the bank current account. When this occurs it may be called the *Bank Cash Book*.

Analysis columns in the Bank Cash Book are useful in providing details of individual amounts banked and the breakdown of payments where one cheque is used to draw money for several purposes. This use arises from the fact that, when a business examines its bank statement, the bank shows only the total of a payment into the account, although that payment may consist of cash and several cheques received from customers. The Bank Cash Book is entered from bank paying-in counterfoils, cheque counterfoils, and bank statements, in the same way as the normal Cash Book. The improved layout is shown below. It can, of course, be used in any Cash Book.

On 24 May, a payment into the bank consisted of five cheques. The paying-in slip counterfoil showed the total to be £187.25, but also recorded the individual cheque values enabling the cashier to record the amounts. **Example**

Bank Cash Book

		Details	Bank			Details		Bank
May 24	P. Harwood	92.15		May 24	Petty Cash	30.43		
	R. T. Corker	16.45			Drawings	66.00		
	Maypole Ltd.	25.65				———		96.43
	K. P. Walters	18.70						
	Niger Containers	34.30						
		———						
			187.25					

Also on 24 May, the owner drew a cheque value £96.43—this was for reimbursement of petty cash £30.43, and drawings £66.

The individual accounts are posted in the usual way, but the amount actually banked, £187.25, and the cheque drawn, £96.43, will appear on the bank statement. The blank column could be used to record cash discounts.

21.04 Write up a trader's Bank Cash Book from the following information.

(a) His balance at the bank at the close of business on 26 May according to his Cash Book was £983.77.

(b) The counterfoils of his paying-in book give the following details.

May 29   Total paid in £197.16, consisting of cash from sales £49.66, a cheque from J. Izzard for £50, and a cheque from L. Waterlow for £97.50. Waterlow's cheque was accepted in full settlement of £100 owed by him.

30   Total paid in £48.46, consisting entirely of cash from sales.

31   Total paid in £75.48, consisting of cash from sales £39.50 and a cheque from H. Benskin for £35.98.

(c) The counterfoils of his cheque book show the following details.

		£
May 29	J. Ormerod and Co. Ltd.	327.67
30	Ivens and Co.	195.00
31	Petty cash	29.92
	Self	100.00
	Ashton's Garage	18.34

The cheque to Ivens and Co. was accepted in full settlement of £200 owing to them.

The cheque to Ashton's Garage was for petrol, oil, repairs, etc., for the previous month, and no previous record of this transaction had gone through the books.

The Particulars column of the Cash Book should indicate clearly which ledger account should be debited or credited in respect of each Cash Book entry. Rule off and balance the Cash Book at the close of business on 31 May.

(RSA 1)

Sammy Makeaste has a wholesale business selling goods for cash and credit. He   **NA 21.05**
keeps a Petty Cash Book, a Bank Cash Book and a daily cash sales record, as well as
the other normal books. On 1 May his accounts contained the following balances:
Petty cash £27; Bank £849; Stock £3,840; Creditors—XY Manufacturers Ltd.
£895, T.T. Textiles Ltd. £634; Debtors—Jon White £144, P. Billings £97; Fixtures
and fittings £775.

(a) Calculate Sammy Makeaste's capital and open the accounts in his ledger.
During May the following transactions occurred.

May	2	Drew a cheque for £58; £8 for petty cash and £50 drawings.
	4	Invoices received from T.T. Textiles £146 and Manny Edwards & Co. £73. Petty cash payments of £1.40 for stamps and 65p travelling.
	5	Cash sales totalling £642 were banked on the same paying-in slip as a cheque for £95 received from P. Billings.
	8	Sales on credit made to Jon White £38 and Kenny Williams £64.
	10	Cash sales of £491 banked. Petty cash payments of £3.45 for stationery and 72p for groceries.
	12	Drew a cheque for £38 as follows: £28 for wages, £10 drawings. Petty cash expenses of £1.48 were paid for stationery.
	15	Cash sales banked £536, together with cheques value £144 from Jon White and Kenny Williams £64.
	18	Invoices received from M. L. King £59 and F. S. Stanley £193.
	21	Drew a cheque £49 to pay £19 repairs to the office, £26 wages, and £4 petrol.
	24	Cash sales banked £299.
	27	Sent cheque value £895 to XY Manufacturers Ltd., and £634 to T. T. Textiles Ltd.
	28	Paid rent by quarterly cheque £400. Cash sales banked £588, plus cheque received of £38 from Jon White.
	31	Drew one cheque for drawings £25, wages £36 and to reimburse petty cash to the float of £35.

(b) Enter these transactions in the books of original entry, post to the ledger, and
take out a trial balance.

Purchases Day Book

Do you recall the advantage of having analysis columns in the Petty Cash Book? If
you do not, look back at page 178. This advantage can also be gained if similar
analysis columns are used in all the books of original entry except the Journal. Can
you recall the books of original entry other than the Purchases Day Book and the
Journal? There are five others—if you have forgotten them, turn to the answers
(**21.06**). The reason why Joe is now explaining the use of analysis columns in the

Purchases Day Book is because his business is expanding and in addition to selling carpets he is going to sell furniture. Let Joe explain.

I shall be receiving invoices from suppliers of furniture and I shall want to know how much I am buying so that I can work out whether or not I am making a profit on selling the furniture.

Purchases Day Book (With Analysis Columns)

										1
Date	Supplier	Invoice No.	Purchase Ledger Folio	INVOICE TOTAL	CARPETS	FURNITURE				V.A.T.
May 2	TKM Ltd.	92 A	T1	148.00	148.00					
4	SHILLERS Ltd.	0641	S2	79.00		79.00				
5	MICKER Ltd.	9132	M3	91.00		91.00				
14	SKP & Co.	849	S5	493.00	493.00					
18	ABC Ltd.	71834	A4	175.00	75.00	100.00				
23	CEEDY Ltd.	S 921	C9	147.00	147.00					
28	S & K Ltd.	498	S3	88.00		88.00				
				1221.00	863.00	358.00				
				GLP7	GLP1	GLP2				

Date (on invoice)
Supplier's invoice number

Creditor's account number (folio reference) to which invoice total is posted

Analysis columns

Credit to Purchase Ledger Control Account (memo only)

I have got a new Purchases Book (see illustration above) which is bigger than the one you have been using so far, because it has a lot of analysis columns which are used in the same way as the analysis columns in the Petty Cash Book. I have already entered the invoices received today and you can see how the invoice total is entered in the Total column and also written in the proper analysis column. Look at the invoice from ABC Ltd. The total is £175.00 but it is made up of carpets priced at £75.00 and furniture priced at £100.00. This needs the use of both analysis columns. Look at page one of the new book. I have also totalled the three columns being used and you can see that the two analysis columns added together equal the Invoice Total column.

$$Carpet + Furniture = Total$$
$$£863.00 + £358.00 = £1,221.00$$

Look at the reference number written under the totals.

GL P1 means what?

GL P2 means what?

It means that now we are going to open two Purchases Accounts. P1 is for purchases of carpets and P2 is for purchases of furniture, and as you already know, GL means the General Ledger, in which the nominal (impersonal) accounts are kept.

The creditors' accounts are entered in the normal way. In the illustration on page 186, the posting has already been done.

Illustration of the Double Entry Posting
From the PURCHASES DAY BOOK — To CREDITOR'S ACCOUNTS
— To PURCHASES ACCOUNT

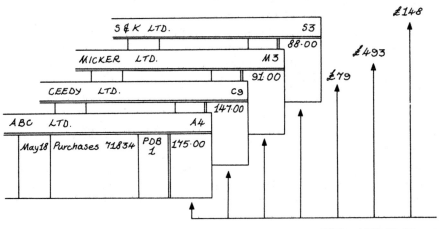

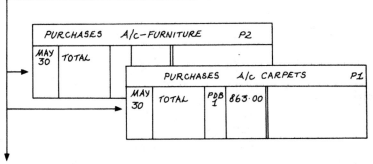

21.07   How can you tell this?

Check the double entry by my illustration. I will explain the use of the other analysis columns when you have got used to entering this new book using the three columns.

Note   An analysed Purchases Returns Book would be ruled in the same way as the analysed Purchases Book.

21.08   Here are invoices received during the following day. Enter them in the Purchases Day Book. Total the three columns and check your arithmetic by making sure that the two analysis columns equal the total column.

Note   You may have to rule your own paper—with only two analysis columns at the moment.

2.5.19–7   Invoice No. 1250 from Bolker Carpets Ltd. £408.00.
Invoice No. 109A from TKM Ltd. for carpets £79.00.
Invoice No. 9171 from Micker Ltd. for furniture £17.50.
Invoice No. PZ914 from Kellers & Co. for furniture £92.75.
Invoice No. 71896 from ABC Ltd. total £147.50. (Carpets £29.00, Furniture £118.50)
Invoice No. 5942 from Ceedy Ltd. for carpets £84.50.

Do not post entries to the ledger.

Check your answer to the above question and then try this more difficult question.

21.09   T. Woods Ltd. operates a garage which sells petrol, oil, some spares, and also repairs and services motor cars. The following invoices were received by T. Woods Ltd. during the first week of November. Enter in the Purchases Day Book with three analysis columns, post to the ledger, and post the totals of the analysis columns to the General Ledger.

Invoice No.	Supplier	Goods/Services	Prices
1P 321	Transworld Tyres	12 tyres	£10 each less 25% trade discount
N43	S.O. Oils	2,000 litres petrol	£210 net
6738	Repair-Speed	Assorted spare parts	£55 net
9321846	Battery Builders	12 batteries (super)	£15 each less $33\frac{1}{3}$% trade discount
78574	Conoco Company	20 litres oil	68p per litre net
N48	S.O. Oils	2,000 litres oil	£210 net

A/342	Parkins Motors	Panel beating	£88 net
22532/M	Larkswood Tyres	Car towing	£15 net
6941	Repair-Speed	48 sparking plugs	30p each less 25% trade discount

Sales Day Book

If we are *buying* furniture as well as carpets, then obviously we are also *selling* furniture. So you will also need an analysed Sales Day Book. Having learned how to enter the Purchases Day Book, this new, analysed, Sales Day Book is easily understood, as Joe explains.

The ruling is the same as the Purchases Day Book—although this book only needs two analysis columns—unless we start selling other goods later on. It is entered from our copy invoices. The customer's account is debited in the usual way—the only difference is that *two* Sales Accounts are opened in the General Ledger and the totals posted from the analysis columns. So all the debit entries in the debtors' accounts are represented by two credit entries in the Sales Accounts. Here is my illustration to explain the entries.

Entering and Posting the Analysed Sales Day Book

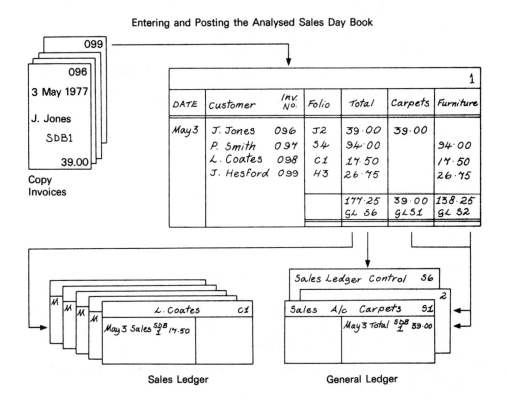

189

Note An analysed Sales Returns Book could be ruled in the same way.

Miscel-laneous sales Although not shown in the illustration, additional analysis columns can be provided if required for regular recurring income arising from the sale of scrap and waste, the disposal of assets, the charging of rents for office or factory space sublet—all of which will require the raising of a sales invoice.

21.10 E. Smithson is a wholesaler whose sales ledger showed the following amounts owing to him on 31 May 19–6.

J. Ford £190; M. Abbott £410; P. Smith £590; S. Lanter £770.

His Sales Book for June 19–6 showed the following.

Sales Day Book

Date	Details	Folio	Total	Furniture	Carpets	Hardware	Carriage & cases
			£	£	£	£	£
June 3	J. Ford		348	250	80		18
10	P. Smith		172	160			12
17	S. Lanter		391		210	170	11
18	M. Mumms		645	30	340	230	45
24	H. Rankin		516	480			36

During the month the following additional transactions took place.

June 9	J. Ford returned goods valued at £80 (all furniture) and cases valued £10.
14	Cheques were received from J. Ford and P. Smith in settlement of the amounts owing by them at 31 May less 5 per cent cash discount.
18	S. Lanter returned cases valued at £18.

Required:

(a) Open personal accounts in the Sales Ledger and record the June transactions, carrying down the balances where necessary on 30 June 19–6.

(b) Post from the Sales Day Book to the nominal ledger.

Note Entries in the Cash Book and Returns Book are not required.

NA 21.11 (a) What do the following indicate?

(i) a debit balance on a personal account,
(ii) a credit balance on a capital account,
(iii) a debit balance on a partner's current account,
(iv) a credit balance on a rent payable account.

(b) L. Davies is a trader whose Sales Ledger showed the following amounts owing to him on 30 June 19–4.

F. Jordan £120. A. Moor £140. S. Payne £59. L. Stanton £70. His Sales Book for the month of July 19–4 was as follows.

Sales Day Book

		Total	Glass	China	Hardware
		£	£	£	£
July 6	F. Jordan	48	12	20	16
10	S. Payne	21	—	—	21
18	L. Stanton	80	60	—	20
22	A. Moor	30	—	30	—
24	R. Hanks	100	40	32	28
		279	112	82	85

During the month of July 19–4 the following additional transactions occurred.

July 8   F. Jordan returned goods valued at £8.

12   Cheques were received from F. Jordan and S. Payne in settlement of the amounts owing by them at that date less 5 per cent cash discount.

Required:

Open the personal accounts in the sales ledger and record the additional transactions for the month of July 19–4 in the personal accounts, where necessary carrying down the balances on the personal accounts on 31 July 19–4. Also make the postings from the Sales Day Book to the impersonal ledger.

Note   Entries in the Cash Book or Returns Book are not required.

(AEB '0')

Extended Purchases Day Book

Joe receives telephone bills, stationery bills, electricity bills, and so on. So far he has put all the bills he has received in his file and taken them out only when he has paid them: when he has paid we have entered them in his Cash Book (as a payment) and made the double entry in his General Ledger, in the appropriate expense account. Now that he has decided to use an analysed Purchases Book, we can begin to enter all invoices and bills received in this book.

As Joe says: this means that the Creditors Ledger will now contain accounts for every person or business that is owed money by us (remember that a *creditor* is *someone who is owed money*). So the Electricity Board will have an account opened when we receive the electricity bill. The local authority will have an account when we receive the rates bill. The GPO will have an account when we receive our telephone bill. These creditors are no different from those from whom we have purchased carpets and furniture—they will all have an account in the Creditors Ledger. Posting the invoice or bill total and entering the folio reference is just the same as for

191

Extended Purchases Day Book (with Analysis Columns for Goods and Services)

DATE	Supplier	INV. NO.	FOLIO	TOTAL	CARPETS	FURNITURE	LIGHTING AND HEATING	POSTAGE STATIONERY ADVERTS.	TELEPH. TELEX.	REPAIRS MAINT.	PACKING CARRIAGE	ASSETS MISC.	V.A.T.
May 2	T K M Ltd.	92A	TI	148.00	148.00								
4	SHILLERS LTD.	0641	52	79.00		79.00							
5	N.T. GASBOARD	00971	N4	61.00			61.00						
5	MICKLER LTD.	9132	M3	91.00		91.00							
10	EXPRESS POST	0111	E7	15.50				15.50					
14	SKP & Co.	B49	55	493.00	493.00								
18	G.P.O.		93	37.51					37.51				
18	ABC LTD.	71834	A4	175.00	75.00	100.00							
21	CALOR	77/13	C8	4.32			4.32						
23	CEEDY LTD	S921	C9	147.00	147.00								
28	RAPMEND	291	R7	66.75						66.75			
28	EXPRESS	1441	E7	19.20							19.20		
28	S & K LTD.	498	53	88.00		88.00							
				1425.28 GLP7	GLP1	GLP2	GLL1	GLP3	GLT1	GLR1	GLP4		GLV1

Personal accounts of suppliers credited with invoice totals

Expense accounts debited

creditors for goods. Look at the example of the Purchases Day Book on page 192. Total up the analysis columns and check that the totals of the columns add up to £1,425.28. The analysis columns are used in the same way as the analysis columns in the Petty Cash Book; the total of the expense is posted to the ledger account. In this way it saves posting each individual invoice to the expense account in the General Ledger. Remember that the individual invoice is still posted to the creditor's account.

Assets purchased on credit

Invoices received can be entered in the book and extended to either a separate column or a Miscellaneous column. Either way, the posting should be made to the appropriate asset account from the column total. Even with a separate column, the total may need analysing if different assets have been purchased.

21.12

Rule up a Purchases Day Book with eight analysis columns and enter the following invoices. Total all the columns and check your arithmetic.

May 1 Smith & Co. 24 pocket calculators at £5 each. Stationery £61 net Invoice No. S 114.

4 B. M. Carpets Ltd. Assorted carpets £149.00; 10 Rolls of hand-woven Indian carpets at £85 each. Invoice No. BX 176.

8 Whitewood Furniture Ltd. 10 bookcases at £24.15 each; 6 chairs at £5 each, and 1 set of coffee tables for £36. Invoice No. Y 007.

16 F.T. Hardwares. 50 tins of 5 litre gloss paint at £4.60 per tin; 2 boxes of nails at £10.50 per box. Invoice No. 114.

17 Jones & Jones Ltd. 1,000 metres of curtain materials at 75p per metre; 650 metres lining materials at 30p per metre. Invoice No. J 0751.

20 S.T.C. Ltd. 10 Sankey saws at £15 each; 18 hammers at £2.50 each; 20 screw drivers at £1.25 each. Invoice No. 74 X.

28 Smith & Co. 10 pocket calculators at £5 each. Invoice No. S 128.

30 F.T. Hardwares. 25 tins paint at £2.50 per tin. Invoice No. 2104.

21.13

The business of Ro-Go operates a fruit machine arcade and has the following accounts in its books on 1 January.

Creditors Property Racketeers Ltd. £4,000; Quick Profit Machine Ltd. £850; Conning Advertisers Ltd. £98; SWEEB (Electricity Company) £325.

Assets I. M. Broke (debtor) £3; cash £41; bank balance £82; fruit machines (WDV) £1,950; property £6,000; capital £2,803.

The following transactions took place in January.

Jan. 1 Invoice received from Maik-nu Repairs for the repair of broken machines £750.

3 Invoice received from Plate-Glass Window Co. for replacing smashed windows £82.

Jan. 4   Cash sales banked £623.

5   Cheque paid to Quick Profit Machine Ltd. (to keep them quiet) £400.

6   Wages paid in cash £4.

7   Invoice received from Securearms Co. (for supplying bouncers) £42.

10   Cash sales banked £749.

12   Invoice received from the GPO for telephones £143.

13   Cheque paid to SWEEB (to keep the lights on) £325.

14   A letter from the Magistrates Court informed Ro-Go that I. M. Broke had been deported to Eyeland.

18   Invoice received from Junk Toys Ltd. £98.

20   Cheque paid to Property Racketeers Ltd. £1,000.

25   Cheque paid on 20 January returned by bank who refused to pay it.

26   Some old fruit machines with a written down value (WDV) of £90 were sold for £15 cash.

Open the ledger accounts.

Enter these transactions in the books of original entry and post to the ledger accounts.

Prepare a trial balance at 31 January.

Analysed Cash Book

Analysis columns can be used for any number of purposes, but the main object is to enable totals of similar transactions to be obtained, such that the posting of a total saves the posting of numerous individual entries. This is the same principle that is applied in the Petty Cash Book; the analysis extends not only to payments but also to receipts. The layout below illustrates the Bank Cash Book that could be used in the situation outlined in question **21.04**.

Bank Cash Book (Receipts Side Only)

Date	Details	FOLIO	Misc.	Disc.	Reciepts From Debtors	Cash Sales	VAT	Bank
May 29	Sales	—				49·66		—
	J. Izzard	SL IL		2·50	50·00 97·50			—
	L. Waterlow	SL WI						197·16
30	Sales	—				48·46		48·46
31	Sales	—				39·50		—
	H. Benskin	SL B2			35·98			75·48
				2·50 PLD1	183·48 PLC4	137·62 PLS1		321·10

Note that debtors' accounts are posted directly

Discounts allowed are posted in total

Cash sales are posted in total

Note that the column for receipts from debtors is totalled and posted to the credit of the control account (memo only). Should the business have a number of sales ledgers (A–G; H–M; N–R; S–Z) then the Receipts from Debtors column would need to be extended to four columns to allow control account totals for each ledger to be collected. Although control accounts are not dealt with in this book, students should nevertheless be aware that such analysis columns are used in practice. This posting to a control account does not replace individual postings of receipts to the credit of debtors' accounts. The Folio column entries indicate the individual postings.

If daily cash sales were to be entered directly into the Cash Book, particularly if some form of analysis is required, the Cash Book might become congested by so many entries. This can be eased by the use of a Cash Received Book, whose sole purpose is to record and analyse cash receipts, and provide the book of original entry from which the debtors' accounts are posted. This book is totalled at the point of banking cash, so that the entries in the Cash Book are the summary totals of the Cash Received Book. **Cash Received Book**

Again, using **21.04**:

Cash Received Book — Page 6

Date	Details	Folio	Total	Disc	Debtors Receipts	Cash Sales	VAT
May 29	Sales	–	49.66			49.66	
	J. Izzard	SL I1	50.00		50.00		
	L. Waterlow	SL W1	97.50	2.50	97.50		
May 29	Cash Book	CB 41	197.16	2.50	147.50	49.66	

Note
Discount is not received and therefore is not added in cross casting the column totals.

Cash Book (Receipts Side) — 41

Date	Details	Folio	Misc	Disc.	Receipts From Debtors	Cash Sales	VAT	Bank
May 29	Cash Received Book	CRB 6		2.50	147.50	49.66		197.16

Again, the totals of the columns would then be used as the amounts to post to the various ledger accounts, the total of the Receipts from Debtors column being used to credit the Sales Ledger Control Account.

The analysed (multi-column) Cash Book

For a small business that pays cash (or cheque) for most items it buys, a cash book with analysed columns is often the most useful type of cash book to use. The analysis columns operate in exactly the same way as those in the Petty Cash Book. When the payment is made, the credit entry in either the Cash or Bank column is also made in the appropriate analysis column. A Bought Ledger column is used to record payments to creditors, a Sales Ledger column is used for receipts from debtors, and a Contra column on either side of the book records contra transfers. The columns themselves can be totalled and cross cast to verify the accuracy of the arithmetic. If insufficient analysis columns are available, a Miscellaneous or Sundries column can be used, but items recorded therein are preferably posted direct to the appropriate nominal ledger account, otherwise the total itself may need to be analysed.

In the illustration opposite, telephone bills, electricity bills, and other expenses for which a column was not available would need to be recorded in the Miscellaneous column.

NA 21.14   Using the details in question **21.05**, assume that Sammy Makeaste uses an analysed Cash Book instead of separate Petty Cash and Bank Cash Books. Draw up his Cash Book for May.

You will need at least nine analysis columns on the payments side, which together with Cash and Bank gives eleven columns. On the debit side you will need at least five columns altogether.

21.15   The information required to make the entries into the business books will come from documents received or prepared by the business. Give the name of the documents used for each of the following books.

(a) Analysed Purchases Book.
(b) Petty Cash Book.
(c) Analysed Cash Book.
(d) Cash Received Book.
(e) Sales Returns Book.

Analysed Cash Book (Credit Side Only)

		FOLIO	RENT	WAGES	MOTOR EXP.S	CASH PURCHASES	BOUGHT LEDGER	CONTRA	MISC.	V.A.T.	CASH	BANK
July 1	Rent	√	20.00									20.00
4	Wages	√		89.45							89.45	
6	Bank	C						109.00			109.00	
8	Rent	√ BL	20.00									20.00
8	R. Taylor & Co.	T4					42.50					42.50
11	Wages	√		97.66							97.66	
12	Petrol	√			10.00						10.00	
15	Rent	√	20.00									20.00
18	Wages	√		94.73							94.73	
22	Bank	C						285.75			285.75	
22	Rent	√	20.00									20.00
25	Wages	√		110.40							110.40	
25	T.T. (Spares) Ltd.	√				96.80						96.80
	Stationery	GL 53							5.45		5.45	
31	Balance	c/d							1752.61		94.98	1657.63
			80.00 GL R3	392.24 GL W1	10.00 GL M1	96.80 GL PI	42.50 GL B2	394.75	1758.06		897.42	1876.95

ANALYSED BOOKS

Notes

1 Folio column entries represent items posted directly to the General Ledger, for miscellaneous items, and the Bought Ledger, to creditors' accounts.

2 Analysis column totals are posted to the General Ledger. The Bought Ledger column is posted to the Bought Ledger Control Account (memo only).

3 The total balance carried down is entered in the Miscellaneous column so that the cross casting of the totals can be carried out at the month end. Total Cash + Total Bank = Other column totals added together.

22. Value Added Tax (VAT)

Value Added Tax, widely referred to as VAT, is a tax payable on goods and services supplied by a registered trader. VAT began on 1 April 1973. At present (1978) there are three rates of tax: the standard rate of 8 per cent, the higher (or luxury) rate of $12\frac{1}{2}$ per cent, and the zero rate. There are also some exemptions.

We do not intend to give you all the detailed information about VAT, as this is beyond the scope of a book of this nature. In this chapter we shall concern ourselves with the calculation of VAT, the preparation of the VAT invoice, and recording in the accounts. Students who wish to know more about VAT should read VAT Notice Nos. 700 and 701 issued by HM Customs and Excise.

Registration

Everyone carrying on a business whose value of taxable supplies is above a certain limit (given by the VAT provisions) must complete Form VAT 1 and send it to Customs and Excise in order to be registered.

Persons supplying taxable goods and services are called *taxable persons*. Besides sending off Form VAT 1, the taxable person must do the following.

1   Record his outputs and the VAT he has added to them (called *output tax*).
2   Issue tax invoices showing the VAT charge.
3   Record his inputs and the VAT he has paid on them (called *input tax*).
4   Work out, for each tax period, the difference between his output tax and his deductible input tax, in order to complete his VAT return.
5   Keep records and accounts.
6   Keep a VAT account.

How VAT Works

VAT is collected at each stage of the process of producing and distributing goods and services. The consumer pays the final tax. Let Joe explain how it works.

At each stage, the taxable person is charged by his suppliers with VAT on the goods and services they supply to him for his business. These goods and services are called his *inputs*, and the tax on them is his *input tax*. When we in turn supply carpets, or any of the goods we sell to our customers, we charge the customers with VAT. The goods and services we supply are called our *outputs*, and the tax we charge is our *output tax*. At intervals, when we have to make a return to Customs and Excise, we add up all our output tax and all our input tax and deduct the smaller amount from the larger; the difference is the amount we have to pay to Customs and Excise or which will be repaid to us.

Zero-rating and exemptions

On supplies that are zero-rated and those that are exempt no output tax is chargeable. But there are the following important differences.

1 Zero-rated supplies are technically taxable (though the rate of tax is nil), and the VAT charged on inputs relating to them can be reclaimed by a registered trader, together with all other input tax. Exempt supplies, on the other hand, are outside VAT and input tax cannot be reclaimed in respect of the activities of the business.

2 A person who makes zero-rated supplies will generally be registered with Customs and Excise and make VAT returns. A person who makes only exempt supplies does not have to register or make returns.

Recording output and input tax

When we sell goods to our customers, the VAT charged is based on the value of the goods.

Joe Wynn sells carpets at a price of £100 plus VAT at 8 per cent to John Winters. John Winters will buy the goods at £108, made up as follows.   **Example 1**

The value of the supply	= £100
The tax chargeable at 8 per cent	= 8
Total payable by J. Winters	= £108

The output tax is £8.

Supposing Joe Wynn buys £50 worth of goods during this same period and pays 8 per cent tax on the value, the total cost to Joe Wynn will be £54, made up as follows.   **Example 2**

The value of the goods bought	= £50
The tax chargeable at 8 per cent	= 4
Total payable by Joe Wynn	= £54

The input tax is £4.

Tax periods

At the end of a tax period (the standard tax period is three months, but can be one month) Joe Wynn will send a return to the Customs and Excise, showing the net amount of VAT payable by him or repayable to him. Suppose in a tax period the only transactions made by Joe were those recorded in Examples 1 and 2 above; his net amount will be worked out as follows.

Total output tax	= £8
Total input tax	= 4
Net amount of VAT payable by J. Wynn	= £4

Sometimes goods and services are supplied at a cost which already includes the VAT. For example, entrance fees charged at football matches are inclusive of VAT, and goods and services supplied in the supermarkets and other retail shops are priced with the VAT included. The amount of VAT due is found by using the following fraction.

$$\frac{\text{Rate of tax}}{100 + \text{Rate of tax}} \times \frac{\text{Price paid for the goods}}{\text{or services}}$$

Example 3 Joe Wynn sells carpets, rugs, and paint to Edward Rockbottom. The total value of the goods, including VAT at 8 per cent, is £432. The tax to be accounted for as output tax is:

$$\frac{8}{100 + 8} \times 432 = \frac{8}{108} \times 432 = 32$$

Therefore:

Value of the goods without the VAT	= £400
VAT at 8 per cent	= 32
Amount paid by Rockbottom	= £432

Example 4 Joe Wynn paid £90 for a radio to be used in the shop. The rate of VAT on the radio is $12\frac{1}{2}$ per cent. What is the VAT paid by Joe Wynn? Using the fraction:

$$\frac{12\frac{1}{2}}{100 \times 12\frac{1}{2}} \times 90 \quad \text{we get} \quad \frac{1}{9} \times 90 = £10$$

Therefore: Value of the goods without VAT	= £80
VAT at $12\frac{1}{2}$ per cent	= 10
Amount paid by Joe Wynn	£90

Tax invoices

Examples of tax invoices are shown below.

A tax invoice must show clearly the following.

1 Identifying number.
2 Time of supply (the tax point).
3 Supplier's name, address, and VAT registration number.
4 Customer's name (or trading name) and address.
5 Type of supply.
6 Description sufficient to identify the goods or services supplied.
7 For each description, the quantity of the goods or the extent of the services, the rate of tax, and the amount payable.
8 Total amount payable (excluding VAT).
9 Rate of any cash discount offered.
10 The total amount of tax chargeable.

VAT Invoice

A. Wholesaler Ltd.
123 The Broadway
Dock Green RA1 4AA

Invoice No. 4654
Date: 24 June 19–7

VAT Registration No. 723 456 789

To: Joe Wynn
  17 High Street
  Notown N7 2DD   Tax Point:
Delivery Note No. XP10   24 June 19–7   Term: Strictly net.

Quantity	Description and Price		Cost £	Total	VAT rate	VAT	
						Std.	Higher
2	Radios LW17	@ £45	90.00				
1	Toaster M122	@ £18	18.00	108.00	$12\frac{1}{2}$%	—	13.50
25	Paint 5 litre	@ £4	100.00				
50	Door mats	@ £1	50.00	150.00	8%	12.00	–
	Delivery charges		5.00	5.00	8%	0.40	–
	Total goods		263.00			12.40	13.50
	Total VAT		25.90				
	SALE TOTAL		288.90				

VAT Account

TAX DEDUCTIBLE			TAX DUE				
Input Tax	£ p	£ p	Output Tax	Std. Rate	Higher Rate	£ p	£ p
April	149.10		April	204.60	194.60		
May	270.30		May	150.70	145.40		
June	216.90		June	140.50	92.20		
Total		636.30	Total @ Std	495.80	–	495.80	
			Total @ Higher	–	432.20	432.20	
			Total				928.00
Overdeclaration and/or overpayments of tax in respect of previous periods	171.60		Underdeclarations and/or underpayments of tax in respect of previous periods			113.70	
		171.60					113.70
TOTAL TAX DEDUCTIBLE TAX PAYABLE		807.90 233.80					
		1041.70					1041.70

Tax returns and payments of tax

Tax returns are made on Return Form VAT 100. Customs and Excise will send each registered person one of these forms, three-monthly or monthly as necessary, with notes explaining how to fill it in.

Payment can be made either by cheque or by credit transfer. Customs and Excise will make repayment of tax by credit transfer and advise the taxable person of any amount transferred. Repayment can also be made direct to the taxable person by payable order.

Special cases

Losses No output tax is chargeable where a taxable person can show to the satisfaction of Customs and Excise that goods belonging to him have been accidentally lost or destroyed. Therefore, if carpets belonging to Joe Wynn fall out of the back of a van, no output tax will be charged. However, if tax-paid goods belonging to a non-taxable person are lost, stolen, or destroyed, no refund of tax can be allowed.

Bad debts VAT cannot be waived on a taxable supply on the ground that the taxable person has not received the due payment from his customer. So, if John Wilson owes Joe Wynn £54, being value of goods of £50 on which VAT of £4 is payable, and Wilson is declared bankrupt, the £4 is payable by Joe Wynn. Where a customer returns goods to a taxable supplier and is given a credit or refund of their value, the supplier may credit or refund VAT and adjust his record of output tax. **Credit for returns**

Discounts

If a supplier allows a customer a discount on condition that payment is made immediately or within a specified time, he must calculate the VAT on the discounted amount, not on the gross amount, whether or not the customer takes advantage of the discount. **Cash**

Joe Wynn sells a quantity of carpets to Sunspot Hotels as follows. **Example 5**

Gross value of goods £700
VAT at 8 per cent
Terms 5 per cent for 7 days settlements, otherwise strictly net.

Sunspot Hotels' VAT invoice will show the following calculations.

Value of goods	= £700.00
less Cash discount at 5 per cent	35.00
	665.00
VAT at 8 per cent (calculated on £665)	53.20
	£718.20

Where a trade discount is allowed tax must be calculated on the discounted amount. **Trade**

Tax on the money removed from telephone coin-boxes installed in business premises is accounted for by the Post Office. Renters of coin-box telephones should, therefore, not include this money in the VAT output records. **Telephone coin-box**

The tax point for goods or services supplied through vending machines and for services through gaming and amusement machines is to be taken as the time when any amount is removed from the machine by the *supplier* or *his agent*. Takings should be treated as tax-inclusive, and the supplier must calculate the output tax as a fraction of the amount removed. **Vending and gaming machines**

Teamatic Ltd. have installed an automatic tea machine in the warehouse of Joe Wynn. The cash is removed on each Monday morning. In February the following amounts were removed: **Example 6**

	£
First Monday's takings	4.80
Second Monday's takings	3.70
Third Monday's takings	4.20
Fourth Monday's takings	3.50

Find the VAT on the takings.

Total takings:

£	Using the VAT fraction on page 200 we get:
4.80	
3.70	$\dfrac{8}{108} \times 16.2 = £1.20.$
4.20	
3.50	Therefore VAT on the takings = £1.20.
16.20	

Bookkeeping procedures for VAT

Having already dealt with analysed books, the procedures for recording VAT are not difficult to understand. Essentially, all that is required is an additional column in the books of original entry.

Purchases Day Book

Purchases Day Book

Date	Details	Folio		Purchases	VAT	Invoice Total
4.1.–3	A. B. Carter & Co.	(d)	Further analysis column as required	150.00	12.00	162.00
	C. Taylor Ltd.	(d)		92.00	7.36	99.36
10.1.–3	Roger Knight & Co. Ltd.	(d)		76.00	6.08	82.08
				318.00	25.44	343.44
				PL P1	PL V1	BL C4
				(a)	(b)	(c)

Notes

(a) Total is debited to Purchases Account.

(b) Total is debited to the VAT Account (this is the input tax).

(c) Control account total, memo only, credited to the Purchases Ledger Control Account.

(d) Individual purchases are credited to creditor's personal account: the *invoice total* is credited, since that is the sum due to the supplier.

This is ruled in exactly the same way as the Purchases Day Book. The total of the output VAT is credited to the VAT Account.

Payments made to creditors are entered in the Cash Book, the total amount being shown in the Creditors Ledger column. The fact that a certain portion of the payment may be for VAT is immaterial, since the VAT was recorded in the Purchases Day Book upon receiving the supplier's invoice. The VAT column in the Cash Book on the credit side will be used only in circumstances where bills, with VAT included, are paid without having been passed through the Purchases Day Book. The column for VAT on the debit side will be used where cash sales arise to which VAT has been added.

Payments received from debtors are recorded in full in the Sales Ledger column, since the output tax on credit sales was recorded in the Sales Day Book.

Cash Book (Credit Side Only)

Date	Details	Folio		Expenses	Creditors Ledger	VAT	Bank
17.1.–3	A. B. Carter & Co.	(a)			162.00		162.00
18.1.–3	Petrol	(b)		8.00		1.00	9.00
21.1.–3	Stationery	(c)		6.00		0.42	6.42
					162.00 (d)	1.42 (e)	

Notes

(a) Posted to A. B. Carter & Co. £162.00.
(b) and (c) Motor expenses debited £8 and stationery debited £6.
(d) Purchases Ledger Control Account, memo only, debited £162.00.
(e) VAT debited £1.42.

The net effect of entries (b), (c) and (e) is the following.

Bank is credited with £15.42

and the debits total:

VAT	1.42
Motor expenses	8.00
Stationery	6.00
	£15.42

Cash Book (Debit Side Only)

Date	Details	Folio	Cash sales	Misc.	Sales Ledger	VAT	Bank
13.1–3	Sales		200.00			16.00	216.00
14.1–3	Commission received	(a)		10.00		0.80	10.80
19.1–3	P. Sharp	(b)			49.00		49.00
			200.00	10.00	49.00	16.80	275.80
			(c)	(d)	(e)	(f)	(g)

Notes
(a) Commission Received Account credited with £10.00.
(b) P. Sharp (debtor) credited with £49.00.
(c) Total of cash sales credited to Sales Account.
(d) Total not posted since individual entries have been posted as arising.
(e) Total credited to Sales Ledger Control Account, memo only.
(f) Total credited to VAT Account.
(g) Total of cash banked, used to cross check arithmetic.

The net effect of these entries regarding VAT is the following.

Bank is debited with a total of £226.80
of which   Sales is credited with   £200.00
           Commission is credited with   10.00
           VAT is credited with   16.80
                                         £226.80

Petty Cash Book
All payments should be checked to see if VAT has been paid. If so, the bill needs to be analysed between the expense and the VAT. An additional column is required to record the sums of VAT paid. When the Petty Cash Book is balanced and the individual analysis columns totalled, the VAT column is posted to the debit side of the VAT Account. Chapter 21 contains an illustration of a Petty Cash Book with a VAT column.

Journal
If VAT arises on a transaction that is recorded in the Journal (such as the purchase or sale of assets if an analysed Purchases Book is not kept) the entries necessary are as follows.

Suppose that an asset costing £907.20 is purchased from the Machine Supply Group Ltd. The price consists of Cost £840 + VAT £67.20.

Journal Entries

	Machinery Account Dr		840.00	
	VAT Account Dr		67.20	
	Machinery Supply Group Ltd.			907.20

Tom Woodpecker, a furniture manufacturer, is a registered taxable person for VAT purposes. He made the following transactions. **22.01**

(a) He sold furniture for £750 less settlement discount of 5 per cent to A. Wholesaler, who did not take advantage of the discount.
(b) He sold furniture for £300 to S. Rockbottom, who was later declared bankrupt. The trustee in bankruptcy will pay a dividend of 20p in a £.
(c) He hired bandsmen to play at a staff party at a cost of £60.
(d) He bought petrol for the delivery van, £13.50 including VAT at $12\frac{1}{2}$ per cent.
(e) He paid his solicitor legal charges of £30.

All items exclude any addition of VAT (except (d)) and the standard rate is to be taken as 8 per cent.

Work out, in respect of each item, the amount of VAT chargeable and state who would be responsible for accounting for it to the Customs and Excise.

(a) Who is a taxable person for VAT purposes? **22.02**
(b) What is a tax point for VAT purposes? Indicate precisely by using the following example. On 22 November 19–1, Chris Locksmith sold two door locks to John Carpenter; the transaction took place in Locksmith's shop.

On 1 March 19–6, A. Bembridge & Son, Maldon Way, Swansea, sold the following **NA 22.03** goods on credit to James Foster, 26 Broad Street, Birmingham 4: Order No. 162.

   10,000 coils sealing tape @ £4.46 per 1,000 coils.
   20,000 sheets Bank A5   @ £4.50 per 1,000 sheets.
   12,000 sheets Bank A4   @ £4.20 per 1,000 sheets.

All goods are subject to VAT at 8 per cent.

(a) Prepare the sales invoice to be sent to James Foster.
(b) Show the entries in the personal ledgers of James Foster, and A. Bembridge & Son.

(RSA 1)

Explain (a) zero rate, and (b) exemption, and show their differences. **NA 22.04**

D. Jones, a wholesale dealer in electrical goods, has three departments: (a) Hi-Fi, (b) **NA 22.05** TV, and (c) sundries. The following is a summary of D. Jones's sales invoices during the period 1 to 7 February 19–7.

	Customer	Invoice No.	Department	List price less trade discount £	VAT £	Total invoice price £
Feb. 1	P. Small	261	TV	2600	208	2808
2	L. Goode	262	Hi-Fi	1800	144	1944
3	R. Daye	263	TV	1600	128	1728
5	B. May	264	Sundries	320	Nil	320
7	L. Goode	265	TV	900	72	972
	P. Small	266	Hi-Fi	3400	272	3672

(a) Record the above transactions in a columnar book of original entry and post to the General Ledger in columnar form.

(b) Write up the personal accounts in the appropriate ledger.

Note Do *not* balance off any of your ledger accounts.

(RSA 1)

22.06   (a) Enter the following transactions in the appropriate accounts in the Sales and Purchases ledgers. Balance the accounts at the end of May 19–6.

			List price £	VAT %
19–6				
May	1	Bought goods from P. Ellison (20 per cent trade discount is allowed).	150	10
	3	Sold goods to G. Brandon.	300	10
		Sold goods to R. Strong.	200	10
	7	Returned goods to P. Ellison.	50	10
	8	G. Brandon returned goods.	40	10
	10	Settled P. Ellison's account less $2\frac{1}{2}$ per cent cash discount.		
	13	Sold goods to R. Strong.	200	10
	18	Sold goods to G. Brandon.	300	10
	24	G. Brandon settled his account.		
	28	Received information that R. Strong's premises had been completely destroyed by fire. The premises were not insured and R. Strong had disappeared.		
	29	Bought goods from P. Ellison (this transaction subject to 25 per cent trade discount).	200	10

208

(b) Write up the VAT Account in the General Ledger. (*Note* Ten per cent may not be the rate ruling at the present time, but it is selected for its convenience in calculations.)

(RSA 1)

23. Recording Wages and Salaries—PAYE

Gross wages and employer's National Insurance Contributions

In all the exercises in the book so far, wages and salaries are given as a specific figure. In practice, the amount shown in the accounts comprises the gross (total) amount payable to the employees (before stoppages for tax, etc.) together with the employer's proportion of national insurance contributions (NIC). The payroll sheet used to calculate wages will need to show the employer's NIC. A simple example follows.

Payroll Sheet Wk 22	*Gross Salary*	*Employers NIC*
Employees: 1 A. Brown	49.92	4.50
2 B. Carruthers	53.64	4.90
	103.56	9.40

The Journal entries will be:

	Wages Account (note 1) Bank Inland Revenue Being wages and employer's NIC for Week 22	Dr	112.96	103.56 9.40

Note 1 This is the total labour cost to the employer.

Income tax and employee's NIC

If everything were as simple as the example above then the operation of a wages system would be very easy. Unfortunately, further complications arise, since the employer must deduct from employees' wages those amounts due for taxation and also the employees' proportion of NIC. To do this we need a more detailed payroll sheet as follows.

	(a)	(b)	(c)	(d)	(e)	(f)
Payroll sheet Wk 22 *Employees*	Gross salary	Tax deducted	NIC deducted	Total deduction	Net pay	Employer's NIC
1 A. Brown 2 B. Carruthers	£49.92 £53.64	5.35 3.40	5.30 5.70	10.65 9.10	39.27 44.54	4.50 4.90
	£103.56	8.75	11.00	19.75	83.81	9.40

Always check arithmetic: (b) + (c) = (d)

(a) − (d) = (e)

The Journal entries will be:

Wages		Dr	112.96	
Bank	(Note 1)			83.81
Inland Revenue	(Note 2)			29.15
Being wages and employer's NIC for Week 22				

Note the following points.

1   The employees do not receive all their wages and therefore it is only necessary to draw from the bank the net wages payable.

2   Both tax and National Insurance contributions are paid to the Inland Revenue. Since the amount is always required to be paid about four weeks in arrears, the Inland Revenue Account is credited at this point. When the cheque is sent for payment, the entry will be:

Debit Inland Revenue Account: Credit Bank Account.

Calculation of gross pay

This calculation depends upon the wage agreement. Salaried staff usually receive a fixed weekly or monthly sum—so no calculation is required unless they work overtime. For weekly paid employees who can earn a bonus, depending upon output, and can also earn overtime payments, it is necessary to have a detailed wages sheet.

Wages Sheet Week 22
Hours Worked

Name	Sat.	Sun.	Mon.	Tue.	Wed.	Thu.	Fri.	Total	Rate of pay	Basic earnings	Bonus	Gross pay
A. Brown	–	–	8	8	8	8	8	40	1.15	46.00	3.92	49.92
B. Carruthers	4	–	8	8	8	8	8	44	1.10	48.40	5.24	53.64
												103.56

It is not possible to illustrate every type of wages sheet that exists. Wages systems vary from firm to firm. Sometimes employees earn additional rates for working overtime, or night work, or special shifts. Often this extra pay is required to be shown to the employees and therefore provision must be made on the wages sheet for this calculation. Whatever system is operated, it is usual to calculate the gross pay and then transfer this figure to a *payroll sheet*.

Payroll sheet

Having calculated the gross pay, the employer will need to calculate the deductions for each employee. These are recorded on the payroll sheet. In addition, those required by law—income tax and National Insurance contribution—are recorded on a special Deduction Card provided by the Inland Revenue. It is important to keep a record of employees' wages and deductions, and the payroll sheets, bound together, will provide a permanent record. Alternatively, a small firm would use a Wages Book, which normally contains the equivalent of fifty-three payroll sheets bound together. (Fifty-three because in some tax years the employee will receive fifty-three pay cheques.)

An explanation of the calculation of the amount of tax to be deducted is beyond the scope of this book, but an outline of how PAYE works follows.

The operation of PAYE (Pay As You Earn)

Code numbers
Based on the annual return sent by a taxpayer to the Inland Revenue, he will be given a *code number*. This represents the total allowances to which he is entitled in that year. This means that he can earn up to his allowances before he starts paying income tax. The system provides for allowances to be divided by 52 to give weekly allowances (or divided by 12 to give monthly allowances for monthly paid employees).

Consequently, an employee who earns in one week more than his 'weekly' allowance will have to pay tax. The code number is made up of the total allowances without the last digit. For example a single man with no allowances other than his personal allowance of £945 (1977/78) is given the code 94 (94).

Tax tables
Each employer is supplied with a printed set of tax tables which comes in two parts: Free Pay Table (Table A) and a Taxable Pay Table (Tables B, C and D).

From Table A the employer can calculate the total allowances or 'free pay', to which the employee is entitled up to that week. The free pay deducted from the total pay will give the taxable pay.

From Table B the employer calculates the tax payable on the taxable pay. The calculations are based on cumulative free pay and taxable pay totals, so the employer needs to keep a weekly record of his calculations. He must also keep a record for each employee on the Inland Revenue's tax deduction card, No. P11, of tax and National Insurance deducted, together with the employer's National Insurance contribution. These cards are returned to the Inland Revenue who can then verify the calculations and check that the sums due to them have been paid.

Other deductions from gross pay

Employees may wish to join a pension scheme and make weekly contributions. Also, many firms run savings schemes for employees, who authorize certain amounts to be taken from their weekly wages. Other sums deducted may include trade union subscriptions, subscriptions to the company sports and social club, payments for tools and overalls, and repayments of loans from the company. In all cases, the employer will need to record the deduction on the payroll sheet. As with income tax, deductions will be credited to the appropriate account.

John Hop gives you the following information regarding his income tax. **23.01**

(a) He is single person.
(b) He is married.
(c) He is married with one child aged 6 months.
(d) He is married with one child aged 2 years.
(e) He is married with two children both under 11.
(f) He is married with two children both over 11 but under 16.
(g) He is married with three children, two under 11 and one of 15.

For each of the above situations work out John Hop's PAYE code number using the following figures:

Single Person Allowance, £945.

Married Person Allowance, £1,455.

Child Allowance child under 11—first £196, subsequent £170.
                   11–15   —first £231, subsequent £205.
                   16 or over   —first £261, subsequent £235.

(a) Make a list of the deductions which an employer is required by law to make from **23.02**
his employees' wages.
(b) Write down three deductions which an employer will make at the employee's request.
(c) What is the importance of an employee's code number

(RSA 1)

Telly Vission has four employees: Sharples, Regan, Rippon, and Watts, each of **23.03**
whom works a 40-hour week. Time worked in excess of this is paid at 'time and a half'. The hourly rate for Sharples and Regan is £1.50, for Rippon £1.40, and for

Watts £1.60. During the week ending 14 May 19–5 the following hours were worked.

Sharples	35
Regan	50
Rippon	40
Watts	45

You calculate the following.

	Tax	Employee NIC	Employer NIC	Other deductions
Sharples	17.30	3.15	4.20	2.50
Regan	24.75	4.95	6.60	—
Rippon	19.00	3.35	4.50	1.40
Watts	21.30	4.55	6.00	—

(a) Draft a payroll sheet for the week recording the above details and showing for each employee gross wages, deductions, and net wages.

(b) Total your columns to cross check your arithmetic.

NA 23.04   From the payroll sheet prepared in answer to **23.03** journalize *all* the bookkeeping entries required.

Answers

Chapter 1

1.01 Pieces of paper are easily lost, while a proper book will record transactions over a long period of time.

1.02 My accountant: so it has got to be correct.

1.03 If you do not, you will not be able to add up the figures correctly.

1.04 You will not go home until I get a satisfactory answer. And if it happens again—I think you know what will be the result.

1.05 £1,761.75.

1.06

	£	£	This is the layout you should use for such
Total		1,761.75	calculations. It is quicker and neater than
Less	54.68		taking each amount away separately.
	12.35		
	87.06		
	———	154.09	
		————	
		£1,607.66	

1.07

Row	Total	Column	Total
1	21.37	1	24.29
2	78.59	2	180.55
3	75.86		
4	29.02		
	———		
1.08	204.84		

1.09

Row	Total	Column	Total
1	175.45	1	208.94
2	246.43	2	194.36
3	235.63	3	443.19
4	188.98		
	846.49		846.49

Chapter 2

2.01　Small shops will put all takings into a till. The amount in the till at the end of the day will be the takings for the day plus any amount in the till to begin with. Large shops will have a till which automatically records the amount entered on the till register on a till roll within the machine. At the end of the day, this till roll is totalled and the total should be the same as the cash in the till.

2.02　(a) (b) (e).

2.03　(a) 12 (b) 29 (c) 42 (d) 39.51.

2.04　(a) £20.00 (b) £23.00 (c) £98.00 (d) £104.50 (e) £176.40 (f) £184.27.

2.05　Just the same as a cash payment. Simply write the details of the payment on the credit side of the Cash Account.

2.06　Debit balance.

Chapter 3

3.01　A loan made to our business.
Amounts owed to suppliers of goods.
Amounts owing for services—for example, the GPO (telephone bill), the area electricity board.
A mortgage granted by a building society. (A mortgage = a loan.)
A bank loan.

3.02　It should be entered in the Cash Account as a cash receipt. If it is then paid into the Bank Account, a contra entry will record such a transfer from cash to bank.

3.03

Cash

Mar. 3	Bank	c 80	Mar. 4	Office		
6	Sales	72		Cleaner		15
10	Sales	116	8	Stationery		14
			11	Purchases		100
			12	Bank	c	129
			12	Bal. c/d		10
		268				268
Mar. 12	Bal. b/d 10					

Bank

Mar. 1	A. Smith	500	Mar. 2	Rent		25
12	Cash	c 129	3	Cash	c	80
			5	Purch.		385
			12	Drgs.		15
			12	Bal. c/d		124
		629				629
Mar. 12	Bal. b/d 124					

3.04

		Cash					Bank			
Bal.	b/d	75	Wages		48	Bal.	b/d	455	J. Walker	86
Sales		16	Window cleaner		2	Cash	c	179	Cash	c	50
Bank	c	50	Wages		49	F. Taylor		64	Drawings	20
Sales		163	Groceries		3	Cash	c	175	Telephone	31
Sales		192	Bank	c	179				Bal.	c/d	686
			Drawings		25					
			Bank	c	175			873		873
			Bal.	c/d	15	Bal.	b/d	686		

Chapter 4

4.01	Star Hotel	60.00
	ABC Carpets	160.00
	Popular Treads	18.75
	Sounds International	86.00
4.02		324.75

4.03   (a) £90; £47.50; £71.50.
       (b) £40; £31.25; £18.25.
       (c) £20; £15.62½; £9.12½.
       (d) £30; £19.50; £12.75.
       (e) £1.25; 50p; 5p.
       (f) £2.25; 60p; 12½p.

4.04   (a) £1.10; £11.80.
       (b) £11.00; £30; £24.60.
       (c) £22.00; £24.00; £6.30.
       (d) £31.50; £40.50; £58.50.

Chapter 5

5.01   Bank Book; Cash Book; and Sales Day Book.

5.02   Cash Book and Bank Book.

5.03   Sounds International £76.00 (Dr).
       Hotel Swanlake £72.00 (Dr).

5.04   Bow Office Furnishers Ltd. £171.50 (Dr).
       Hotel Swanlake £47.80 (Dr).

5.05	Metro Shopfitters	Gross	583.40		
	less Trade disc.	116.68		Net goods	466.72
	Containers				15.00
					————
	Invoice Total				481.72

	Bow Office Furnishers Ltd.				
		Gross	607.00		
	less Trade disc.	121.40		Net goods	485.60
	Containers				12.50
					————
					498.10

Chapter 6

6.01   Sales Account.

6.02   Cash Account balance £48.70 (Dr).
Bank Account balance £319.50 (Dr).
Metro Shop Fitters A/c balance £481.72 (Dr).
Bow Office Account balance £498.10 (Dr).

6.03   Sales Day Book total £516.82.
Cash Account   £92.50   (Dr).
Bank Account   £873.00 (Dr).
W. Ing   £349.25 (Dr).
Garner   £16.85   (Dr).
Office furn.   £317.68 (Cr).
Shop fitts.   £404.60 (Cr).

6.04   Cr Cash Account: Dr Sales Returns Account.

6.05   £218.50 (Dr).

6.06   £116.00 (Dr).

Chapter 7

7.01   (a) Rent Account   (e) Sales Account.
(b) Wages Account   (f) Insurance Account.
(c) Motor Running Expenses Account   (g) Discounts Allowed Account.
(d) Fixtures and Fittings Account   (h) Rent Received Account.

7.02   Credit the Bank Account.

7.03   Mar. 5   Motor Running Account.
5   Wages Account
5   Purchases Account

7.04

	Debited	Credited
(a)	Motor Van	Bank
(b)	Purchases	Cash
(c)	Rent	Bank
(d)	Cash	Sales
(e)	A. Smith	Sales
(f)	P. Taylor	Sales
(g)	Insurance	Bank
(h)	Wages	Cash
(i)	Drawings	Cash

7.05 (a) Sales—Nominal Ledger.
(b) Purchases—Nominal Ledger.
(c) A. Smith—Sales Ledger.
(d) Machinery—Nominal Ledger.
(e) Wages—Nominal Ledger.
(f) Commissions received—Nominal Ledger.
(g) Losses on till takings—Nominal Ledger.
(h) Discounts—Nominal Ledger.
(i) D. Jones—Bought Ledger.

7.06 Sales Day Book total   £192.80.
Cash Book balance   £236.20 (Dr).
Bank Book balance   £35.00 (Cr).

7.06 (c) List of balances

Debits Cash £236.20; Wages £88.00; Printing expenses £15.50; Discount allowed 75p; Drawings £10.00; Rent £48.00; Sales returns £8.00; Shaw £107.55; Miller £8.50; Shop fittings £18.90; Purchases £265.00.
Credits Bank £35.00; Sales £771.40. Trial balance total £806.40.

7.07 Sales Day Book page 10.

7.08

	Dr	Cr
(a)	Motor Van	R.A. Garage Ltd.
(b)	Shop Fittings	Shop Fitters Ltd.
(c)	Shop Fitters Ltd.	Bank
(d)	B. Worth	Cash
(e)	Bank	Office Equipment

7.09 Sales Day Book total £322.70.
Balances on Accounts
Debits Cash £315.85; Warehouse fittings £285; Bank charges £28.50; Office

machine rental £18.70; Drawings £75; P. Carter £88.75; F. Taylor £28.45; P. White £56; Wages £231.45; Forklift truck (asset) £1,950; S. Bond £19.50. *Credits* Bank £739.20; Sales £1,008; Forklifts Ltd. £1,700.

Chapter 8

8.01 List of balances
Debits Cash £277.45; P. Rowler £93; Office equipt. £425; Discount allowed £3; Motor running expenses £27; Drawings £35; Stock £500; Motor car £1,450; Bank £3,497; Rent £55; Purchase £611; Lease £3,500; Stationery £4.25; Postage 85p; Packing material £12.45.
Credits T. Taylor £6,950; Sales £616; Bank loan £2,500; London Supply Co. £425.
Trial balance total £10,491. Sales Day Book total £135.

8.02

R. Bell Capital Account

Aug. 31 19–8	Drawings		2760	Sept. 1 19–7	Bal.	b/d	2845
	Bal.	c/d	3235	Aug. 31 19–8	Net profit		3150
			5995				5995
				Sept. 1 19–8	Bal.	b/d	3235

Drawings Account

Aug. 31 19–8	Cash	1980	Aug. 31 19–8	Capital A/c		2760
	Rates	200				
	Motor Exp.	500				
	Heating	80				
		2760				2760

8.03 Capital = £7,515.

8.04 List of balances
Debits Cash £25; S. Bade £48.75; Stock £285; Fixtures £290; Motor vehicles £800; Purchases £370; Telephone £46.75; Trade expenses £19.50; Drawings £103; T. Tynn £98.42; Wages £128.20; M. Mynn £57.60; F. Fynn £147; P. Pynn £107.65; Bank charges £5.50.
Credits Bank £2.10; K. Hick £43; S. Hoe £33.45; Sales £883.97; Dividends £16.80; Capital—C. Camp £1,553.05.
Trial balance total £2,532.37.
Note Owner's drawings of stock are credited to Purchases Account.

Chapter 9

9.01 Trial balance total £55,690.

9.02 Trial balance total £45,949.

9.03   Trial balance total £5,299.

9.04   (a) Profit £705.
        (b) Profit £2,420.
        (c) Loss £80.

Chapter 10

10.01   Cash balance £368.50 (Dr). Bank balance £212.00 (Dr).

10.02   Cash balance £176.00 (Dr). Bank balance £380.50 (Dr).

10.03   Cash balance £193.10 (Dr). Bank balance £403.60 (Cr).

10.04   Cash balance £191.37 (Dr). Bank balance £222.00 (Dr).
        Discount Allowed total £26; Discount Received total £8.

10.05   Cash balance £40 (Dr). Bank balance £383 (Dr).
        Discount allowed £6. Post to debit side of Discount Allowed Account.
        Discount received £7; Post to credit side of Discount Received Account.

10.09   List of balances
        Debits Cash £343.89; Stock £931; Fixtures £1,297.65; P. Steele £77; M. Hart
        £90; Purchases £687; Rent £100; Motor expenses £75.50; Stationery £2.15;
        Drawings £62; B. Reeves £86.50; Bank charges £14.86; Hire charges £46;
        Sales returns £10; Motor van £860; Discount allowed £6.75.
        Credits Bank £392.26; J. Dove £96.50; Sales £1,336.54; Capital £2,110;
        Bank loan £750; Discount received £5.
        Trial balance total £4,690.30.
        Note   Drawings of stock are posted to Sales Account since the question
        states the goods are valued at selling price. Otherwise it is assumed that they
        are cost price, in which case the value would be credited to Purchases
        Account.

Chapter 11

11.01   Credit Cash £85.
        Debit supplier's account £85.

11.02

Allweather Covers	Cr	£140.00
Allday Protectors	Cr	112.50
All purpose Sheeting	Cr	316.20
Bought Day Book total		£568.70

11.03   List of balances
        Debits Bank £2,053.20; Motor running expenses £55; Wages £166.85;
        Debtors: Tubular Poles £76, Wheeltappers £100; Purchases £1,134.50; Rent
        £19.50; Discount allowed £4.90.

Credits Capital £2,648; Creditors: Round Wheels £256, Rollover £157, Square Way Dealers £73; Sales £475.95.
Sales Day Book total £274.
Bought Day Book total £486.

Chapter 12

12.01 Purchases Account.

12.02

Syd Cellar, The Cave Mountainside, Wasteshire					*Statement*
To: Bill Byer					Date
Date	Details		Debit	Credit	Balance
Oct. 5	Goods Inv. SC/432		36.00		36.00
12	Credit–Cheque			34.20	
	Credit–Discount			1.80	Nil
18	Goods Inv. SC/443		63.00		63.00
21	Debit Note–Containers		10.00		73.00

12.03

F. Lower Miller Account

Jan. 12	Returns—Goods	PRB	25.00	Jan. 1	Bal.		b/d	98.00
20	Bank	CB	98.00	5	Purchases	BDB		96.00
	Returns—			8	Containers	BDB		7.50
	Containers	PRB	7.50					
28	Bank	CB	69.23					
	Discount Recd	CB	1.77					
			201.50					201.50

12.04 List of balances

Debits Cash £40.50; Motor £800; Equipment £590; Wages and casual labour £158; Misc. material £14; Stationery £7; Motor running expenses £89.50; Materials £321.50; Drawings £90; Debtors £937.
Credits Bank £108; N. Evans & Co. £250; A. Garage Ltd. £39.50; Capital £1,380; P & D. Supplies £166; Allday Services £42; Sales £1,062.
Sales Day Book total £1,025.
Bought Day Book total £288.
Trial balance total £3,047.50.

Chapter 13

13.02 *Totals on 31 January* Sales Day Book £294.50; Bought Day Book £1,011; Sales Returns Book £57; Purchases Returns Book £16.50.

Balances on 31 January Cash Book £30; Bank Book £780.25; Sales £1,433.70; Sundry expenses £15.25; Discount allowed £1; Wages £187.50; Purchases £1,261; Sales returns £57; Purchases returns £16.50.

Debtors R. Rawson £219.50, P. Sharp £4; A. Cowley £49.50.

Creditors Allday Services £828.50; G. Grove £166.

Stock £889; Premises £10,800; Fixtures £1,500; Capital £13,428; Drawings £78.70. Trial balance total £15,872.20.

13.01

Cash Book

	Disc.	Cash	Bank		Disc.	Cash	Bank
Balance		78	4,154	Gibbon	29		551
Thomas	9		171	Hall			30
Gaddes	20		380	Jackson			225
Middleditch			100				

Personal accounts balances Middleditch £75 (Dr).
Jackson £43 (Cr).

Chapter 14

14.01 (a) £13,740, (b) £13,360, (c) £13,740, (d) £4,520, (e) £4,370.

14.02 (1) £3,750, (2) £9,200 (assuming FIFO).

14.03 Gross profit £4,584; Net profit £2,046.

14.05 (a) (i) 1 To determine the quantity of stock actually held to form the basis of the closing stock valuation required for the accounts.
2 To check that stock has not been lost or stolen.
3 To find any old/obsolete/deteriorated stock which will have lost value.

(ii) The stock value is deducted at the year end from the cost of purchases. A lower stock value leaves a higher cost of purchases. This in turn leads to a lower profit.

(b)   *Trading Account*

Opening stock	£8 × 1,000 =	8,000	Sales (i)	£10 × 2,500 =	25,000	
Purchases	£7 × 2,000 =	14,000	less Returns	£10 × 10 =	100	
	3,000 =	22,000		2,490	24,900	
Closing stock	£7* × 500 =	3,500	Sales (ii)	£4 × 10 =	40	
	2,500	18,500		2,500	24,940	
Gross profit		6,440				
		24,940			24,940	

* It is assumed that the items remaining in stock were a part of the latest purchase at £7 each.

14.07 Gross profit £1,783; Net loss £1,219. Trial balance total £11,125.

Chapter 15

15.01 *Balance Sheet items*
   Liabilities side Capital 31 Dec. 19–5 £6,647; Mortgage £5,000; Current liabilities £1,860; Total £13,507.
   Assets side Fixed assets £8,080; Current assets £5,427; Total £13,507.

15.03 (a) Corrected net profit £680.
   (b) Balance Sheet totals £3,440.
   Assets side Fixed assets £560; Current assets £2,880.
   Liabilities side Capital £1,780; Current liabilities £1,660.

15.05 (a) Capital £6,255.
   (b) Balance Sheet totals £6,975.

15.06 Balance Sheet totals £31,244.
   Assets side Fixed assets £19,460; Current assets £11,784.
   Liabilities side Capital £24,364; Current liabilities £6,880.

Chapter 16

16.01 Insurance Account: Dr balance b/d £39 (amount transferred to Profit and Loss Account £102).
   Commission Receivable Account: Dr balance b/d £25 (amount transferred to Profit and Loss Account £100).
   Telephone Account: Cr balance b/d £76 (amount transferred to Profit and Loss Account £369).
   Carriage Expenses Account: Cr balance b/d £15 (amount transferred to Profit and Loss Account £92).

16.02

Wages Account

Dec. 31 19–9	Bal.	b/d	9,174.62	Jan. 1 19–9	Bal.	b/d		87.55
	Bal.	c/d	110.76	Dec. 31	P. & L. A/c			9,197.83
			9,285.38					9,285.38

16.04

Advertising Revenue Account

June 1 19–7	Bal.	b/d	885	May 30 19–8	Bank		9,742
May 30 19–8	Revenue A/c		9,884		Discount		376
					Bal.	c/d	651
			10,769				10,769
June 1 19–8	Bal.	b/d	651				

16.05

Rent Account

19–7				19–7			
Feb. 28	Bank		200	Dec. 31	Profit & Loss A/c		1,200
May 31	Bank		300				
Aug. 31	Bank		300				
Nov. 30	Bank		300				
Dec. 31	Bal.	c/d	100				
			1,200				1,200
19–8				19–8			
Feb. 28	Bank		300	Jan. 1	Bal.	b/d	100
May 31	Bank		360	Dec. 31	Profit & Loss A/c		1,400
Aug. 31	Bank		360				
Nov. 30	Bank		360				
Dec. 31	Bal.	c/d	120				
			1,500				1,500
				19–9			
				Jan. 1	Bal.	b/d	220

Rates Account

19–7				19–7			
Mar. 20	Bank		60	Dec. 31	Profit & Loss A/c		360
Apr. 29	Bank		200		Bal.	c/d	100
Nov. 18	Bank		200				
			460				460
19–8				19–8			
Jan. 1	Bal.	b/d	100	Dec. 31	Profit & Loss A/c		415
Apr. 3	Bank		210		Bal.	c/d	105
Nov. 25	Bank		210				
			520				520
19–9							
Jan. 1	Bal.	b/d	105				

16.08 Gross profit £2,880; Net profit £1,130.
Balance Sheet items:

Capital at beginning + Profit − Drgs.	£2,530
Current liabilities	3,820
Fixed assets	3,000
Current assets	3,350

16.11 Capital in trial balance £2,884.
Cost of food and drinks sold £4,979.
Gross profit £5,691 (kitchen wages and depreciation included in Trading Account).
Cost of china, glass and crockery lost/broken £176.
Net profit £3,177.
Balance Sheet totals £7,471.

Chapter 17

17.01 (a) Office equipment; motor lorries; land and buildings; and machinery.
   (b) Extensions to buildings; replacement of accounting machine by computer; new engine for a vehicle; and replacement of old lighting system by a new system.
   (c) Wages; rent; insurance; and petrol.

17.02 Real = assets. Nominal = incomes and expenses. Personal = of a person. Profit would be £400 too little. No effect on Balance Sheet except that assets would be understated (offset by a lower profit).

17.03 (a) £1,600, (b) £145, (c) £140, (d) £50.

17.04 (a) Year 1 = £300, Year 2 = £255, (b) Year 1 = £1,600, Year 2 = £1,280.
   (c) Year 1 = £60, Year 2 = £54, (d) Year 1 = £40, Year 2 = £37 (to the nearest £).

17.05 (a) £35, (b) £20, (c) £40, (d) £3,500.

17.06 (a) WDV end Year 1 = £450, Year 2 = £400, Year 3 = £350.
   (b) WDV end Year 1 = £450, Year 2 = £405, Year 3 = £364.

17.12 (a) See text book page 140.
   (b) Motor Vans Account balance 31 Mar. 19–4 = £15,200 (Dr).
   Provision for Depreciation Account balance 31 Mar. 19–4 = £9,200 (Cr).
   Profit and Loss Account £50 (Cr) (profit on disposal).
   Note Depreciation in year = £3,800.
   Provision Account balance = 6,000 + 3,800 − 600 = £9,200.

Chapter 18

18.01 (a)

Trading Account for year ended 31 May 19–6

Stock 1 June 19–5	8,500	Sales	37,000
Purchases	29,000		
	37,500		
less Stock 31 May	7,900		
	29,600		
Gross Profit	7,400		
	37,000		37,000

(b) Debtors at 31 May 19–6 = 3,400 + 37,000 − 36,000 = £4,400

18.02 (a) Cost of goods sold = £24,000.
Gross profit   = £12,000.
Net profit   = £5,400.
Expenses   = £6,600.

(b) Cost price of average stock held = £2,000. (Divide turnover at cost price by rate of stock turnover = £24,000 ÷ 12 = £2,000.)

18.05

Cash Flow Statement

	£	£
Bank and Cash balance 1 Jan. 19–9		1,840
add Net profit	4,500	4,500
		6,340
less Increase in fixed assets	600	
Increase in Stock	150	
Increase in Debtors	110	
Decrease in creditors	450	
Drawings	5,000	6,310
Balance 31 December 19–9		30

Chapter 19

				£	£
19.01	(a)	Office Equipment Account	Dr	75.00	
		B. Kirkland and Co.			75.00
		Credit purchases per Invoice No. .... dated			

	(b)	Safeway Insurance Co.	Dr	750.00	
		Motor Vehicle Disposal Account			750.00
		Loss claim agreed per letter ref. .... dated			

	(c)	Bank Deposit Account	Dr	23.00	
		Interest Received Account			23.00
		Per statement No. .... dated			

	(d)	P. Carter	Dr	4.50	
		Discount Allowed Account			4.50
		Discount now disallowed upon return of Cheque No. ... marked R/D			

	(e)	B. Waltham—Drawings Account	Dr	18.50	
		Purchases Account			18.50
		Value of stocks withdrawn by owner			

19.02	1 June 19–6	Premises Account	Dr	10,000	
		Stock Account		1,500	
		Motor Van Account		700	
		Cash Account		70	
		Bank Account		150	
		Rates Account		80	
		Mortgage Account			2,000
		Creditors			250
		S. Trader—Capital Account			10,250
				12,500	12,500

Opening assets and liabilities of the business on
1 June 19–6

19.03	(a)	C. Shell—Drawings Account	Dr	800	
		Wages Account			560
		Materials Account			240
		Private expenditure transferred			

	(b)	A. H. Clark	Dr	84	
		H. Clarkson			84
		Correction of the misposting of cheque payable to A. H. Clark			

	(c)	Office Equipment Account	Dr	300	
		Purchases Account			300
		Transfer of asset purchases, wrongly debited to Purchases Account			

19.07	1 June 19–7	Motor van	Dr	850	
		Fixtures		700	
		Stock		4,950	
		Debtors		3,400	
		Goodwill*		1,300	
		Provision for doubtful debts			150
		Creditors			2,750
		T. Brown			8,300
				11,200	11,200

Assets and liabilities acquired upon purchase of business.
(* Balancing figure)

Balance Sheet of J. Parker on 1 June

Capital	8,750	Goodwill			1,300
		Fixed assets			
		Motor van		850	
Current liabilities		Fixtures		700	1,550
Creditors	2,750	*Current assets*			
		Stock		4,950	
		Debtors	3,400		
		less Prov.	150	3,250	
		Bank		450	8,650
	11,500				11,500

Chapter 20

20.02 (a) Cash Book balance = £413 (£390 + 48 − 25).

   (b) *Bank Reconciliation Statement 30 Apr. 19–6*   £

Balance per statement	414
less Unpresented cheques (21 + 42)	63
	351
add Item not credited	62
	413

20.04 (a) Cash Book balance = £55 (overdrawn) (£40 + £15).

   (b) *Bank Reconciliation Statement 30 June 19–6*   £

Balance per statement	75	OD
add Unpresented cheques (35 + 25)	60	
	135	OD
less Item not credited	80	
	55	**OD**

   (c) To prove the accuracy of the figures both in the Cash Book and on the statement.

20.06 *Bank Reconciliation Statement 31 Jan. 19–4*   £

Balance per bank statement	1,512
less Cheques unpresented (83 + 95 + 162)	340
	1,172
add Item not credited by bank	422
	1,594
Note 1 Add Fire insurance premium, paid by bank but not in Cash Book	120
	1,714
Note 2 Add Bank interest, charged by bank but not in Cash Book	86
Balance per Cash Book (before correction)	**1,800**

Notes 1 and 2 These two items would not normally appear in a Bank Reconciliation Statement. Since the question says that the statement should end with the balance according to the Cash Book, the two items are added back to the balance shown on the statement. The Cash Book balance of £1,800 would normally be adjusted by deducting the two items shown in the question under (b) and (c), leaving the corrected Cash Book balance of £1,594.

20.08 Corrected Cash Book total = £1,363.25.

Bank Reconciliation Statement	£
Bal. per statement	1,134.00
add Items not credited	473.75
	1,607.75
less Unpresented cheques	244.50
	1,363.25

Chapter 21

21.01 Petty Cash reimbursed—1 March £30.27; 1 April £33.14.
Wages column £22.05; Postage and telegram £4.44; Stationery £3.85; Ledger £2.80.

21.04 Bank Cash Book balance £633.94.

21.06 Cash Book; Sales Day Book; Petty Cash Book; Sales Returns Book; Purchases Returns Book.

21.07 Folio reference is entered.

21.08

Total	Carpet purchases	Furniture purchases
829.25	600.50	228.75

21.09 Total Purchases = £812.40 (Credited to individual suppliers)
Analysis Repairs—£103.00 (Debit Repairs Account)
Petrol, Oils—£433.60 (Debit Petrol, Oils Account)
Spares—£275.80 (Debit Spares Account)

21.10 Personal accounts balances (all debits)—Ford £258; Abbott £410; Smith £172; Carter £1,143; Mumms £645; Rankin £516.
Nominal accounts—Furniture sales, credit £920; Carpet sales, credit £630; Hardware sales, credit £400; Carriage and cases, credit £122, debit £28; Balance—credit £94.

21.12 Total purchases = £3,016.

21.13 *Trial Balance of Ro-Go at January 31*
Debit balances Repairs £832; Wages £4; Gifts £98; Bouncers £42; Telephone £143; Loss on asset disposal £75; Property £6,000; Fruit machines £1,860; Bank £729; Cash £52; Bad debts £3.
Credit balances Property Racketeers £4,000; Quick P.M. Ltd. £450; Conning Advertisers Ltd. £98; Securearms £42; Maik-nu £750; Plate Glass £82; GPO £143; Sales £1,372; Junk Toys £98; Capital £2,803. Trial balance totals: £9,838.

21.15 (a) Invoices received for goods, services, assets.
(b) Vouchers signed by persons using the cash.
(c) Receipts: (i) Cash till rolls; salesman's receipts—for cash sales.
(ii) Bank paying-in book for contras and cheques received.
(iii) Cash Received Book—if used.
Payments: Cheque counterfoils; bank statements; petty cash vouchers.
(d) As (c) (i) and (ii) above.
(e) Copy credit note sent to customer.

Chapter 22

22.01 (a)

	VAT		Payable by
Amount		£750.00	
Less 5 per cent		37.50	
		712.50	

	VAT at 8 per cent	= £57.00	Tom Woodpecker
(b)	8 per cent of £300	= £24.00	Tom Woodpecker
(c)	8 per cent of £60	= £4.80	Bandsmen
(d)	$£13.50 \times \dfrac{12\frac{1}{2}}{112\frac{1}{2}}$	= £1.50	Garage owner
(e)	8 per cent of £30	= £2.40	Solicitor

22.02 (a) A taxable person is a person who makes, or intends to make, taxable supplies. (Taxable supplies are goods and services which are subject to VAT.)

(b) A tax point is the date on which a taxable supply is made. Tax point 22 November 19–1.

22.06 (a) *Purchases Ledger P. Ellison Account* Debits: Returns + VAT £44; Bank £85.80; Discount received £2.20. Credits: Purchases + VAT £132; Purchases + VAT £165.
Balance £165 (Cr).

23.03 (1) Simplified payroll sheet

Department:: Packing				PAYROLL					Week No. 6	Week Ending: 14 May 19–5	
NAME	HOURS WORKED		RATE OF PAY	GROSS WAGE	DEDUCTIONS				NET PAY	EMPLOYER N.I.C.	TOTAL N.I.C.
	NORMAL	OVERTIME			TAX	N.I.C.	OTHER	TOTAL			
Regan	40	15	1.50	82.50	24.75	4.95	–	29.70	52.80	6.60	11.55
Rippon	40	–	1.40	56.00	19.00	3.35	1.40	23.75	32.25	4.50	7.85
Sharples	35	–	1.50	52.50	17.30	3.15	2.50	22.95	29.55	4.20	7.35
Watts	40	$7\frac{1}{2}$	1.60	76.00	21.30	4.55	–	25.85	50.15	6.00	10.55
PAGE TOTAL				267.00	82.35	16.00	3.90	102.25	164.75	21.30	37.30
				1	2	3	4	5	6	7	8

(2) *Note* Column 5 = Col. 2 + Col. 3 + Col. 4.
Column 6 = Col. 1 – Col. 5.
Column 8 = Col. 3 + Col. 7.

233

Sales Ledger G. Brandon Account Debits: Sales + VAT £330; Credits: Returns + VAT £44; Bank £616; Balance nil.

R. Strong Debit balance £440 (2 × Sales + VAT of £220).

(b) *VAT Account* Debits: Ellison £12; Returns Brandon £4; Ellison £15. Credits: Brandon £30; Strong £20; Returns Ellison £4; Strong £20; Brandon £30.

Balance £73 (Cr).

Chapter 23

23.01 (a) 94, (b) 145, (c) 165, (d) 165, (e) 182, (f) 189, (g) 202.

23.02 (a) Income tax; National Insurance Contributions. (Additional deductions can be required under a Court Order.)

(b) Savings; Sports Club subscription; Trade Union subscription.

(c) Determines the employee's 'free pay'.

Index